THE OFFICIAL TOUR DE FRANCE RECORDS

First published in 2012

Copyright © Carlton Books Limited 2012

Carlton Books Limited
20 Mortimer Street
London W1T 3JW

A CIP catalogue record for this book is available from
the British Library

10 9 8 7 6 5 4 3 2 1

ISBN: 978-1-78097-009-7

Editor: Martin Corteel
Project Art Editor: Luke Griffin
Designer: Brian Flynn
Picture Research: Paul Langan
Production: Rachel Burgess

Printed in Dubai

le TOUR de france

THE OFFICIAL TOUR DE FRANCE RECORDS

CHRIS SIDWELLS

CARLTON

CONTENTS

⬇ *From left to right: Stan Ockers (partially obscured), Gino Bartali, Fausto Coppi, Eddy Merckx, Bernard Hinault, Miguel Indurain and Lance Armstrong.*

Introduction

The Tour de France is approaching its 100th edition, creating a history spread over three million kilometres of cycling by hundreds of racers, each one trying to do his best. All that distance on open roads, fighting terrain and nature, as well as each other, has generated a mass of facts, figures and human stories. Not all are honourable, some involve sharp practice and even downright cheating, but the bad as well as the good are part of the rich tapestry that is the Tour de France. And they certainly haven't affected its popularity.

The Tour de France is the biggest annual sporting event in the world. For the first three weeks of July it takes over the roads of France like a moving state, applying its own rules and stopping everyday life in its tracks. It even has its own police force, a bank, and a huge mobile village that is erected and taken down in every stage town, every day.

The Tour is a spectacle, a phenomenon even, but it is also a very tough race. It's so tough that stage distances have slowly decreased, but the Tour has become faster and more spectacular as a result, while still preserving its rock-hard core. Tour de France racers are among the fittest athletes on the planet.

The Tour has never produced a fluke winner, although some have won by guile as much as by strength. A few names appear in the records more than once, yet single and multiple winners, and those who have dominated one of the auxiliary competitions like the King of the Mountains, are the legendary riders of the Tour de France. Although the Tour is not just about winners.

Anyone who makes it through three weeks of racing, across at least two huge mountain ranges, through heat and cold, through wind and rain, downhill and up, has a story to tell. I've enjoyed telling their stories as much as those of the yellow jerseys, the Kings of the Mountains and the green jersey winners. Every Tour finisher is as important as the stage winners, the great cycling nations and the iconic teams. And they are as important as the Tour's legendary riders and the great climbs.

I hope you enjoy reading about all the facts and figures, and about the characters that make up the chapters of the Tour de France, as much as I've enjoyed writing *The Official Tour de France Records*.

Chris Sidwells January 2012

PART 1
TOUR DE FRANCE ALL-TIME RECORDS

The Tour de France is the people's race. Unlike other sports, people don't go to see the Tour de France – the Tour comes to them, to their towns and their villages, using their mountains, their country roads and city streets. This is the reason why a publicity stunt, thought up in 1903 to advertise a newspaper, has captured the hearts of a country, then a continent and now the world. The Tour de France is a nation's gift to the planet.

The Tour de France finishes each year on the Champs Elysées, right in the heart of Paris. It is one of only two days out of 365 that this iconic avenue is closed to traffic.

THE YELLOW JERSEY

The yellow jersey is the symbol of race leadership in the Tour de France. It's awarded after the first stage, and as the race goes on it shows who has completed the route in the shortest time so far. The final yellow jersey is awarded to the rider who has won the race overall – by completing a whole lap of France quicker than anyone else.

The first man to win five Tours de France, Jacques Anquetil, is one of the legends who are the story of the yellow jersey. In this picture the first Irishman in yellow, Anquetil's team-mate Shay Elliott, rides on Anquetil's right.

YELLOW JERSEY

The first winner of the Tour de France, Maurice Garin, didn't get a yellow jersey. He quickly became famous, as did the whole race, but it was difficult for fans to follow. The Tour de France is a stage race, so the winner is the man who rides all of the stages together in the shortest total time, but he might not lead when it passes any particular point on the route. Fans needed to see who was leading overall at any stage of the race, so in 1919 the man who invented the Tour, Henri Desgrange, decided that the overall leader should wear a distinctive jersey.

FIRST TOUR

At the turn of the 20th century a new sports newspaper called *L'Auto* needed to boost its circulation. The editor, Henri Desgrange, asked his entire staff to put on their thinking caps and come up with a publicity stunt. His cycling reporter, Geo Lefèvre, was into long-distance bike races, like Paris to Brest and back (1,400 kilometres), so he suggested a race around the whole of France. Desgrange liked the idea, but it was too much in one go, so he split Lefèvre's 2,428-kilometre route into six stages, with a few days' rest between each one. It was a success, and over the next few years the number of stages grew as their distances came down.

WHY YELLOW?

There are two stories. One is that yellow was chosen because the pages of *L'Auto* were printed on yellow paper. The other is that Desgrange didn't make up his mind about a leader's jersey until the 1919 race was already in progress. At that point the Tour had 12 stages left, so to get through to the end of the race Desgrange needed a dozen sets of cycling jerseys in small, medium and large – making a total of 36 jerseys, all the same colour. The only colour his supplier had in such bulk was yellow.

⬆ *Henri Desgrange, the father of the Tour, was an accomplished racer in his youth and set the first world hour record.*

EUGÈNE CHRISTOPHE

Between 1903 and 1913 the Tour grew towards being an international event, but the 1919 Tour was the first race after the First World War, so the field was predominantly French with a scattering of Belgians, one Italian and one Spaniard. The chances of a Frenchman wearing the first yellow jersey were high, and Eugène Christophe didn't disappoint. He didn't win the 1919 Tour, however – a Belgian did, Firmin Lambot. In fact Christophe was one of the best and bravest racers never to win the Tour, but at least he was the first in yellow.

⬅ *The front page of* L'Auto *on the first day of the first ever Tour de France.*

Most Tour victories

1	Lance Armstrong (USA) –	7 wins	(1999, 2000, 2001, 2002, 2003, 2004, 2005)
2	Miguel Indurain (Spain) –	5 wins	(1991, 1992, 1993, 1994, 1995)
=	Bernard Hinault (France) –	5 wins	(1978, 1979, 1981, 1982, 1985)
=	Eddy Merckx (Belgium) –	5 wins	(1969, 1970, 1971, 1972, 1974)
=	Jacques Anquetil (France) –	5 wins	(1957, 1961, 1962, 1963, 1964)
6	Greg LeMond (USA) –	3 wins	(1986, 1989, 1990)
=	Louison Bobet (France) –	3 wins	(1953, 1954, 1955)
=	Philippe Thys (Belgium) –	3 wins	(1913, 1914, 1920)

WHAT ABOUT THE OTHER WORDS?

They are the names of sponsors of the jersey, plus the sponsors of the team the race leader rides for. The jersey sponsors are printed before the Tour starts, and they used to be embroidered or flocked on to the yellow jersey. However, there's no telling before each stage who'll wear the yellow jersey at the end of it, so all the team sponsors' names were stitched on to individual cloth rectangles and the appropriate one was pinned to the jersey before the presentation ceremony. Now they are ironed on to the yellow jersey from pre-prepared transfers after each stage.

→ *Cadel Evans was Australia's first Tour winner in 2011.*

WHAT DO THOSE INITIALS MEAN?

When the Tour de France resumed after the Second World War, every yellow jersey bore the initials HD in honour of its founder, Henri Desgrange. The tradition was dropped between 1984 and 2003, but it's back now and HD is printed on each sleeve.

PRIZE MONEY

The first winner of the Tour de France, Maurice Garin of France, received 6,000 gold francs. The 2011 winner, Cadel Evans from Australia, won 450,000 euros. In addition the man wearing the yellow jersey gets paid every day he wears it. The total prize purse for the yellow jersey is 1,005,000 euros.

ZIP AT THE BACK

The yellow jersey that's presented on the podium at the end of each stage has a full zip up the back, so the rider can just put his arms through it, and someone behind him (usually the five times Tour winner Bernard Hinault, who works for the organizers) zips it up at the back. This jersey is just for show; for the following day the leader receives a proper yellow jersey in which to race.

← *The name of the rider's team sponsors and the sponsor of the overall Tour, plus the logos of the jersey sponsors, are prominent on each yellow jersey.*

WOOL TO LYCRA

The first yellow jerseys were woollen and heavy. They got lighter as textile technology improved, and a light, wool-like material called Ryovil was used until the late 1970s, when acrylic fibres began to be used. Nowadays lycra mixed with other man-made fibres makes the yellow jersey a light garment that dries quickly and fits well.

COLOUR CLASH

There's nothing to prevent a professional team having yellow kit, and where yellow is part of the sponsor's logo it happens. It isn't a problem in other races, but in the Tour de France the only racer allowed to wear yellow is the race leader. Teams with yellow kit have to change colour for the Tour, recent examples being the Spanish teams Kas and ONCE. Kas raced in yellow jerseys with blue sleeves, so swapped the colours around for the Tour. ONCE raced the rest of the year in all-yellow kit, but wore all-pink during the Tour.

THE BUTTERCUP

In 1951 Dutchman Wim van Est crashed down a ravine on the Col d'Aubisque while wearing the yellow jersey. He fell about 20 metres and got stuck on a ledge. When his team-mate Gerrit Peeters stopped to help him he shouted, "What are you doing down there? You look like a buttercup." The Dutch team rescued Van Est by tying all their spare tyres together to form a rope and haul him up. Unfortunately this ruined their tyres, and the yellow jersey and his whole team had to withdraw from the race.

YELLOW LUCK

Wim Van Est is one of 14 riders who have dropped out of the Tour while wearing the yellow jersey. Most of them were injured in racing crashes, like Britain's Chris Boardman in 1998. Others, like Francis Pélissier in 1927, were forced out by illness, whereas inter-country rivalry forced out Belgium's Sylvère Maes in 1937. To his exasperation, throughout the race French fans had pushed their compatriot Roger Lapébie up the hills, while Maes had even been stopped by closed level crossings when no train was in sight. "I'm not going to continue while being steadily robbed of my lead," Maes told journalists as he packed to go home.

⬆ *Chris Boardman was the second British racer to wear the yellow jersey.*

YELLOW SHORTS

No matter what their jersey colour or design was, up until the late 1970s teams had to race in black shorts it was the international rule of cycling. Then shorts matching team colours were allowed, but it still wasn't permitted to wear shorts to match the yellow jersey. Finally in the 1990s Mario Cipollini of Italy started flouting the rules by wearing all-yellow kit when he led the Tour. After fining Cipollini and anyone who copied him, the organizers eventually relented, and now the Tour de France leader can wear shorts to match his yellow jersey.

⬆ *Van Est (left) abandoned the Tour, but made a lucrative advert for his Pontiac watch, saying, "My heart nearly stopped on the mountain but not my Pontiac."*

MOST YELLOW JERSEYS

1 Eddy Merckx (Belgium) – 96 from 1969 to 1975
2 Lance Armstrong (USA) – 83 from 1999 to 2005
3 Bernard Hinault (France) – 73 from 1978 to 1986
4 Miguel Indurain (Spain) – 60 from 1991 to 1995
5 Jacques Anquetil (France) – 50 from 1957 to 1964
6 Antonin Magne (France) – 38 from 1931 to 1934
7 Nicolas Frantz (Luxembourg) – 37 from 1927 to 1929
= Philippe Thys (Belgium) – 37 from 1913 to 1920
9 André Leducq (France) – 35 from 1929 to 1938
10 Louison Bobet (France) – 34 from 1949 to 1955
= Ottavio Bottecchia (Italy) – 34 from 1923 to 1925

← *Eddy Merckx dominated cycling from the late sixties to the mid-seventies, winning nearly everything, including five Tours.*

YELLOW MYTH

Although it's generally accepted that Eugène Christophe was the first yellow jersey, the first triple winner, Philippe Thys, told a cycling magazine in the 1950s that he had worn one before him. He said that Henri Desgrange had asked him to wear a distinctive yellow jersey when he led the 1913 Tour. He refused at first but was talked into agreeing by his team manager a few days later. The problem is that there's no account of this in any newspaper or journal from the time to corroborate his story. However, those who knew him said that Thys was an honourable person who wouldn't lie about such a thing.

COLLAR BUTTONS

The original yellow jersey had a traditional collar, like a shirt, and buttons up to the neck. This was replaced by a round collar and a zip in the 1960s.

YELLOW FROM START TO FINISH

Italy's Ottavio Bottecchia in 1924, Nicolas Frantz (Luxembourg, 1928), Roman Maes (Belgium, 1935) and Jacques Anquetil (France, 1961) are the only men who, after winning the first stage and being awarded the first yellow jersey of that Tour de France, have kept it until the end.

A LA WALKOWIAK

Seven men have won the Tour de France without winning a stage, but only one cyclist has ever won it without managing to win a single stage in any Tour de France. This man was Roger Walkowiak, who won in 1956 largely because of rivalry and complacency within the French national team. He was far from the strongest man in the race, and his legacy is that when anyone looks like winning who isn't the strongest, journalists say he's winning "à la Walkowiak".

→ *History might say Roger Walkowiak was lucky to have won the Tour, but everyone who finishes a single Tour de France is a fabulous athlete.*

FIRST FOREIGNER

Firmin Lambot of Belgium won the 1919 Tour de France on the penultimate day when bad luck ripped the yellow jersey from Eugène Christophe's shoulders. Christophe, a Frenchman, had worn the jersey since it was introduced on stage 4, but this stage ran from Metz to Dunkirk, right across what had been the Western Front of the First World War only a year before. The roads were terrible, cratered by bombs and chewed by tank tracks. Christophe's bike broke, and because the rules stated that a racer had to finish on the bike he started with, Christophe lost hours repairing his. It wasn't the first time bad luck like that struck him either.

← *Firmin Lambot was from Florennes, near Namur, in Belgium. Between his two Tour victories (1919 and 1922) another racer from the same town, Leon Scieur, won in 1921.*

HE WON'T WEAR IT

Louison Bobet was very particular about his health. His dedication took him to three Tour de France victories between 1953 and 1955, but he came to the organizers' attention long before that. In 1947 they secured sponsorship for the yellow jersey, for the first time in Tour history, from a firm called Sofil, who made artificial yarn. Sofil yarn was added to wool to make the 1947 yellow jersey, but when Bobet took over the race lead he refused to wear it, pointing out that only pure wool was healthy to race in and that artificial fibres made the racers sweat too much. The organizers had a pure wool one made for him overnight.

→ *Tom Simpson's Tour story began with glory but ended in tragedy when he died during the 1967 Tour.*

RED LAMP

While the leader of the Tour is referred to as the yellow jersey, the man at the back is called the Lanterne Rouge, or red lamp, so named after the red light that was hung on the back of French trains. He was a figure for sympathy, often an unsponsored racer struggling along on his own. Over time being Lanterne Rouge began to attract fame, and with it contracts to appear in show races, and riders would slow down to win it. The organizers thought this demeaned the Tour, and in 1939 and 1949 under a new rule the last man each day was disqualified. Now the last man in the Tour hardly gets a mention.

FIRST BRITISH YELLOW JERSEY

Tom Simpson took over the lead on stage 12 of the 1962 Tour. He lost the yellow jersey next day, but finished sixth overall, the highest British placing until Robert Millar finished fourth in 1984 and Bradley Wiggins did the same in 2009. Simpson loved playing English stereotypes for the French press, so photographs of him wearing a bowler hat and sipping tea in the yellow jersey appeared in every newspaper in France next day. No other British racer wore yellow until Chris Boardman in 1994. Since then only Sean Yates (1994), Boardman again (1997 and 1998) and David Millar (2000) have worn it.

Not only was Greg LeMond's 1989 victory amazing because of how close it was, but because he'd come back from near death after being shot in a hunting accident.

NARROWEST EVER VICTORY MARGIN

That happened in 1989 when Greg LeMond beat Laurent Fignon by just eight seconds after 3,285.3 kilometres of racing. Fignon led by 58 seconds going into the final stage, a short time trial of 24 kilometres. It ran from Versailles to the Champs-Elysées, a route that recalled a famous march by revolutionaries after the storming of the Bastille 200 years before, and a French victory would have added to the celebrations of 200 years of France as a republic. Fignon was French, from Paris in fact, and his defeat caused intense disappointment – some say that French cycling has never recovered. What's not in doubt is that no Frenchman has won the Tour since 1985.

TOUR WINS BY NATIONS

1.	France	36 wins
2.	Belgium	18 wins
3.	Spain	13 wins
4.	USA	10 wins
5.	Italy	9 wins
6.	Luxembourg	4 wins
7.	Holland	2 wins
=	Switzerland	2 wins
9.	Australia	1 win
=	Denmark	1 win
=	Germany	1 win
=	Ireland	1 win

MELLOW JOHNNY

Yellow jersey is "maillot jaune" in French, which seven times winner Lance Armstrong heard being pronounced as "mellow Johnny" in his native Texas. When Armstrong opened a bike shop in Austin, he called it Mellow Johnny's.

NO YELLOW JERSEY

Five riders have refused to wear the yellow jersey, and on each occasion it was because the former leader had suffered a setback, causing him to leave the race. Each new leader chivalrously waited a day before wearing it, except for one who was not allowed to. Growing increasingly unhappy about the tradition because it deprived the yellow jersey sponsors of publicity, in 2005 the organizers insisted that Lance Armstrong wear the jersey after he started a stage in his normal team kit. He had to stop on the road, get changed and sprint back to the race.

EIGHT CHANGES

The record number of different racers wearing the yellow jersey in a single Tour is eight, and it happened in 1958 and 1987. On the second occasion, when Stephen Roche won for Ireland, he wore the jersey early on, lost it and then regained it, so it actually changed hands ten times during the race.

FIRST AMERICAN

In 1986 Alex Stieda became the first rider from North America to wear the yellow jersey. Stieda was Canadian and racing for the first American team to enter, 7-Eleven, who were also making their Tour debut that year. He took it by finishing fifth on stage 2, but lost it during the next stage, a team time trial. He wore all four jerseys at various times in his first and only Tour de France.

→ *Alex Stieda was derided for wearing a skinsuit, most often used for time trials. But, on the short stage 2, it made him more aerodynamic and gave him a place in history.*

THE KING OF THE MOUNTAINS

Other prizes are awarded in the Tour de France, and the one for King of the Mountains is the most prestigious after the yellow jersey. Riding up hills is difficult, so everyone, even if they don't regularly ride a bike, can imagine that cycling over mountains is incredibly hard. That's why the best climbers in the Tour de France command respect, and of all the riders they are among the most popular with the fans.

Lucien Van Impe wears the polka-dot jersey of the King of the Mountains. Of all the great climbers who have ridden the Tour, Van Impe is arguably the best.

THE KING OF THE MOUNTAINS

There has always been a fascination with the climbing aces of the Tour de France. Slight of build, with a taste for heroics and high theatre, they are cycling's most enigmatic characters. A true climber seems to sprout wings and fly upwards, defying the very gravity that binds the rest of us to the earth.

↑ *The 'Angel of the Mountains' (Charly Gaul, middle) leads while the 'Eagle of Toledo' (Federico Bahamontes) watches in yellow from behind.*

THE ANGEL OF THE MOUNTAINS

Charly Gaul of Luxembourg won the Tour a year before his great Spanish rival Bahamontes. The "Angel of the Mountains" was a small man with thinning hair who excelled in bad weather. Unusually for a great climber, Gaul could also time trial, and in 1958 he beat Bahamontes against the watch up Mont Ventoux and then gained over 14 minutes on race favourite Raphaël Géminiani after an epic escape across the Chartreuse mountains in torrential rain. Unpredictable and secretive, Gaul only won the mountains prize twice, in 1955 and 1956, and became a recluse in retirement, putting on weight and looking like Burl Ives with his long beard.

THE SPANISH FLEA

Vicente Trueba of Spain, riding as an independent touriste-routier, was the first winner of the grand prix de la montagne in 1933. He did not win a stage but was first over the Cols d'Aspin, Aubisque, Peyresourde, Tourmalet, the Vars, Ballon d'Alsace and the mighty Col du Galibier, and had he been less of a nervous descender the "Spanish Flea" might well have achieved more than his best overall finish of sixth. He did not wear the dazzling white and red spotted top either, as the introduction of the polka-dot jersey did not take place until many years later in 1975.

➜ *Tiny Trueba had the almost skeletal physique that many climbers share.*

RETAINING THE TITLE

Charly Gaul of Luxembourg was the first rider to succeed in retaining the mountains title (1955 and 1956). Since then seven men have achieved the feat, with Richard Virenque of France the record holder, winning four consecutive mountains titles between 1994 and 1997, as well as one in 1999, and two more in 2003 and 2004.

MOUNTAIN KING

Belgium's Félicien Vervaecke was the first rider to win the mountains title twice (1935 and 1937). He also finished on the Tour podium three times, but never won overall. However, when he stopped racing, Vervaecke opened a bike shop called Le Roi des Montagnes in the Brussels suburb where a young Eddy Merckx lived. Vervaecke became Merckx's first coach and set him on his way to winning five Tours.

TOP OF THE WORLD

Richard Virenque holds the outright record for polka-dot wins, a record that was previously shared between two of the all-time great climbers of the Tour: Federico Bahamontes and Lucien van Impe. Van Impe claims that he could have won more, but stopped trying after he'd equalled the six wins of Bahamontes, out of respect for his hero, and the man who helped him early in his career. Van Impe is also quite scathing of Virenque's triumphs, suggesting that modern Tours don't favour true climbers, and that Virenque wasn't a true climber. "True climbers can change pace, once, twice, three times on the same mountain, and when they do, no one can follow," he says. "Virenque couldn't do it. A true climber can win the Tour like that. Virenque didn't win."

← *Richard Virenque won the most mountains titles because it was largely what he focused on, but he did finish second overall in 1997. Others have won the King of the Mountains, but also tried, sometimes successfully, to win the Tour as well.*

YELLOW CLIMBERS

Lucien van Impe won six polka-dot jerseys between 1971 and 1983, winning the Tour in 1976. He made full use of his compact physique and hard training on the short cobbled climbs of his native Flanders. In the modern era it is much harder for pure climbers to win the Tour, such is the all-round prowess of the overall contenders over the big mountains and especially in the time trials, which never favour lightweight climbing aces. Only two climbing specialists have won the Tour since van Impe: Carlos Sastre of Spain who won on one climb, Alpe d'Huez in 2008, and Italy's Marco Pantani in 1998. His electrifying attack in pouring rain to Les Deux Alpes toppled Jan Ullrich with enough of a margin for him to hold off the German in the final week. Pantani is the finest climber never to have won the polka-dot jersey.

THE KINGS OF THE MOUNTAINS

Year	Rider	Country	Year	Rider	Country	Year	Rider	Country
2011	Samuel Sanchez	Spain	1987	Luis Herrera	Colombia	1963	Federico Bahamontes	Spain
2010	Anthony Charteau	France	1986	Bernard Hinault	France	1962	Federico Bahamontes	Spain
2009	Franco Pellizotti	Italy	1985	Luis Herrera	Colombia	1961	Imerio Massignan	Italy
2008	Bernard Kohl	Austria	1984	Robert Millar	Great Britain	1960	Imerio Massignan	Italy
2007	Juan-Mauricio Soler	Columbia	1983	Lucien van Impe	Belgium	1959	Federico Bahamontes	Spain
2006	Michael Rasmussen	Denmark	1982	Bernard Vallet	France	1958	Federico Bahamontes	Spain
2005	Michael Rasmussen	Denmark	1981	Lucien van Impe	Belgium	1957	Gastone Nencini	Italy
2004	Richard Virenque	France	1980	Raymond Martin	France	1956	Charly Gaul	Luxembourg
2003	Richard Virenque	France	1979	Giovanni Battaglin	Italy	1955	Charly Gaul	Luxembourg
2002	Laurent Jalabert	France	1978	Mariano Martinez	France	1954	Federico Bahamontes	Spain
2001	Laurent Jalabert	France	1977	Lucien van Impe	Belgium	1953	Jésus Lorono	Spain
2000	Santiago Botero	Colombia	1976	Giancarlo Bellini	Italy	1952	Fausto Coppi	Italy
1999	Richard Virenque	France	1975	Lucien van Impe	Belgium	1951	Raphaël Géminiani	France
1998	Christophe Rinero	France	1974	Domingo Perurena	Spain	1950	Louison Bobet	France
1997	Richard Virenque	France	1973	Pedro Torres	Spain	1949	Fausto Coppi	Italy
1996	Richard Virenque	France	1972	Lucien van Impe	Belgium	1948	Gino Bartali	Italy
1995	Richard Virenque	France	1971	Lucien van Impe	Belgium	1947	Pierre Brambilla	Italy
1994	Richard Virenque	France	1970	Eddy Merckx	Belgium	1939	Sylvère Maes	Belgium
1993	Tony Rominger	Switzerland	1969	Eddy Merckx	Belgium	1938	Gino Bartali	Italy
1992	Claudio Chiappucci	Italy	1968	Aurelio Gonzalez	Spain	1937	Félicien Vervaecke	Belgium
1991	Claudio Chiappucci	Italy	1967	Julio Jimenez	Spain	1936	Julian Berrendero	Spain
1990	Thierry Claveyrolat	France	1966	Julio Jimenez	Spain	1935	Félicien Vervaecke	Belgium
1989	Gert-Jan Theunisse	Netherlands	1965	Julio Jimenez	Spain	1934	René Vietto	France
1988	Steven Rooks	Netherlands	1964	Federico Bahamontes	Spain	1933	Vicente Trueba	Spain

HOME ON THE RANGE

The Vosges proved that cyclists could climb mountains, so in 1910 the Tour de France went to the Pyrenean mountain range, and in 1911 it visited the highest road passes in the Alps for the first time.

⬆ *Not only did the Tour pioneers have to cope with mountain terrain on totally unsuitable bikes, they had to cope with roads made for horse and carts.*

WHO'S THE DADDY?

There's a lot of debate about who was the best King of the Mountains. Richard Virenque won the title seven times, but although he was a very good climber he won because he went for every point on every hill he could, which some climbers think is not how to get the job done. Charly Gaul only won the title twice, but he was a far better climber than Virenque. Federico Bahamontes won six titles so has a bona fide claim, but he also has an opinion about who should get it. "The greatest climber of all time is Lucien van Impe of Belgium," says the Eagle of Toledo.

POLKA DOTS

Since 1975 the leader of the King of the Mountains competition always wears a white jersey covered in red spots. In French it's the Maillot à Pois, and English speakers call it the polka-dot jersey. The colours and design were chosen by the then joint race organizer, Félix Lévitan, who had seen the same jersey being worn by a track racer at the Paris indoor track, the Vélodrome d'Hiver, during the 1930s and liked it.

➡ *Olympic road race champion, Samuel Sanchez was the 2011 King of the Mountains, the latest in a long line of top Spanish climbers.*

POINTS MEAN PRIZES

All the mountains, plus some of the longer or steeper hills, on the Tour route are classified according to how difficult they are, where difficulty is a function of steepness and length. The climbs are then awarded points, the fourth-category climbs being worth the lowest number of points and the first-category climbs the highest – except that there is also another category, Hors Catégorie, meaning beyond category, and these climbs get the most points of all.

MOUNTAIN POINTS

This is how the points were awarded during the 2011 Tour de France:

Hors Catégorie:

20, 16, 12, 8, 4 and 2 points to the first six racers to the summit

First category:

10, 8, 6, 4, 2 and 1 point to the first six racers to the summit

Second category:

5, 3, 2 and 1 point to the first four racers to the summit

Third category:

2 and 1 point to the first two racers to the summit

Fourth category:

1 point to the first racer to the summit

THE GIANT OF PROVENCE

Climbing heroes of the Tour de France are not always lightly built sparrows. Some are cart horses who throw everything into a single day of glory over the mountains. One such rider was Eros Poli, one of the tallest and heaviest riders in the 1994 Tour, who attacked early on stage 15 and went on a long lone breakaway from Montpellier to Carpentras (231km). The final obstacle was the fearsome Mont Ventoux, the "Giant of Provence", and Poli arrived at its foot with 22 minutes in hand over the bunch. He needed every second of that advantage as he winched his way agonizingly up the moonscape flanks of the mountain pushed up by volcanic swell or action. At the top he had just four minutes in hand over the field and plummeted into Carpentras for an emotional, and highly improbable, mountain stage win.

➔ *No Tour racer was built less like a climber than Eros Poli, but he won where many great climbers can only dream of doing the same.*

MOUNTAIN TOP TEN

The ten highest climbs in the Tour are:

1.	The Col de la Bonette	2,802 metres	Alps
2.	Col d'Iseran	2,770 metres	Alps
3.	Col d'Agnel	2,744 metres	Alps
4.	Col du Galibier	2,646 metres	Alps
5.	Grand St-Bernard	2,470 metres	Alps
6.	Port d'Envalira	2,408 metres	Pyrenees
7.	Col du Granon	2,404 metres	Alps
8.	Val Thorens	2,275 metres	Alps
9.	Col d'Allos	2,250 metres	Alps
10.	Arcalis	2,240 metres	Pyrenees

BEAR ATTACK

Henri Desgrange was a worrier, and one of the things that worried him most during stage 10 of the 1910 Tour, the one that climbed the highest peaks the race had so far, the Peyresourde, Aspin, Tourmalet and Aubisque, was attacks on the riders by bears. Bears were quite common in the Pyrenees in those days, and on the highest slopes, where there would be no spectators for miles on end, the prospect of a bear picking off a back-marker was real. There are still some indigenous bears high in the Pyrenees today, plus some imported Slovenian bears in the Col de Marie Blanque area.

➔ *Henri Desgrange worried when his race first entered the mountains, but he grew to love them. He's remembered by this huge memorial on the south side of the Col de Galibier.*

FASTER THAN A CAR

The first Tour de France route in 1903 included a number of hills, but the organizers didn't deliberately seek them out. They wanted to, though, and in 1905 they routed the Tour over a genuine mountain called the Ballon d'Alsace in the Vosges range. Henri Desgrange thought the riders would have to get off and walk up at least some of it, but instead René Pottier rode all the way to the top, beating Desgrange in his race official's car.

SOUVENIR HENRI DESGRANGE

This prize is awarded each year to the rider who crosses the highest point of the race in the lead. In 2011 it was awarded to Maxim Iglinsky of Kazakhstan for leading over the Col d'Agnel.

BRITISH KING OF THE MOUNTAINS

Robert Millar is the only British racer to win the King of the Mountains title. He achieved it in 1984 when he was also fourth overall in the Tour. Millar, who was born in Glasgow, won three Tour stages, all of them in the mountains. He is one of the great climbers of cycling, having also won the King of the Mountains competition in the Tour of Italy.

← *Robert Millar, Britain's only true "grimpeur", racing in his element.*

LOAD OF BOTTLE

The key to being a good climber in the Tour de France is to have a high power to weight ratio. There are limits on how much power a human being can put out, which is why the weight side of that equation is crucial to a climber. The lightest are often the best, and good climbers try to make their bikes as light as possible too. This can be a disadvantage when descending, and it's one that an excellent climber called Jean Robic, who won the 1947 Tour, tried to counter by having a bottle filled with lead shot handed to him by a helper at the top of climbs. He claimed the extra weight on his bike helped him descend quicker, although some Tour historians think Robic made up the story to enliven an interview. He was a bit like that.

⬇ *Colombians from the high peaks of the Andes added South American spice during the 1980s.*

EXTREME WEATHER

During the summer, when the Tour de France is held, the high mountains have a very capricious climate. On the same day in different years the same mountain can be bathed in sweltering heat or be blocked by snow. The King of the Mountains must be able to deal with both conditions. In addition the Pyrenees in particular are noted for thunderstorms that can strike at any time.

IMPROVING ROADS

When they first climbed the mountains, the roads the riders raced on in the Pyrenees and Alps were just muddy, rutted farm tracks. These were replaced over the years by hard-packed gravel, and later by tarmac and other metalled surfaces. The solid surfaces allow fans to paint the names of their favourites, and any other slogan or funny picture they can think of, on the road. One of the best road paintings was picked up on a mountain pass a couple of years ago by one of the TV helicopters that follow the Tour. It read: "Hello Mum, don't say I never write you."

EL JARDINIERO

This was the nickname of Colombia's finest Tour de France cyclist, Lucho Herrera. He won three mountain stages in the Tour, and was King of the Mountains in 1985 and 1987, when he also finished fifth overall. Herrera got his nickname because before his cycling career he was a flower picker in Colombia.

HEAVYWEIGHT KINGS

Not all Kings of the Mountains have the archetypal bird-like climber's build. Eddy Merckx, who as well as winning the Tour five times also took the mountains title twice, was six feet tall and weighed more than 12 stone. The 2001 and 2002 mountains king, Laurent Jalabert of France, was another bigger racer. Jalabert started his cycling career as a sprinter and won the green jersey, the Tour's sprint award, in 1992 and '95 before changing the kind of racer he was and becoming a better climber.

⬇ *Laurent Jalabert changed from being a sprinter to a climber and also became King of the Mountains.*

RATIO OF CLIMBS

Figures taken from the 2010 Tour

Fourth category	20 climbs
Third category	12 climbs
Second category	9 climbs
First category	10 climbs
Hors Catégorie	6 climbs

CATEGORY CHANGES

It's rare but some climbs change category from year to year depending on which side they are climbed from. For example, the Col du Petit St-Bernard in the Alps has been in four Tours, but it was second category in 1949, first in 1959, second in 1963 and first in 2009. Obviously the climb didn't change its gradient or character in all those years: categorization is basically just an arbitrary decision made by the organizers at the time.

COLOMBIAN COFFEE

In 1983 the Colombian national team took part in the Tour de France for the first time, backed by the Café de Colombia coffee company. With a background of racing in the Andes their riders made a big impression on the Tour de France over the following ten years, and Café de Colombia became a sponsor of the polka-dot jersey.

CLIMBING STYLE

Even among the best climbers of the Tour de France, styles have differed a lot. Riders like Lucien van Impe and Charly Gaul used low gears, spinning their legs quickly. They were capable of searing changes of pace, which their competitors could not match. Sports science theory says their way is best, as quickly revving a low gear puts less strain on muscles, and if the rider stays seated, this method of pedalling is energy efficient too. But there are great climbers who went against that theory, notably the two Spaniards, Julio Jimenez and Federico Bahamontes. They used higher gears, grinding out their attacks and making them stick by pedalling out of the saddle for lengthy uphill bursts.

↗ *No appliance of science for Julio Jimenez as he grinds out another leg-breaking attack.*

CLIMATE CHANGE

If you want evidence of the changing global climate, all you need to do is study pictures of the Tour de France. In the 1920s and '30s almost every picture from the high mountains shows riders racing between high banks of snow. These begin to disappear during the fifties, although they can still be seen in some shots from the 1960s. You never see this now, and even the glaciers in the background on climbs like the Col de Galibier, which is climbed in most Tours, have clearly retreated up their valleys.

➔ *When you see numerous fans at the top of mountain passes today, dressed in shorts and T-shirts (often a lot less), it's hard to believe this is how the same places used to look.*

THE GREEN JERSEY

Points are awarded to the riders as they cross the finish line at the end of each stage, and at intermediate points along the route. More points are awarded on the stages raced over flat or rolling terrain than in the mountains or time trials, and flat or rolling stages tend to be won by the sprinters, so the green jersey is the sprinter's prize in the Tour de France.

Mark Cavendish was the green jersey in 2012, and is the fastest sprinter in the world today. His prodigious list of stage wins has already made him part of the records of the Tour de France.

THE GREEN JERSEY

In 1953, to celebrate the Tour's 50th birthday, the organizers decided to award points on each stage for the first finishers across the line, and give a prize to the racer who amassed the highest number of points through the three weeks of the race. The points contest was called the Grand Prix Cinquantenaire, and a green jersey was used to denote the leader, so it became called the green jersey competition. It proved popular with the riders, because it gave them something else to go for in the race. It was a chance to earn more money.

FIRST WINNER

A Swiss racer, Fritz Schaer, won the first Grand Prix Cinquantenaire. He was a good sprinter, and sprinters tend to win the green jersey simply because more stages suit them in the Tour than suit the climbers and those who are trying to win the race overall.

WHAT MAKES A TOUR SPRINTER?

Because a racer saves energy by slipstreaming it's very difficult to get significant time gaps on flat stages. In the mountains, where slipstreaming is a lesser factor, or in individual time trials, where it's not a factor at all, it's possible for talented climbers or time triallists to gain time on the rest. This means that on a flat or rolling stage, where riders are able to follow each other relatively easily, it's quite common for the stage to be decided by a big sprint at the end involving the whole field. This favours riders who have an explosive turn of speed. If they save energy following in the bunch and then use their speed at the end they can win the stage.

↑ *Switzerland's Fritz Schaer leads the peloton on the stage between Pau and Cauterets in 1953, on his way to winning the inaugural points race.*

ALL THREE JERSEYS

Eddy Merckx is the only man ever to win all three jerseys in one Tour de France. It happened during Merckx's first Tour, in 1969, when he won overall by over 20 minutes. He dominated the race totally. Merckx is accepted by many experts to be the greatest male road racer ever.

← *Eddy Merckx displays all three jerseys in 1969. the white jersey is for leader of the defunct combined classification, there was no climber's jersey until 1975.*

2011 TOUR DE FRANCE POINTS DISTRIBUTION

Stage Type	1st	2nd	3rd	4th	5th	6th	7th	8th	9th	10th	11th	12th	13th	14th	15th
Flat	45	35	30	26	22	20	18	16	14	12	10	8	6	4	2
Medium mountain	30	25	22	19	17	15	13	11	9	7	6	5	4	3	2
High mountain	20	17	15	13	11	10	9	8		7	6	5	4	3	1
Time trial	20	17	15	13	11	10	9	8	7	6	5	4	3	2	1
Intermediate	20	17	15	13	11	10	9	8	7	6	5	4	3	2	1

→ *No one has rivalled Erik Zabel's dominance of the green jersey yet.*

CHOOSING THE COLOUR

Green was chosen as the colour for this jersey because it was the predominant colour used by first sponsors La Belle Jardinière in their logos and advertising. All other sponsors of the points competition have gone along with this, except for Sodas Sic in 1968 who insisted on the jersey being red.

GREEN CAP

During the 1970s there was a team points competition, and the members of the leading team were given a green racing cap to wear.

↑ *Britain's Barry Hoban decorates his green cap with cabbage leaves, an old Tour trick to help keep the sun off.*

MOST VICTORIES

Erik Zabel of Germany won the green jersey six consecutive times: in 1996, 1997, 1998, 1999, 2000 and 2001. The rider who has come closest to matching him is Irishman Sean Kelly, who won four: in 1982, 1983, 1985 and 1989.

WHY CAN'T SPRINTERS CLIMB?

It's that power to weight thing again. Riders who can sprint tend to be heavily muscled, and heavily muscled riders find their weight a handicap when climbing. They have plenty of power but it's at the cost of heavy muscles. There is also a difference in muscle fibre type between sprinters and climbers: a sprinter's muscle is less able to maintain the high constant pace required for success in the mountains. Again, sprinters have the power but it tends to come all in one burst, and doesn't spread over an entire mountain or series of mountains.

SPRINTER'S WEIGHTING

The green jersey competition has became more weighted towards sprinters over the years by the awarding of more points on flat and rolling stages than in the mountains or in a time trial. There are also intermediate points along the route where points are awarded, and these suit sprinters too. Even on a mountain stage there might be some points available early on, and if the climbing hasn't started the sprinters will win them. The green jersey was given the ultimate sprinter weighting in 2011 when the points for an intermediate sprint were made the same as for a high mountain or time trial stage.

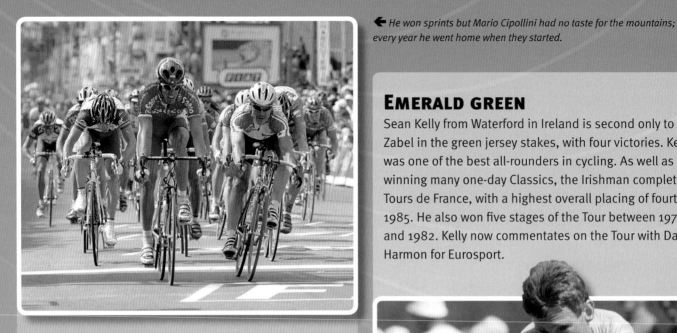

He won sprints but Mario Cipollini had no taste for the mountains; every year he went home when they started.

EMERALD GREEN

Sean Kelly from Waterford in Ireland is second only to Erik Zabel in the green jersey stakes, with four victories. Kelly was one of the best all-rounders in cycling. As well as winning many one-day Classics, the Irishman completed 12 Tours de France, with a highest overall placing of fourth in 1985. He also won five stages of the Tour between 1978 and 1982. Kelly now commentates on the Tour with David Harmon for Eurosport.

JULIUS CAESAR

Not all the great sprinters of the Tour de France have won the green jersey. Mario Cipollini was one of the fastest ever sprinters in cycling. He won 12 stages in the Tour de France but never made it to the finish of the whole race. Cipollini was a poor climber, and the Alps and Pyrenees always proved too much for him. However, he enlivened the Tour in other ways. For example, in 1999, to celebrate Julius Caesar's birthday, he came to the start line dressed as the Roman emperor. He often disregarded the rules of the Tour regarding team strip, and was fined several times for wearing non-approved kit. Cipollini exasperated the organizers of the Tour so much that he wasn't invited to the race between 2000 and 2003, although his team also wasn't thought to be strong enough to take part.

The racers head through Cannes in 1910. This image is one of the first colour pictures of the Tour.

Sean Kelly was a tough sprinter who always fought through to the finish in Paris. He finished 12 times out of 14 starts.

ALL ON POINTS

Between 1906 and 1912 the points winner was also the Tour de France winner. The organizers thought that deciding the race on points would stop what had happened during the first two Tours. Partisan fans had ambushed riders, holding them back until their favourite built up a big lead. Deciding the race on points reduced the instances of this, because it didn't matter if someone won a stage by one hour or a second; he was still only one point ahead. The problem was that the points system favoured consistent rather than brilliant racers, so in 1913 the race was decided on elapsed time and it has been ever since.

WINNERS OF THE POINTS RACE (GREEN JERSEY)

Year	Rider	Country	Year	Rider	Country
1953	Fritz Schaer	Switzerland	1983	Sean Kelly	Ireland
1954	Ferdy Kubler	Switzerland	1984	Frank Hoste	Belgium
1955	Stan Ockers	Belgium	1985	Sean Kelly	Ireland
1956	Stan Ockers	Belgium	1986	Eric Vanderaeden	Belgium
1957	Jean Forestier	France	1987	Jean-Paul van Poppel	Holland
1958	Jean Graczyck	France	1988	Eddy Planckaert	Belgium
1959	André Darrigade	France	1989	Sean Kelly	Ireland
1960	Jean Graczyck	France	1990	Olaf Ludwig	Germany
1961	André Darrigade	France	1991	Djamolidine Abdoujaparov	Uzbekistan
1962	Rudi Altig	Germany	1992	Laurent Jalabert	France
1963	Rik van Looy	Italy	1993	Djamolidine Abdoujaparov	Uzbekistan
1964	Jan Janssen	Holland	1994	Djamolidine Abdoujaparov	Uzbekistan
1965	Jan Janssen	Holland	1995	Laurent Jalabert	France
1966	Willy Planckaert	Belgium	1996	Erik Zabel	Germany
1967	Jan Janssen	Holland	1997	Erik Zabel	Germany
1968	Franco Bitossi	Italy	1998	Erik Zabel	Germany
1969	Eddy Merckx	Belgium	1999	Erik Zabel	Germany
1970	Walter Godefroot	Belgium	2000	Erik Zabel	Germany
1971	Eddy Merckx	Belgium	2001	Erik Zabel	Germany
1972	Eddy Merckx	Belgium	2002	Robbie McEwen	Australia
1973	Herman van Springel	Belgium	2003	Baden Cooke	Australia
1974	Patrick Sercu	Belgium	2004	Robbie McEwen	Australia
1975	Rik van Linden	Belgium	2005	Thor Hushovd	Norway
1976	Freddy Maertens	Belgium	2006	Robbie McEwen	Australia
1977	Jacques Esclasson	France	2007	Tom Boonen	Belgium
1978	Freddy Maertens	Belgium	2008	Oscar Freire	Spain
1979	Bernard Hinault	France	2009	Thor Hushovd	Norway
1980	Rudy Pevenage	Belgium	2010	Alessandro Petacci	Italy
1981	Freddy Maertens	Belgium	2011	Mark Cavendish	GB
1982	Sean Kelly	Ireland			

⬆ *Thor Hushovd won the green jersey in 2005 and 2009, so far the only Norwegian to do so.*

MIGHTY THOR

For the 2011 Tour they changed the green jersey rules slightly to favour the fastest sprinters. This made the competition less open, which some fans don't like. However, it reverses a recent trend for all-round racers to be winning green. Thor Hushovd of Norway, for instance, won in 2009 by finishing consistently just behind Mark Cavendish in the sprints, then making a long breakaway in the mountains to gain points that a racer like Cavendish had no chance of getting because he's not such a good climber. Hushovd was helped by the race judges relegating Cavendish to last on one stage for appearing to impede Hushovd.

NOTHING IN IT

The narrowest winning margin in the green jersey competition was two points. It happened in 2003 when Australian Baden Cooke beat his countryman and arch-rival Robbie McEwen. It took the final sprint on the Champs-Elysées to separate them. It wasn't the first time they clashed either – in one 2002 stage finish they were leaning on each other as they crossed the line at over 40 miles per hour, each trying to lever himself ahead of the other.

⬅ *The sprint rivalry between Baden Cooke and Robbie McEwen (far right) boiled over at times.*

THE WHITE JERSEY

The white jersey in the Tour de France goes to the highest-placed young rider in the overall standings. The first white jersey of each Tour is awarded to the fastest young rider after the first stage, and the competition continues until Paris, where the young rider who has completed the whole route in the lowest time wins the classification overall. The white jersey is a good guide to future success, and a number of winners have later won the Tour de France, but it's not infallible because more white jerseys haven't won the Tour than have.

Because the Tour de France tends to favour experience, the white jersey competition was created for younger riders. Some winners have gone on to win the yellow jersey, and a few have even won both at the same time.

THE WHITE JERSEY

As well as being for younger riders, the white jersey is the youngest competition in the Tour de France. It was first awarded in 1975, dropped from the Tour in 1989, only to be reintroduced in 2000. Before 1975 there was a different white jersey competition, for the highest combined points total in the overall and King of the Mountains competitions. It was called the "combine" competition, and when the white jersey was switched to the best young rider, the combine jersey became a mix of the yellow, green and polka dots. It was confusing, and so was the competition. The combine competition was dropped in 1989.

YOUNG PRIZES

The winner takes 20,000 euros from a purse of 66,500 euros. The sponsors of the white jersey competition are Skoda, who also supply vehicles for the Tour de France.

⬆ *In 1983 Laurent Fignon of France (far left) became the first cyclist to win the white and yellow jerseys in the same Tour.*

JAN THE MAN

Jan Ullrich of Germany is the king of the white jersey, winning it three times in a row, 1996, 1997 and 1998. He also won the yellow jersey in 1997. Ullrich shares the record for white jerseys with Luxembourg's Andy Schleck (2008, 2009 and 2010). Schleck was awarded the 2010 Tour in 2012 after Alberto Contador had been stripped of the win for a doping offence.

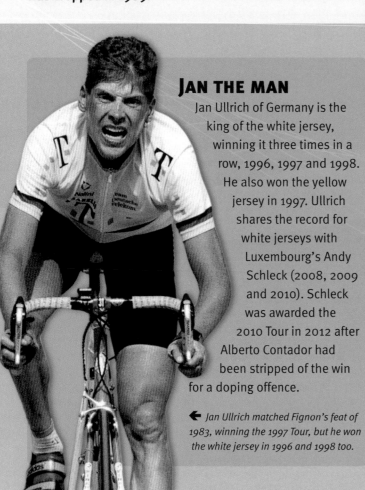

⬅ *Jan Ullrich matched Fignon's feat of 1983, winning the 1997 Tour, but he won the white jersey in 1996 and 1998 too.*

YELLOW AND WHITE

When Laurent Fignon of France won the white jersey in 1983, he also won the Tour de France overall. His feat was equalled by Jan Ullrich in 1997, Alberto Contador in 2007 and Andy Schleck in 2010. Fignon was called "the Professor" by bike fans, simply because he wore round, steel-framed spectacles. He was famous later in his pro career for wearing his long blond hair in a ponytail. He won the Tour again in 1984. Sadly, Laurent Fignon died from cancer in 2010. The only other riders to win both white and yellow jerseys, though not in the same year, were Greg LeMond and Marco Pantani.

THE CYCLING POLITICIAN

The 1985 white jersey, Fabio Parra, was thought at the time to be a potential Tour de France winner for Colombia. The South American country had produced a number of great climbers, but none of them could time trial very well and some weren't adept at riding in fast groups on flat stages. Tour winners need both those skills, and Parra had them. However, third in 1988 was the highest he ever got in the yellow jersey stakes, which still makes Parra the highest overall Tour de France finisher from South America. After he stopped racing, Parra did an MBA and opened a plastics business. Now pursuing a political career, he ran for the Colombian senate in the Cambio Radical party in 2011, but was defeated.

Up or Down

Since the competition started, the average overall position of the white jersey winner in the Tour de France has been ninth. The lowest placing overall was Fabrice Philipot in 1989, who came 24th. Seventeen racers have finished worse than ninth, and 17 have finished better than ninth. The worst periods for young riders in the Tour were between 1988 and 1993 and between 2002 and 2006, when no white jersey winner finished in the top ten.

← *The first ever white jersey winner was Francesco Moser in 1975.*

White Jersey Winners

Year	Rider	Country	Overall position
1975	Francesco Moser	Italy	7th
1976	Enrique Martinez-Heredia	Spain	23rd
1977	Dietrich Thurau	Germany	5th
1978	Henk Lubberding	Holland	8th
1979	Jean-René Bernaudeau	France	5th
1980	Johan van der Velde	Holland	12th
1981	Peter Winnen	Holland	5th
1982	Phil Anderson	Australia	5th
1983	Laurent Fignon	France	1st
1984	Greg LeMond	USA	3rd
1985	Fabio Parra	Columbia	8th
1986	Andrew Hampsten	USA	4th
1987	Raul Alcala	Mexico	9th
1988	Erik Breukink	Holland	12th
1989	Fabrice Philipot	France	24th
1990	Gilles Delion	France	15th
1991	Alvaro Mejia	Columbia	19th
1992	Eddy Bouwmans	Holland	14th
1993	Antonio Martin Velasco	Spain	12th
1994	Marco Pantani	Italy	3rd
1995	Marco Pantani	Italy	13th
1996	Jan Ullrich	Germany	2nd
1997	Jan Ullrich	Germany	1st
1998	Jan Ullrich	Germany	2nd
1999	Benoit Salmon	France	16th
2000	Francisco Mancebo	Spain	9th
2001	Oscar Sevilla	Spain	7th
2002	Ivan Basso	Italy	11th
2003	Denis Menchov	Russia	11th
2004	Vladimir Karpets	Russia	13th
2005	Yaroslav Popovych	Ukraine	12th
2006	Damiano Cunego	Italy	12th
2007	Alberto Contador	Spain	1st
2008	Andy Schleck	Luxembourg	12th
2009	Andy Schleck	Luxembourg	2nd
2010	Andy Schleck	Luxembourg	1st
2011	Pierre Rolland	France	11th

First Youngster

Francesco Moser of Italy was the first rider to win the white jersey for best young rider. He did it in 1975, when he finished a promising seventh overall and won the prologue time trial plus one other stage. Moser was a better rider in single-day races than he was at Grand Tours like the Tour de France, although he did win the 1984 Tour of Italy. He was world champion in 1977, and broke Eddy Merckx's world hour record in 1984. He won the Paris–Roubaix Classic three times, and won a number of other big single-day races.

↑ *Henk Lubberding, seen here following the yellow jersey Bernard Hinault on the final stage, took the white jersey home to Holland in 1978.*

⬆ *France hasn't won the Tour de France for more than 25 years. Will the 2011 white jersey Pierre Rolland break the trend?*

THE HOPE OF FRANCE

France has not won its biggest bike race since 1986, but 2011 saw Pierre Rolland become the first Frenchman since Gilles Delion in 1990 to win the white jersey. He achieved this at 24, having been a pro for four years, and as well as his high overall placing of 11th in what was his first Tour de France in 2011, Rolland won the stage that finished on Alpe d'Huez. That is one of the most famous stages in the Tour de France, and only the best racers win on top of the Alpe, but Rolland did so while trying to help his team-mate Thomas Voeckler hang on to the yellow jersey. He is definitely a candidate for winning of the Tour one day.

EASTERN PROMISE

All the western European nations apart from Great Britain have won at least one Tour de France, but there has never been a winner from the former eastern bloc. This is despite Denis Menchov and Vladimir Karpets of Russia winning the white jersey in 2003 and 2004 respectively, and Yaroslav Popovych taking the title for Ukraine in 2005.

FIRST FOR MEXICO

Raúl Alcála was the first Mexican racer to ride the Tour. His debut year was 1986, and in 1987 he finished ninth overall and won the white jersey. Alcala finished another six Tours, winning two stages and finishing eighth overall in 1989 and 1990.

JOBS FOR THE BOYS

A lot of former Tour de France riders still work on the race, either for the organization, in the media or as team managers. The 1979 white jersey winner, Jean-René Bernaudeau, is one of the longest-serving team managers. For over 20 years he has been attracting sponsors to fund his team. It's based in the Vendée, his home region on France's Atlantic coast, and where possible Bernaudeau prefers to employ Vendean racers. Pierre Rolland races for Bernaudeau's current team, which is sponsored by car hire firm Europcar.

➡ *Jean-René Bernaudeau rode the 1979 Tour. He's now behind the wheel of a team car.*

MANY COLOURS

As well as yellow caps for the overall team leaders on time, green ones for the team leading on points, and a combined jersey for the race's best all-rounder, who was most often the yellow jersey anyway, another Tour de France competition that is no more is the red jersey. This was given to the leader of a competition based entirely on points awarded for the intermediate sprints on each stage.

← *Greg LeMond (riding behind Urs Zimmerman) wore the combined jersey in 1986.*

RED NUMBER

This is still awarded, and it's the Prix de la Combativité award, going to the rider who spends the longest time on the attack, away from the peloton during a stage. Instead of the usual black number on a white background, this aggressive racer is given a black number printed on a red background to wear during the next stage. At the end of the Tour the most combative racer gets awarded the overall prize. It has a long history: during the first Tour in 1903, a prize of 100 old francs was given to the rider who in the opinion of the race judges "finished the course, even if unplaced, who is particularly distinguished by the energy he has used". Nowadays the combativity prize is 20,000 euros for first overall from a purse of 56,000 euros, because like the yellow, green and polka-dot jersey wearers, the red number gets paid each day it is on his back. The red number competition sponsors are Brandt.

TEAM AWARD

The winning team in the Tour de France is the one whose best three riders complete the entire route in the shortest total added time. There's nothing to wear that shows who is leading (although at one time yellow caps were sported), but among the teams this competition is treated as a matter of pride. And, of course, there's prize money that's worth having too – 50,000 euros for first team out of a total of 176,000.

AUSSIE, AUSSIE, AUSSIE

The first native English speaker to win the white jersey was Phil Anderson of Australia. His country has a long relationship with the Tour de France: the first Australians, Don Kirkham and Ivor Munro, rode the Tour in 1914, long before any British or American racer. And a little later, Hubert, later Sir Hubert, Opperman was one of the best racers in Europe. He competed in the 1928 and 1932 Tours, but was hampered by lack of team support in races that were decided on a complicated team scoring basis. Anderson was a still a pioneer when he won white in 1982. He was fifth overall that year, and fifth again in 1985. His success spurred more Aussies on to live and race in Europe, and Cadel Evans eventually won the Tour in 2011.

→ *Phil Anderson played a huge part in the Australian cycling story that led to Cadel Evans winning the Tour in 2011.*

GRANDS DÉPARTS

The start of each Tour de France is called the Grand Départ. This is the place where the Tour starts its annual trip around France, nowadays often visiting one or more neighbouring countries. The first Grand Départ was from the Paris suburb of Montgeron, and the race started and finished in the French capital every year until 1926, when the Grand Départ was in Evian. Since then, although the Tour always finishes in Paris it has only started there once, in 2003, and the Grand Départ shifts every year. On several occasions it has even been staged outside of France.

The Grand Départ is a chance for a different region and, increasingly, a different country to show itself off against the backdrop of the world's biggest annual sports event.

GRANDS DÉPARTS

In the beginning it was just the start of a race; now the Grand Départ costs a fortune to put on, commands world attention for months and can put millions into a local economy. Towns and cities all through Europe vie for the honour of staging the start of each Tour, submitting plans and feasibility studies as if they were hosting a mini-Olympics. No other place on the route gets the race for as long: teams arrive throughout the preceding week; the atmosphere builds to an opening ceremony to introduce the riders on the day before the prologue time trial; then the city gets at least the prologue and the start of the first road stage. The Grand Départ is a very big deal.

FIRST TIME OUTSIDE PARIS

The first Grand Départ outside Paris was from Evian, a town at the foot of the Alps, in 1926. The official history records that Henri Desgrange, dissatisfied with the racers' apathy in the Tour after the last mountains, told one of his assistants to make the Alps the last climbs of the 1926 Tour, as they were the nearest to Paris, and to cut the stages between them and the finish down to two. "It's a pity we can't move the Alps nearer Paris," his assistant replied, joking, but it made Desgrange think. "We can't, but we can move the race to the Alps," he said. So they did – they made the route go around France, anti-clockwise, before returning to Evian, then doing the distance left to Paris in two stages.

TOUR GETS ITS CLOGS ON

Desgrange's Evian adventure didn't really work; the 1926 Tour was raced more cautiously than ever before. The start returned to Paris until 1951, when Metz in eastern France hosted the Grand Départ. Desgrange was no longer the organizer; by then a young and highly educated journalist called Jacques Goddet had taken over the Tour, bringing fresh ideas. In the following two years the Grand Départ toured France, visiting Brest, then Strasbourg, before finally leaving the country to start in Amsterdam in 1954. The first stage went to Braaschaat in the northern Flanders province of Limburg. The Tour stayed in Belgium for next day's start at Beveren, and from there they raced into France to finish at Lille. A Dutch racer called Wout Wagtmans won the first stage and wore the yellow jersey for the next three days.

↑ *The Netherlands broke out the bunting when Amsterdam hosted the 1954 Grand Départ.*

HISTORY BEGINS

The first Tour start was a long way from the razzmatazz of today's Grands Départs. Sixty men and their machines assembled at the crossroads of the Avenue de Paris and the Rue de Corbeil in Montgeron, outside a café called Au Reveil Matin (which means the alarm clock) at three o'clock in the afternoon of 1 July 1903. Twenty-one were professionals, the rest hopeful amateurs or enthusiastic adventurers. A few spectators, their interest spiked by Henri Desgrange's inspiring editorials in *L'Auto* magazine, gathered to watch. Desgrange gave the men a final briefing, and then at 3.16 he waved the French flag and they were off.

← *Au Reveil Matin as it looked in 1903.*

COUNTRIES WHO'VE HOSTED THE GRAND DÉPART

France	79	Switzerland	1
Holland	5	England	1
Belgium	4	Monaco	1
Germany	3	Ireland	1
Luxembourg	2	Spain	1

CYCLING BY GASLIGHT

Until 1967 every Tour started with a normal road race stage, apart from 1927 and 1928 when all the flat stages were run as team time trials. It was felt, though, that this lacked a bit of theatre, and the Tour de France loves theatre. So in 1967 the organizers decided to tack a short time trial on to the Tour, running it the evening before the first stage proper. They called it the prologue time trial, and the first one was run in Angers on a race circuit lit by camping lamps supplied by the French company Gaz. It was regarded as a way of introducing the racers to the public, and it decided who wore the yellow jersey on the first day, but was thought of simply as that – a prologue to the main event. Things have certainly changed. There are racers today who train specifically to win the prologue, which is usually only between six and ten kilometres long.

⬇ *Ireland made the Tour very welcome in 1998, when Dublin was the site of the Grand Départ.*

LONDON CALLING

The 2007 Grand Départ was in London. The prologue time trial started in Whitehall, went through Parliament Square, then past Westminster Abbey, up Constitution Hill, did a loop around Hyde Park and finished on the Mall with Buckingham Palace in the background. The first road stage started in London and finished in Canterbury. After that the race used the Channel Tunnel to journey to France.

⬇ *The 2007 Grand Départ couldn't have had a more British backdrop as the prologue time trial went past the Houses of Parliament.*

GRAND DÉPART 2012

The 2012 Tour de France will start in the Belgian city of Liège. The prologue will start on one side of the Parc d'Avroy, go north through the city streets, then along the banks of the River Meuse. After three kilometres there is a full 360-degree turn and the riders will race back to finish on the opposite side of the Parc. The full distance will be 6.1 kilometres. The first road stage starts next morning and goes through the Ardennes hills in a big loop to Seraing, which isn't far from Liège.

BOARDMAN LEADS IN IRELAND

The 1998 Grand Départ was hosted by Dublin. The British racer Chris Boardman took the third of his three Tour de France prologue wins, so it was also the second time he took the yellow jersey. Tom Steels of Belgium then won a road race stage that started and finished in Dublin. The third and final Irish stage was from Enniscorthy to Cork. It was won by Jan Svorada, a Czech, but Boardman crashed and was too injured to continue. The team cars and race vehicles left Cork by ferry to the next stage start in the Breton port of Roscoff, while the racers and key team and race staff travelled to France by air.

↑ *Glasgow is all go for the 2017 Tour start.*

What's it cost?

It cost London £1.5 million to host the Grand Départ in 2007, but it's estimated that the event put £80–90 million into the local economy. Glasgow hopes to host the Grand Départ in 2017, and they have a £5 million budget to do it.

More for their money

As hosting the Grand Départ has become more expensive, the places it goes to want more of the race. It's not enough to have the prologue and first stage start; recent Grands Départs have seen three days of racing in a region, and sometimes twists to the Tour's format. For example, the 2011 Grand Départ in the Vendée region of France saw a road stage go across the region as stage 1, then a team time trial on a circuit as stage 2. The start of stage 3, a road stage, was also in the Vendée. Stage 3 in 2012 starts in Vise, which is in the Belgian province of Liège.

First for Corsica

The Tour de France has never visited the French island of Corsica, but now Corsica is going to host the Grand Départ in 2013. Logistics cannot explain the long absence of the Tour: Corsica is only 100 miles from the mainland – Ireland was much further away. The real reason is that the Tour feared that the Corsican separatist movement would disrupt the race. That now seems less of a threat, while the Tour organizers also point out that by starting in Corsica the race will connect Napoleon's birthplace with his resting place in Paris.

Bad start

When Leiden in Holland hosted the Grand Départ in 1978, torrential rain fell during the prologue time trial. It was so bad that all the team managers, except one, asked the organizers not to let the times count towards the overall standings. They agreed, but they also decided not to award the yellow jersey. On hearing this, the manager who hadn't agreed to annulling the times, Peter Post, whose TI Raleigh racers had taken the top four spots, was livid. His riders attacked all through the next stage, again run in awful conditions, and the prologue winner, Jan Raas, won the stage and took the yellow jersey.

Blessing

When the Tour used to start with a road race stage, a local dignitary would wave the start flag or cut a ceremonial ribbon, often while the French national anthem was played. The riders would also be blessed en masse by a priest. A film made by French film director Claude Lelouch called *Pour un Maillot Jaune* (For a Yellow Jersey), set in the 1965 Tour, graphically depicts these ceremonies as well as the whole atmosphere of the race in that era.

← *Spectators used to throw water over the racers on hot days, but this Spanish racer wants to grab a whole bucket of holy water.*

THE FUTURE

It's probably only a matter of time before the Tour starts on another continent. As far back as 1986, when Greg LeMond became the first American, the first non-European in fact, to win the Tour de France, the idea was mooted to stage a Grand Départ in New York. The logistics aren't insurmountable. The riders would need two rest days after it, one to fly and one to recover, and hire cars would have to act as race vehicles, but if the will and money are there it could happen. A Russian start has been mooted too, and countries like Qatar and Dubai have expressed an interest.

SHORTEST APPEARANCE

Britain's Chris Boardman crashed on a slippery corner during a downpour of rain just minutes into the prologue time trial of the 1995 Tour de France in St Brieuc, Brittany. He was too badly injured to continue. It's the shortest time anyone has ever raced in the Tour.

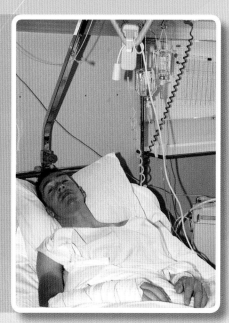

➜ *Chris Boardman's 1995 Tour lasted about 90 seconds before a bad crash put him in hospital.*

BEHIND THE WALL

The 1987 Tour started in West Berlin. Europe was still divided then, and the German city was both the symbol and the ultimate reality of that division because it was separated by a wall into East and West Berlin. However, the old enmities which created a divided Europe were thawing, and the Cold War was coming to an end. The Berlin Wall fell in 1989 after the communist bloc countries of Eastern Europe relaxed their authoritarian stance. This relaxation had begun in 1987, particularly in Poland. Communist countries didn't allow their athletes to take part in professional events like the Tour de France, but two Poles were in a pro team that started the '87 Tour. After stage 2, a team time trial in Berlin, one of them, Lech Piasecki, took the yellow jersey, the first Eastern European racer to do so.

⬆ *Culture shock, as photographers get Luis Herrera of the Café de Colombia team to stand against the Berlin Wall.*

MISSING THE START

In 1989 the previous year's Tour winner, Pedro Delagdo missed his start in the prologue time trial. The clock starts ticking from the moment every rider is due to start, so by the time the very flustered Spaniard set off he was already 2 minutes on 40 seconds down on the winner. So he started the Tour in last place by some margin. The way he worked his way through the field to finally finish third in the Tour, at 3 minutes 34 seconds was both a gritty and classy performance

YORKIE TOUR

The English county of Yorkshire is bidding for the 2016 Grand Départ. The plan is for two road race stages, the first starting in Leeds before heading to Scarborough via the Yorkshire Dales and North Yorks Moors, the second travelling from Scarborough to Sheffield via Hull.

STARTS AND FINISHES

The only way the Tour de France could work was by splitting its total length into stages. Most start in one place and finish in another, although stages can and do start and finish in the same place. Stages have varied in number and length over time, and they vary in length within each Tour. There are rules today governing how long a stage and how long the Tour can be, but there wasn't when the Tour started. This change has had a dramatic effect on the race.

Every day in a different town or city, the start village, the finish gantry, the stands and crowd barriers have to be put up, taken down, transported and erected again to create the Tour de France starts and finishes.

STARTS AND FINISHES

When the Tour de France began, what excited people about the race was the long-distance element. This meant the stages were incredibly long, sometimes over 400 kilometres, and they took many hours for the riders to complete. Two or three days were needed after each stage, not just for the racers to recover, but to enable some to finish the stage and still have some time to eat, sleep and prepare for the next one. Public tastes changed, bikes improved, racers got fitter and more organized and racing became tactical. Fans wanted speed and action, so stage distances were reduced, producing the aggressive racing we see in the Tour de France today. The modern Tour format is a race over 23 days with 21 stages and two rest days.

LAST TOUR DE FRANCE

Rural France was a rough place at the start of the 20th century. People had very parochial attitudes and were suspicious of anyone who wasn't from their area, which meant that their support for a local cycling champion was total and where possible would be backed by deeds as well as words. This led to several riders being held up in different regions by angry crowds, and only allowed to go when the local champion had gained a lot of time. If the delayed riders struggled, they often got beaten up. Henri Desgrange despaired and wrote in *L'Auto* that the 1904 Tour might be the last unless people could control themselves.

TIMING THEMSELVES

The first stage of the first Tour, from Paris to Lyons, was 467 kilometres long. It took the winner, Maurice Garin of France, 17 hours 45 minutes to complete, but he was still faster than the race officials. Timing was down to staff from *L'Auto*, who set the racers off and then got on the train to wherever the stage finished. However, on the first stage the official got there slightly after the first two had arrived, so Garin and Emile Pagie had to decide between them that 55 seconds separated them at the line. The next man, Emile Georget, was clocked in 39 minutes 54 seconds behind Garin, and 38 hours had gone by before the last man, Eugène Brange, arrived in Lyons.

↑ *Maurice Garin finishes a stage in 1903.*

OH NO NOT HERE AGAIN

The most visited stage town is of course Paris. The Tour started there for many years and has always finished in the capital. Bordeaux fills second place with 80 visits out of 98 Tours. Because the roads around Bordeaux are flat, stages usually end in a bunch sprint there. This led to the Bordeaux stage becoming known as the sprinter's world championships.

← *Belgian Rik Van Looy wins in Bordeaux in 1963.*

First finish on avenue des Champs Elysées

The final stage to Paris used to end on the velodrome that was inside the Parc des Princes stadium. But that was demolished to make way for the capital's "périphérique", or ring road, in 1967. The stage was sometimes a road race, but often it was a time trial. A nearby velodrome called the Piste Municipale in Vincennes hosted the finish for a few years, until the Tour organizers persuaded the city authorities to let the Tour have a much grander finale on the avenue des Champs Elysées. The first one was in 1975, when Walter Godefroot of Belgium won a massed sprint. The Champs Elysées quickly replaced Bordeaux as the unofficial sprinter's world championships. A road stage has rounded off the Tour every year since 1975, except in 1989 when a time trial brought the Tour to the Champs Elysées.

Border crossing

The first time a Tour stage went into a foreign country was on a technicality. On stage 2 in 1907, from Roubaix to Metz, the race had to pass through Alsace-Lorraine, now part of France but then occupied by Germany after they'd annexed it during the Franco-Prussian War of 1870. Ironically, the riders and race officials were waved through by the German border guards when they passed into Germany, but were stopped and searched by French guards when they returned to France.

↑ *A capacity crowd of more than 30,000 specators welcomes a pre-1975 Tour home to Paris in the Parc de Princes.*

Taking the train

There was suspicion that some riders cheated in the first Tour, such a massive race being very difficult to police. The following year there was no doubt: the cheating was so wholesale that the first four overall were disqualified. They had cut the route, been towed by cars for mile after mile, and some had even taken the train to cover sections of the race. Although the Tour finished in July 1904, the disqualification couldn't be announced until December. This was because the race stirred such passionate support that the organizers feared for their safety if they had announced it earlier.

Highest finish

A mountain-top stage finish was first tried in the 1950s, but it didn't catch on in the Tour until the seventies. Now mountain-top finishes make for some of the most exciting stages in the Tour, and are sometimes where the race is decided. The highest ever finish was on top of the Col du Galibier at 2,645 metres in 2011.

→ *Andy Schleck winning at the highest ever Tour stage finish in 2011.*

LOSING HIS BOTTLE

One of the most spectacular disqualifications happened to Tom Steels in 1997. He was a fast sprinter from Belgium who won nine Tour stages. He is a very mild-mannered man but, like most sprinters, saw red in the finale of a race. Coming to the end of a stage in Mayenne, Steels was so frustrated by the tactics of a rival, Frédéric Moncassin, that he pulled his drinks bottle from its cage and threw it at the Frenchman, scoring a direct hit on the back of his head. No one was hurt, no one crashed, but Steels was, quite rightly, disqualified for dangerous riding. He got married that winter, and after the ceremony, instead of confetti, his guests pelted Steels with empty plastic bottles.

← *Belgian sprinter Tom Steels explains to the media why he so publicly lost his temper in 1997.*

JUST SAY NO

The Tour has had a bad history with performance-enhancing drugs. One of the problems was that they weren't illegal in cycling until the Tour had been going quite a few years, and there was no testing anyway. The other problem was that the Tour was so tough that some racers argued that they needed drugs in order to cope, and in Europe many bike fans agreed with them. But ambitious athletes have to be protected from drug abuse, so drug tests were developed and in 1966, after changes in French law regarding drugs in sport, they were introduced to the Tour de France. The racers protested – they said that having to pee into a bottle was an affront to their professional dignity, and at the start of one stage they even demonstrated by walking for a while before eventually starting to race – but the tests stayed.

STRIKE

The idea of split stages began in the 1920s. Towns and cities compete to host Tour starts and finishes, so if you split a stage in two, producing two starts and two finishes in the same day, the organizers double their revenue. The riders put up with this for years, but then triple stages started to creep in: three starts and three finishes in one day. No extra distance, just three sets of clothes, three lots of hassle getting washed, changed and ready again. Eventually it proved too much, and in 1978 the riders went on strike. Shortly before a stage finish in Valence d'Agen, they stopped short of the line and refused to move. The organizers pleaded with them, but they wouldn't play and instead of racing they slowly walked over the line. The crowd weren't happy, but the riders had made their point. Triple stages were out and double stages were reduced.

CRASHES

Many stages end in bunch sprints, and these involve an element of risk. The racers taking part in the Tour are great bike handlers, but everything happens so fast in a bunch sprint and people make mistakes, and not only the bike racers. In 1994 at Armentières a policeman was so keen to get a picture of the racers hurtling towards him that he didn't realize he'd moved slightly out from the barricades he was supposed to be guarding and into the road. Several riders collided at upwards of 60 kph while trying to avoid him. Two of the worst injured were the green jersey, Laurent Jalabert, and the then Belgian national champion Wilfried Nellisen.

→ *The crash at Armentières in 1994 was one of the worst in Tour history.*

STARTS AND FINISHES LEAGUE TABLE

Bordeaux	80	Nantes	30
Pau	58	Belfort	29
Luchon	49	Brest	28
Metz	40	Montpellier	26
Grenoble	40	Roubaix	25
Perpignan	36	Toulouse	26
Nice	35	Aix-les-Bains	22
Caen	34	St-Etienne	22
Bayonne	32	Strasbourg	22
Marseilles	32	Alpe d'Huez	23
Briançon	31	La Rochelle	20

↑ *Frenchman Pierre Rolland, who would go on to claim the white jersey, wins at l'Alpe d'Huez in 2011.*

↑ *Aldo Ronconi with the laurel of victory in Luxembourg in 1947, the first time the capital city of the tiny principality had enjoyed the honour of a stage finish.*

TOUR TRAVELS

The first time a stage finished outside France was in Metz in 1907, followed by Geneva in 1914. The Swiss city became a regular part of the Tour, but the race refused to venture anywhere else for a finish until 1947, when Brussels hosted the end of stage 2. A trend was set, and next day's stage finished in Luxembourg City. Since then stages have started and finished in most European countries.

ON THE BUSES

Every Tour team has a bus, and these buses have grown more expensive and elaborate each year. The riders arrive in them, and use them to get ready and have a final briefing. Then, after the start, the bus motors off on a separate, more direct route to the stage finish, along with many of the press cars and team staff. The buses park near the finish, and that's where the riders head for after each stage, to be whisked away in air-conditioned luxury to their hotels. The buses are equipped with showers, entertainment and media and are often the ultimate in luxury travel. The big drawback is that very often the stars of the Tour stay behind the tinted glass of their buses until the last moment before each stage start. It's understandable, though, as they are under a lot of pressure to perform.

YELLOW DISGRACE

One of the most high-profile disqualifications at a stage finish happened in 1978. Michel Pollentier won the stage to the summit of Alpe d'Huez, taking over the yellow jersey in the process. He had to provide a sample of urine for a dope test, but during the testing procedure it was discovered that Pollentier had a bag of someone else's urine and a tube concealed under his clothes. He was thrown out of the Tour for trying to falsify the dope test results.

➜ *Michel Pollentier was stripped of his glory after winning the Alpe d'Huez stage in 1978 when he tried to provide a false urine sample.*

STAGE WINS

Winning a stage in the Tour de France carries such prestige that it is often the high point of a racer's career. People who've heard of no other bike race have heard of the Tour de France. This has made the race so important, so high-profile in cycling, that every stage is fiercely contested for its own sake as well as for its impact on the overall standings. A stage winner can expect a better contract with his team, he can count on being paid to appear in exhibition races all over Europe, and he will become a celebrity within cycling and within his home region.

Winning a stage is on every Tour racer's wish list, and wearing the yellow jersey is something they all dream of. Fabian Cancellara makes a wish and dream come true as he wins in Compiègne in 2007.

STAGE WINS

It's possible to win the Tour de France without winning a single stage, and it has happened, but while those fighting to win overall must keep their eye on that prize, the glory of winning a stage is still important to them. To the rest, winning a stage can crown a career and assure bigger earnings. Within a team, however, there is little rivalry over winning stages, as all the prize money from every competition in the Tour, including daily stage prizes, is shared equally among all team members at the end.

LONELINESS OF THE LONG-DISTANCE CYCLIST

The longest ever lone breakaway that ended with a stage win was made by a Frenchman, Albert Bourlon, in 1957. He attacked at the start of the stage from Carcassone to Luchon and spent the whole of its 253-kilometre length alone in the lead, winning by 16 minutes 30 seconds.

⬆ *Albert Bourlon in action on his epic breakaway in 1957 when he won the stage by 16 minutes and 30 seconds.*

DOING THE IMPOSSIBLE

The record for the fastest stage won by a rider finishing on his own, in what is called a lone breakaway, is held by Johan Bruyneel, and he did it in 1993. Bruyneel, who is Belgian, later became famous as the man who guided Lance Armstrong to seven straight Tour victories. Bruyneel won two stages but says what he did in 1993 was impossible. It's very hard for a single rider to hold off a chasing bunch, and Bruyneel says: "I was not a classy enough racer to do it, at least not normally. That day was different, though. I lost my father just before the Tour that year. He loved cycling, it was the thing that we shared. My dad wanted to be a pro but couldn't, so he was very proud of me. I felt my dad with me on the road to Amiens that day, he gave me the strength to ride the way I did."

⬆ *Johan Bruyneel crosses the line after his "impossible" stage win at Amiens in 1993.*

SLOWEST TOUR

The 1919 Tour is also the slowest ever overall, with an average of 24.05 kph. It was to be expected really, as the First World War had just finished and many of the field had spent the previous four years fighting or simply trying to stay alive. They weren't really fit enough to race, but it was thought important to the nation's morale that the Tour went ahead. Out of 67 starters only ten men made it to the finish.

➔ *Firmin Lambot won the slowest ever and most attritional Tour in 1919. Only nine other cyclists completed the Tour.*

TOP TEN FASTEST EVER TOUR STAGES

Rider	Ave speed (km/h)	Stage	Distance (km)	Year
Mario Cipollini	50.355	Laval–Bois	194.5	1999
Pablo Lastras	49.938	Bordeaux–St-Maxient-l'Ecole	203.5	2003
Johan Bruyneel	49.417	Evreux–Amiens	158	1993
Adri van der Poel	48.927	Tarbes–Pau	38	1988
Tom Steels	48.764	Tarascon-sur-Ariège–Le Cap-d'Agde	205.5	1998
Patrick Sercu	48.677	Fribourg–Fribourg	46	1977
Robbie McEwen	48.584	Chambond–Montargis	183	2005
Eddy Merckx	48.532	Vouvray–Orléans	112.5	1974
Nico Verhoeven	48.118	Berlin–Berlin	105.5	1987
Eric Zabel	47.904	Sauternes–Pau	161	1997

↑ Mario Cipollini holds the speed record for the Tour by winning the fastest ever stage, the 195.5km from Laval to Bois, in 1999.

SLOWEST STAGE

The slowest ever stage was stage 6 of the 1919 Tour, when 326 kilometres between Bayonne and Luchon were completed by the winner, Honoré Barthelmy, at an average speed of 20.7 kph. Barthelmy had a glass eye, which used to fall out when he raced. He reckoned that he spent most of his winnings on new glass eyes, so eventually he took it out to race, filling his empty eye socket with a lump of cotton wool and covering it with a patch.

➔ Not only does Mark Cavendish hold the British record of stage wins (20), he's young enough and on course to beat the all-time record of Belgium's Eddy Merckx.

EDDY, FREDDY AND CHARLEY

Eight is the most stages any rider has won in a single Tour de France, and the title is shared by three men: Eddy Merckx, who did it twice (1970 and 1974), Freddy Maertens (1976) and Charles Pélissier (1930). Pélissier, who also took second place seven times in the 1930 Tour, finished ninth overall when he set the stage win record; Maertens finished eighth when he equalled it, whereas Merckx won the two Tours when he did so.

TOP SEVEN TOUR DE FRANCE STAGE WINNERS

	Name	Country	Stage wins
1	Eddy Merckx	Belgium	34
2	Bernard Hinault	France	28
3	André Leducq	France	25
4	André Darrigade	France	22
=	Lance Armstrong	USA	22
6	Nicolas Frantz	Luxembourg	20
=	Mark Cavendish	GB	20

BRITISH RECORD

Mark Cavendish holds the record for British stage wins with 20. Barry Hoban fills second place with eight. Sharing third are Robert Millar, David Millar and Michael Wright with three each. Then come Chris Boardman and Brian Robinson, the man who won Britain's first Tour stage back in 1958, with two. Max Sciandri and Sean Yates both achieved one stage win.

TIME GAPS

For those who avoid crashes, and on stages where there isn't one in the final three kilometres, the clock keeps ticking right to the line. Any clear gap between the rear wheel of one rider and the front wheel of the next, or between groups of riders, is timed and counts for the overall standings. This means that the race favourites, even if not contesting a bunch sprint, if that's how the stage ends, must try to stay near the front so as not to get caught behind gaps. Some overall winners, like Eddy Merckx and Lance Armstrong, excelled at causing gaps by going really hard during the run-in to the finish.

← *Eddy Merckx never stopped forcing the pace, neither in the mountains, nor even in the final kilometres of a flat stage.*

WINNING MOUNTAIN STAGES

Tactics in the mountains are complicated by the fact that the best climbers are often those going for the yellow jersey and trying to win the Tour outright. Their attacks depend on where they stand overall: whether they are in front trying to defend or behind trying to gain time. Otherwise climbers tend to fall into two categories: those who set a high constant pace and slowly burn everybody off their wheel, and those who are capable of rapid bursts of speed that distance the rest immediately. Such a rider might attack two or three times, with the others clawing him back, until he attacks a final time and stays clear.

THE PHYSIOLOGY OF WINNING

Whether a climber slowly burns away the opposition or bursts clear of them, he does so by doing what bike racers call putting their rivals "into the red". Those following simply exceed the speed at which their body processes can maintain the power needed to stay with the pace. Although answering rapid bursts of speed may not be beyond the power of those doing it, the attacks exact a physiological cost that the body cannot continue repaying. This is why a third attack is often successful.

NOT LOSING TIME

Crashes are common in stage finishes, and they are often not the fault of those who crash, but the time lost in such a crash could have a big bearing on the overall standings. For the last few years, therefore, the Tour rules have stated that time lost by crashing in the final three kilometres doesn't count when calculating a rider's overall time. Effectively, for those involved in a crash the clock stops with three kilometres to go.

→ *Djamolidine Abdoujaparov has a spectacular crash while sprinting for the finish on the Champs Elysées of the final stage of the 1991 Tour.*

TOP SEVEN STAGE-WINNING MARGINS

	Rider	Margin	Stage	Year
1	José-Luis Viejo	22'50	Montgenèvre–Manosque	1976
2	Pierino Baffi	21'48	Pau–Bordeaux	1957
3	Daan de Groot	20'31	Millau–Albi	1955
4	Brian Robinson	20'06	Annecy–Chalon-sur-Saône	1959
5	Fons de Wolf	17'40	Rodez–Domaine du Rouret	1984
6	Albert Bourlon	16'30	Carcassonne–Luchon	1947
7	Francis Campaner	14'01	Pau–Bordeaux	1974

↑ *Spain's José-Luis Viejo won a stage by the biggest ever margin in 1976. He was 22 minutes and 50 seconds clear of his nearest rival, Gerben Karstens.*

TACTICS

Sprinters want stages to finish in a bunch sprint. That means they can hide for most of the stage, save their strength and then burst for the line inside the final kilometre. Riders who aren't quite as fast but who have a fair burst of speed will try to form a breakaway group to get ahead of the main bunch. Such a group will share the pace to keep their average speed high and steady, which gives them the best chance of gaining time on the rest. Nearer the finish those who aren't so confident of their sprint will attack, aiming to break away alone and win or to help a team-mate by dropping better sprinters from the group.

USING YOUR HEAD

There is sometimes contact between racers in sprint finishes. They will lean on one another with their shoulders to try to take a better position in the mass charge for the line. At the end of stage 11 in the 2010 Tour, Mark Renshaw had his team-mate Mark Cavendish following closely behind him. It was Renshaw's job in their team, HTC Columbia, to lead Cavendish to the finish, and ride as hard as he could to give Cavendish the speed to launch his sprint, but on this stage a rival, Julian Dean, tried to muscle in on HTC's line by leaning on Renshaw's shoulder. As he did this, Renshaw pushed back with his head, which the race judges decided was a head-butt, although even Dean says it wasn't. They disqualified Renshaw from the Tour on the grounds of dangerous riding for what to most observers was a controlled and skilful manoeuvre carried out at more than 60 kph.

NOT PLAYING IT STRAIGHT

When Brian Robinson won the first ever Tour stage for Great Britain in 1958 he actually crossed the line in second place. He had broken away from the main field with an Italian racer, Arigo Padovan, and they sprinted it out for the stage win in Brest at the western tip of Brittany. Although Padovan was leading Robinson when he began to sprint, slowly but surely the racer from Mirfield in West Yorkshire began to edge past the Italian. As he did so, however, Padovan stopped riding in a straight line and kept altering his position on the road to block Robinson's progress. Padovan went across the line first, but the Englishman's protest at his tactics was upheld by the judges, and Robinson was awarded the stage.

→ *Brian Robinson wins his second ever stage – and the second recorded by a British cyclist (this time without controversy) – at Chalon-sur-Saône in 1959.*

TIME TRIALS

Time trials play a crucial role in the outcome of any Tour de France. Riders always gain or lose time in them, because time trials are individual efforts. Whereas on flat or rolling stages it's hard to break away from the main pack, and doing so depends on good tactics, riding alone means a stage is decided purely on physical rather than tactical ability. This is why time trials are often referred to as the race of truth.

Cyclists in individual time trials have to ride alone, with no shelter or hiding place. As the potential to lose time is huge, they are crucial, so anyone with ambitions of winning the Tour must ride well against the clock. To prove their importance, some Tour de France winners have been time trial specialists.

TIME TRIALS

Riders in time trials set off on their own, or in team time trials as a team, at intervals of two minutes, to race over a set distance. The individual or team who completes the distance in the fastest time wins. There is no hiding place in a time trial. Racers must go hard and spread their energy over the whole distance, not a metre more or less. It takes a special mix of muscle fibre and brain power to excel in time trials.

⬆ *Jacques Anquetil was the first time trial specialist to win the Tour, one of the first to really study the event and fully appreciate its demands.*

TEAM TIME TRIALS

Each team sets off as a unit at intervals from the other teams, just as an individual rider does in a normal time trial. They race over the route for the stage and the team's time is taken when one of their riders, usually the fifth one, crosses the line. The whole team are given the time of the fifth rider. This means that riders can get dropped from a team, but with nine riders in each one, teams cannot afford to lose many. Individual time triallists are usually the best at team time trials, but the team event also demands a few different skills. Riders must be precise in the way they set the pace at the front of the team, which rides in line astern, and the rest must be very precise in the way they follow. Once a rider has finished pace setting he moves to one side and slowly drops back, then joins the back of the line, and another rider takes over at the front. All this must be done in an exact way.

➡ *Britain's David Millar holds the record for the fastest ever Tour time trial over 40 kilometres.*

MAÎTRE JACQUES

There have been many great time triallists in the Tour de France, but the first to rely on his time trial ability to win the race was also the first man to win the Tour five times, Jacques Anquetil of France. Of course Anquetil had other racing abilities. When he needed to stay at the front in the mountains for his strategy to work, even the greatest climbers couldn't distance him, or at least not by any more time than he could afford to lose. Anquetil's greatest strength, however, was the time trial. He had the ability to ride at a constant hard pace. His riding style was very aerodynamic, and he seemed to understand the science of air-flow long before the rest of cycling did. Anquetil also had an innate ability to solve the problems of any time trial route, always coming up with an effort that gave him the best time.

MILLAR TIME

Greg LeMond has the absolute speed record for Tour de France time trials, but it was set on a 24-kilometre course that had a drop in elevation along its length. The record for a standard Tour time trial, one of a more usual Tour distance of around 50 kilometres, was set by Britain's David Millar in 2003.

TOP FIVE FASTEST EVER TOUR TEAM TIME TRIALS

Rank	Team	Speed (kph)	Stage	Year
1	Discovery Channel	57.320	Tours–Blois (67.5 km)	2005
2	Gewiss-Ballan	54.930	Mayenne–Alençon (67 km)	1995
3	Carrera	54.610	Berlin (40.5 km)	1987
4	Ariostea	52.919	Chassieu (36.5 km)	1991
5	Panasonic	52.049	Libourne (63.5 km)	1992

TOP TEN FASTEST EVER TOUR INDIVIDUAL TIME TRIALS OVER 20 KILOMETRES IN LENGTH

Rank	Rider	Speed (kph)	Stage	Year
1	Greg LeMond	54.545	Versailles–Paris (24.5 km)	1989
2	David Millar	54.361	Pornic–Nantes (49 km)	2003
3	Lance Armstrong	53.986	Freiburg im Breisgau–Mulhouse (58.5 km)	2000
4	Levi Leipheimer	53.082	Cognac–Angoulême (55.5 km)	2007
5	Miguel Indurain	52.349	Tours–Blois (64 km)	1992
6	Serhiy Honchar	50.554	Saint Grégoire–Rennes (52 km)	2006
7	Miguel Indurain	50.539	Périgueux–Bergerac (64 km)	1994
8	Tony Rominger	50.495	Brétigny–Montlhéry (48 km)	1993
9	Serhiy Honchar	50.480	Le Creusot–Montceau-les-Mines (57 km)	2006
10	Jan Ullrich	50.443	Bordeaux–Libourne (63.5 km)	1996

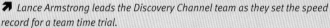

↗ *Lance Armstrong leads the Discovery Channel team as they set the speed record for a team time trial.*

↑ *The last time the final stage of the Tour de France was a time trial in Paris, Greg Lemond won by the narrowest ever margin (eight seconds).*

FIRST TIME TRIAL

The first ever individual time trial was part of the 1934 Tour de France and was won by Antonin Magne of France. He covered 90 kilometres on his own between La Roche-sur-Yon and Nantes at an average speed of 35.5 kph. Magne dominated the 1934 Tour and was already well ahead before the time trial, which contributed to his overall winning margin in Paris of 27 minutes 31 seconds.

TOUR FINALE

From the 1950s to the early 1970s the final stage of the Tour was often run as a time trial. It is an exciting way to finish a three-week race, because if it has been a close struggle the outcome can be in doubt until the last few minutes. The 1964 and 1968 Tours went down to the wire like that. Only once since the Tour switched its final stage on to the Champs-Elysées in 1975 has the final stage been a time trial, although the last day in 1976 had two legs: one lap of the famous finishing circuit run as a time trial, then a multi-lap road race. When they reintroduced the final time trial in 1989, it enabled Greg Lemond to beat Laurent Fignon in the finish straight along the famous avenue by eight seconds, the narrowest ever winning margin of the Tour de France.

↑ *Some Tour riders use wind tunnels to refine their riding position and improve their aerodynamics when cycling at fast speeds.*

CYCLING AERODYNAMICS

The average speed of individual time trials has increased faster than the average speed of road race stages. The main reason for this is a better understanding of aerodynamics in cycling. When a cyclist is cruising on a flat road, aerodynamic drag is the most significant force to overcome. Roughly speaking, aerodynamic drag doubles for every one kilometre per hour increase in cycling speed. At slow speeds the forces involved are very small, but they keep doubling and become significant as speed increases. This is why riding behind someone is so much easier than riding alone. Lone cyclists must make the smallest hole in the air and ensure it passes over and around their body and bike as smoothly as possible. They do this by wearing special one-piece racing suits and tear-drop-shaped helmets, and by riding the most aerodynamic bikes in the world. Some of the best racers spend hours refining their riding position in a wind tunnel.

FOLLOWING CAR

Each racer is followed by one of his team cars, carrying a spare bike and wheels in case of mechanical problems or punctures. The team manager is allowed to give time checks, but must do so from behind, so before radios were used in cycling they would shout these through megaphones. There are motorbike referees on the route too, checking that riders don't get paced by their team cars and that no one settles into the slipstream of another racer if he is caught by him.

REVERSE ORDER

Apart from the prologue, where last year's Tour winner always starts last and the rest of the start order is decided by the organization working with the teams, in Tour time trials the riders set off in the reverse order of the overall standings. The last man overall starts first and the yellow jersey starts last.

BIG MIG

Miguel Indurain of Spain was the modern master of Tour de France time trials. Like Jacques Anquetil, Indurain dominated the Tour by gaining in time trials and not losing much in the mountains. It's a very effective if slightly unspectacular way to win, which Indurain used to such effect that he became the first rider ever to win five Tours in a row. Indurain earned the nickname "Big Mig" because he was just that: big, especially for a cyclist. Well over six feet tall and powerfully muscled, Indurain didn't look like a climber, but he solved the power to weight problem that stops big racers going uphill fast by producing off-the-scale power. Also his big muscles weren't the explosive fast-twitch fibres of a sprinter, but those of a lean-burn endurance racer. Indurain was a physical anomaly with huge lungs and an enormous heart that only beat 28 times a minute at rest.

→ *Miguel Indurain was one of the most powerful racers in Tour history and the first to win five straight Tours.*

THE PROLOGUE

From being a bit of a novelty, the prologue time trial developed through being an event for specialists to become a crucial part of any overall contender's attempt to win the Tour. Modern Tours de France are decided by seconds, or maybe a couple of minutes at most, certainly not the time gaps there were even ten years ago. A contender cannot let a single second go, so they all have to be on it for the prologue. In fact it is often one of the main contenders who wins this short time trial held in the streets of the Grand Départ city. Prologue specialists include Chris Boardman of Great Britain, who won three Tour prologues and has three of the four fastest times (average speeds) in history. Thierry Marie of France is the other racer to have dominated prologue time trials with three wins and the fifth fastest time ever recorded.

← *Britain's Chris Boardman set the fastest and two more of the top five prologue time trial record speeds.*

OFF THE RAMP

An elevated platform with a ramp down to the floor, giving each racer a flying start, was first used in a Tour time trial in Châteaulin in 1965. This has evolved into a custom-made mobile start house. After his warm-up, a rider gets to the start house five minutes before his time slot to go, walks up some steps at the back of it, sits down and waits for his call. When the racer in front sets off, he mounts up and is held steady by an official, while another counts down the seconds to his start. As well as giving each racer a flying start, the start house allows the crowd and the TV audience to get a good look at the racers as they set off.

BROKE BACK MOUNTAIN

Frenchman Roger Rivière was one of the few riders ever to beat Jacques Anquetil in a Tour de France time trial. He did it in 1959 on stage 6 from Blain to Nantes, riding 43.5 kilometres in 56 minutes 46 seconds; 58 seconds faster than Anquetil. Rivière didn't win that Tour, but he was in a great position to win the 1960 Tour de France when he crashed on the descent of the Col du Perjuret, which runs off Mont Aigoual in the Cevennes. Rivière went off the road and fell down the mountainside, breaking his back. He spent the rest of his life in a wheelchair and died at the age of 40.

TOP FIVE FASTEST EVER TOUR PROLOGUE TIME TRIALS

Rank	Rider	Speed (kph)	Stage	Distance	Year
1	Chris Boardman	55.152	Lille–Euralille	7.2 km	1994
2	Chris Boardman	54.193	Dublin	5.6 km	1998
3	Fabian Cancellara	53.660	London	7.9 km	2007
4	Chris Boardman	52.465	Rouen	7.3 km	1997
5	Thierry Marie	52.365	Lyon	5.4 km	1991

↑ *Roger Rivière had the ability to win the Tour, but after his crash in 1960 he spent the rest of his life in a wheelchair.*

THE PELOTON

Peloton comes from a French word meaning little ball – platoon and pellet also come from the same word. Cycling uses peloton to describe the largest group in a road race, but it means much more. As well as being the mobile base of operations in a race, the peleton is also an abstract concept, signifying the fraternity of pro racers and representing the thoughts and attitudes of pro racing. The peloton has an opinion, and nothing in pro bike racing changes unless there is consensus within the peloton.

Peloton is the French word used universally to describe the colourful bunch of racers in the Tour de France, but it means much more.

THE PELOTON

Roads were awful, cycling was young and race bikes were heavy and unreliable when the Tour de France began. The competitors' fitness varied a lot too. A hard core of them were pro racers who trained hard, but the rest were hopeful amateurs training in their spare time or adventurers who thought riding around France might be fun. This meant that once a stage started the field quickly spread out, with everyone doing the best they could to reach the end. However, with roads improving, bikes becoming lighter and more reliable and the Tour contestants' fitness increasing, race speeds grew and the peloton was born.

↑ *With the wind blowing into the riders from the left, the lead racer (green, front left) is riding into it, and the rest shelter to the side or behind him.*

MOBILE BRIEFING

On any stage each team has two team cars following behind that carry spare wheels, bikes, food, drinks and other kit. If there are no breakaways, then all the team cars follow the peloton and are on hand if their riders puncture or need mechanical assistance. If a breakaway gets an advantage of one minute or more, the race referee, who is called a "commissaire" in cycling, calls a team car for each of the racers in the breakaway to move forward and follow the break. If the lead drops below one minute, the cars must drop back behind the peloton. At any time in a stage a racer can drop back to talk to the staff in his team car.

ECHELON

In crosswinds the peloton might fan across the road to form echelons. The front man rides on the side of the road that the wind is blowing from, the others line up inside and slightly behind him. If a rider attacks in a crosswind he'll do so on the opposite side of the road, so as not to offer anyone following him protection from the wind. This tactic is called putting the race in the gutter.

ETIQUETTE

Within the peloton there are a lot of do's and don'ts, most of which are concerned with mutual safety. Riders indicate road hazards to each other, shouting left or right depending on where they are. They never drop a discarded bottle but throw it over the peloton and on to the side of the road, where a spectator will take it home. Racers try to ride straight and steady and corner with control, avoiding making abrupt movements as much as humanly possible. In short, they look after each other's safety, and anyone not doing soon finds himself ostracized by the peloton. Not a good career move.

← *Is there a better setting for a bike race than the French countryside, such as between Epernay and Montargis?*

STICKY BOTTLES

When riders go to their team cars for drinks bottles, they always hold on to the last one they collect for a little longer than necessary. This is called "sticky bottle syndrome", and strictly speaking it's cheating, because the racer is getting a push without pedalling. But the Tour is tough and its commissaires aren't heartless; a certain amount of sticky bottle syndrome is tolerated, so long as it's not abused.

→ *Holding on to the team car isn't allowed, but race officials don't mind if it isn't too blatant.*

ATTACKS AND CHASES

Riding in the Tour de France peloton is never easy for long. Attacks are made early in every stage, and if they are made by riders whom the peloton do not want to see escaping, such as the favourites, it will react to try and chase them down. When this happens the peloton is stretched into a long line, and the slipstream effect is greatly reduced, especially in a crosswind. This also happens towards the end of a stage, where the sprinters' teams might be trying to control the race. They will ride very hard, stretching the peloton again. Tactics differ again in hilly and mountainous stages. Slipstreaming is less important uphill, and talented climbers find it easier to attack and leave the peloton behind. The peloton also fragments on mountainous stages.

FACT OF CYCLING

If one cyclist follows closely behind another, the rider in second place expends about 75 per cent of the energy the front rider is using to pedal. If those two riders are joined by others to become a pack, the amount of energy required to stay in the middle of the pack drops even more. When 100 or more cyclists are bowling along the road, those at the front and the sides of this big bunch will be pedalling furiously while those in the middle are stroking their pedals around or even freewheeling. This is the peloton of the Tour de France, a mobile base from where attacks are made and countered.

↑ *Lilian Jegou collects his food bag or musette at a feed station on the stage between Cholet and Châteauroux in 2008.*

MEALS ON WHEELS

Riders start each stage with two bottles of liquid on their bikes and food in the form of energy bars, gels and sometimes cakes in the three pockets that are stitched in the back of their racing tops. At around half distance they are handed a bag called a "musette", which has replacement bottles and more food in it. The racers put the bottles into carriers on their bikes and the food in their pockets, but this still isn't enough food to last them through a stage. From time to time designated racers from each team drop back through the peloton to collect bottles and food from their team cars. They each carry as many as 12 bottles, tucked in their pockets and up their jersey fronts and backs, then slowly make their way back up through the peloton, distributing the bottles as they go.

↑ *Another day's work in the Tour peloton is done, and everyone who survives is another day closer to Paris.*

THE AUTOBUS

Tactics are important for the best climbers and those going for the overall win, but further down the field Darwinian selection rules the day. Even so, after the favourites dance away from the rest, it isn't as simple as every man for himself. Over a period of several kilometres dropped riders form a large group called the "autobus", and it's really worth catching because its destination is survival. There is a time limit for each stage based on a percentage of the winner's time. Any rider finishing outside the limit leaves the Tour. The autobus always has one or two senior pros in it, and their job is to work out the leader's finish time and the pace the bus needs to do to stay within the limit.

CAFE RAIDS

Keeping the racers fed and watered during each stage is done with great efficiency nowadays. Previously, though, on hot stages the peloton used to stop and riders would rush into cafes to raid their refrigerators for cold drinks. These sometimes included alcohol, and two racers from the 1960s were especially fond of the hard stuff. The great Belgian Classics winner Rik Van Looy enjoyed a beer or two when he raced, and his team-mates carried bottle openers to help him. Jacques Anquetil preferred a glass of chilled Chablis served up while he was riding.

HAND SIGNALS

When they are setting the pace at the front of the peloton, or in a breakaway, riders indicate when they've done their turn by flicking out an elbow. The side of the flick indicates which side of them the following racer should pass to take his turn.

THE BROOM WAGON

When the Tour first climbed into the Pyrenees in 1910 they did so into what the locals called the Circle of Death. These were the highest passes anyone had ever raced over, and every year they took the lives of people who tried to walk them. There wasn't much the Tour could do to keep the riders safe, except have a van follow the last man on the road, so that if he had to stop he could at least be driven to the stage finish behind the rest. It was called the "voiture balai", or broom wagon in English. An upturned broom strapped to the van symbolized sweeping up the last man on the road. The broom wagon can be seen following the Tour today, still with its broom, but it's a long time since a retiring Tour racer graced its seats. Nowadays riders who have to stop get whisked away by team cars, out of the glare of unwanted publicity.

→ *In 1959 Jean Robic was dropped by the peloton on stage 20 to Chalon sur Saône and faced the struggle many face every year. Does he give up and climb into the broom wagon, or battle to the finish? He was swept up.*

⬆ *The TV helicopter goes in low to get some side-on shots of the fast-moving peloton.*

TV COVERAGE

TV cameramen from all the companies who have bought the right to film the Tour capture the action from the pillion seats of motorbikes. Race photographers do the same. It's a skilled job for both the cameramen and the bike pilots, and once accredited the same people do the job for years because of the trust they've built up with the racers. The TV images are beamed to two helicopters that follow each stage. The helicopters then send the images to satellites for distribution around the world. They also contain cameramen who get aerial shots.

⬇ *Crowds watch the action on a giant TV screen during the 2007 prologue, through central London.*

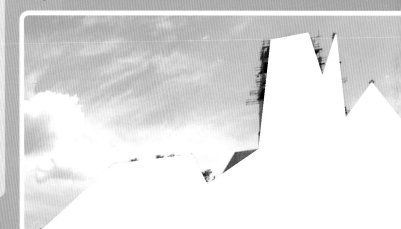

DOMESTIQUE

This French word, which means house servant or maid, is still used to describe a racer in the Tour peloton whose job is to help his team leader. That help includes setting the pace to control attacks by rivals, fetching drinks from the team car and distributing them to their team in the peloton, and pacing his leader back to the peloton if he's had mechanical trouble. Sometimes a domestique may also have to give his leader a push, or even give up his own bike or wheels to help him.

WILL OF THE PELOTON

One of the most striking examples of the peloton acting as an entity is over the question of performance-enhancing drugs. The Tour de France has had its share of drugs scandals and revelations over the years, partly because of the fact that cycling was one of the first sports to test for drugs, and it has led and still leads the sports world in the rigour of its testing. However, there was also an acceptance within the peloton that the Tour de France was so hard that drugs were needed to ride it well. And if members of the peloton didn't accept that, and many didn't, there was still a reluctance to speak out against it. Both the belief and reluctance have largely disappeared now, and that change in collective will as much as anything has led to the fall in positive dope tests in the Tour de France.

PLAYING TO THE CROWD

It's not an exaggeration to say that spectators line the whole Tour de France route, but for most stages the largest crowd is at the stage finish. The Tour is a free show for most, although there are ticket-only areas. A huge TV screen at the finish keeps everyone up to date with what's happening out on the road.

LONGEST AND SHORTEST

The Tour de France started out as a simple
endurance test, but it has changed as bike racing
has got faster and tactics have become more
sophisticated. The Tour also became more
humane, and it has been improved as a spectacle
by the reduction over the years of both its overall
length and the length of individual stages. A
modern Tour de France is an exciting mix of speed,
colour, super-fitness and human endeavour.

The second Tour de France, in 1904, was the
shortest, with six stages averaging just over
400 kilometres each. The longest Tour was in
1926, 5,745km, and it was won by Belgium's
Lucien Buysse, though his brother, Julien
(right, with Ottavio Bottecchia in rear), won
the opening stage from Evian to Mulhausen.

LONGEST AND SHORTEST

The Tour de France is still a supreme endurance test, but modern Tours test speed and tactical intelligence as well. This wasn't so in the early days of the Tour, when distance was paramount and racers would put up with almost anything to win.

↗ *Stages were so long in early years of the Tour de France that the racers often started in the dark.*

SHORTEST TOUR

The second edition of the race in 1904 remains the shortest Tour de France so far, just 2,428 kilometres (1,509 miles).
There were only six stages:

1. Paris–Lyon, 467 km
2. Lyon–Marseille, 374 km
3. Marseille–Toulouse, 423 km
4. Toulouse–Bordeaux, 268 km
5. Bordeaux–Nantes, 425 km
6. Nantes–Paris, 471 km

↓ *Lucien Pothier of France arrives in Bordeaux at the end of stage 4 in 1904.*

MIDNIGHT START

The incredible length of the stages in 1926 (average 337.9 kilometres or 210 miles) meant that some stages started at midnight, like stage 10 from Bayonne to Luchon. By 1926 this stage was a Pyrenean classic – 326 kilometres (203 miles) long, it climbed the highest passes in the Pyrenees – and that year the weather was terrible. Ottavio Bottecchia, winner of the previous two Tours and the first Italian ever to win, suffered so much in the icy torrential rain, thunderstorms, hail and sleet, that he never raced again. Lucien Buysse won by 25 minutes, and an hour later only ten riders had finished. By midnight, 24 hours after they started, 47 had finished, and another 57 struggled home through the rest of that night. Eventually the organizers decided to allow anyone finishing within 40 per cent of the winner's time to continue riding in the Tour, but the remaining 22 left out on the road were collected by car. Their Tour was over.

THE 2012 TOUR DE FRANCE ROUTE

Stage	Date	Route	Length
Prologue	Saturday 30 June	Liège–Liège	6.1 km ITT
1	Sunday 1 July	Liège–Seraing	198 km
2	Monday 2 July	Visé–Tournai	207 km
3	Tuesday 3 July	Orchies–Boulogne-sur-Mer	197 km
4	Wednesday 4 July	Abbeville–Rouen	214 km
5	Thursday 5 July	Rouen–St-Quentin	197 km
6	Friday 6 July	Epernay–Metz	210 km
7	Saturday 7 July	Tomblaine–La Planche des Belles Filles	199 km
8	Sunday 8 July	Belfort–Porrentruy	154 km
9	Monday 9 July	Arc-et-Senans–Besançon	38 km ITT
Rest day	Tuesday 10 July	Mâcon	
10	Wednesday 11 July	Mâcon–Bellegarde-sur-Valserine	194 km
11	Thursday 12 July	Albertville–La Toussuire	140 km
12	Friday 13 July	St-Jean-de-Maurienne–Annonay Davézieux	220 km
13	Saturday 14 July	St-Paul-Trois-Châteaux–Le Cap d'Agde	215 km
14	Sunday 15 July	Limoux–Foix	192 km
15	Monday 16 July	Samatan–Pau	160 km
Rest day	Tuesday 17 July	Pau	
16	Wednesday 18 July	Pau–Bagnères-de-Luchon	197 km
17	Thursday 19 July	Bagnères-de-Luchon–Peyragudes	144 km
18	Friday 20 July	Blagnac–Brive-la-Gaillarde	215 km
19	Saturday 21 July	Bonneval–Chartres	52 km ITT
20	Sunday 22 July	Rambouillet–Paris Champs-Elysées	130 km

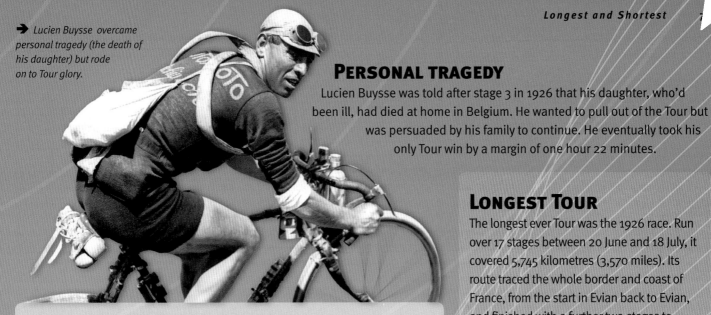

➜ *Lucien Buysse overcame personal tragedy (the death of his daughter) but rode on to Tour glory.*

PERSONAL TRAGEDY

Lucien Buysse was told after stage 3 in 1926 that his daughter, who'd been ill, had died at home in Belgium. He wanted to pull out of the Tour but was persuaded by his family to continue. He eventually took his only Tour win by a margin of one hour 22 minutes.

LONGEST TOUR

The longest ever Tour was the 1926 race. Run over 17 stages between 20 June and 18 July, it covered 5,745 kilometres (3,570 miles). Its route traced the whole border and coast of France, from the start in Evian back to Evian, and finished with a further two stages to Paris. The winner was Lucien Buysse of Belgium at an average speed of 24.064 kph (14.953 mph).

STAGES OF THE LONGEST TOUR

Stage	Route	Length	Winner
1	Evian–Mulhouse	373 km	Jules Buysse (BEL)
2	Mulhouse–Metz	334 km	Aimé Dossche (BEL)
3	Metz–Dunkerque	433 km	Gustaaf van Slumberouck (BEL)
4	Dunkerque–Le Havre	361 km	Félix Sellier (BEL)
5	Le Havre–Cherbourg	357 km	Adelin Bernoit (BEL)
6	Cherbourg–Brest	405 km	Joseph van Dam (BEL)
7	Brest–Les Sables-d'Olonne	412 km	Nicolas Frantz (LUX)
8	Les Sables-d'Olonne–Bordeaux	285 km	Joseph van Dam (BEL)
9	Bordeaux–Bayonne	189 km	Nicolas Frantz (LUX)
10	Bayonne–Luchon	326 km	Lucien Buysse (BEL)
11	Luchon–Perpignan	323 km	Lucien Buysse (BEL)
12	Perpignan–Toulon	427 km	Nicolas Frantz (LUX)
13	Toulon–Nice	280 km	Nicolas Frantz (LUX)
14	Nice–Briançon	275 km	Bartolomeo Aimo (ITA)
15	Briançon–Evian	303 km	Joseph van Dam (BEL)
16	Evian–Dijon	321 km	Camille van de Casteele (BEL)
17	Dijon–Paris	341 km	Aimé Dossche (BEL)

CUTTING A LONG STORY SHORT

Modern Tours are much shorter than the early editions of the race for several reasons. First the organizers cut night starts as they were unsafe and difficult to police. Then they realized that long stages and long Tours made riders race quite conservatively, trying to save their energy for crucial days. Shorter Tours with an increased number of shorter stages created a faster, more exciting spectacle. After the death of the British racer Tom Simpson in the 1967 Tour, the governing body of cycling stepped in to limit stage lengths and the number of days of racing and to stipulate that the Tour had to have two rest days.

21ST-CENTURY TOURS

A Tour de France can now be no longer than 3,500 kilometres (2,200 miles). This has created the transfers by road, rail and air that we see in modern Tours. Given the rule-book constriction it's almost impossible to include the terrain needed to make a good Tour, and visit the places that want to host stages, without exceeding 3,500 kilometres. Some stages are therefore linked by road, rail or air transfers.

← *Racers speed into a tunnel on their way to Sestrières in 2011. The Tour remains a test of endurance and speed.*

... / -Eleven team races through a corner during the shortest ever prologue in 1986.

LE PETIT PROLOGUE

Prologue time trials are short, just a quick shuffle of the pack to find the first yellow jersey and to decide a pecking order for the team cars to follow the race. The order is important because if a rider has a mechanical problem he saves energy if his team car gets to him quickly. Even so, some prologues are shorter than the usual eight kilometres (five miles) that kick off most modern Tours. The shortest ever prologue was just 1 kilometre (0.6 miles) in Pornichet-La Baule in 1988. The longest is a little bit more up for debate. The Tour has started with a longish time trial, like the 19 kilometres (12 miles) that kicked off the 2005 race. But it was called a time trial, not a prologue, so it's generally accepted that the longest true prologue was the 10.4 kilometres (6.5 miles) around Roubaix in 1969.

ADDED EXCITEMENT

One of the reasons why Tour de France stages have got shorter is that long stages can be boring, and very long stages are very boring. They also have a stultifying effect on the race as a whole. Even as late as the 1960s the Tour often had a 300-kilometre stage, and as Eddy Merckx says, "Even though such a stage might have been over easy terrain, riding one is very tiring because of the nervous energy you use, and because of the strain it places everywhere from your hands to your feet." Short stages are exciting because racing starts from the gun and is much more aggressive throughout. Modern Tours have an average stage length of around 160 kilometres (100 miles), but last year there was a stage in the Alps of only 100 kilometres (62 miles). During it the riders tackled three big mountains, and it was brilliant to watch. The organizers intend to repeat this kind of stage in 2012.

⬆ *In the 1920s, the public wanted to see fast racing, not small groups of tired riders plodding through their village in small groups.*

THE LONGEST DAY

The longest ever stage was 482 kilometres (300 miles), from Les Sables-d'Olonne to Bayonne, in 1924. Look at a map of France; that's from the Vendée, tucked just under the outstretched arm of Brittany, down to the western end of the Pyrenees, close to the Spanish border. It was too much, according to one French journalist. Albert Londres, a serious writer who commented on serious matters, said that the Tour was becoming like a ballroom dancing marathon where the winner was the one who stayed awake longest, rather than a race decided by speed and athleticism.

SNOW STOPS PLAY, NEARLY

It rained and was freezing cold during the first part of the 1996 Tour, and got worse as the race moved south. Stage 9 from Le Monetier-les-Bains to Sestrières was due to scale the giant alpine climbs, the Iseran (2,770 metres) and the Galibier (2,640 metres), but they were blocked by snow. The whole race was bussed around the mountains to start in the valley below the uphill finish, for a stage of 46 kilometres (29 miles) won by eventual Tour winner Bjarne Riis – still the shortest road stage ever.

⬆ The riders were taken by car and buses over some of the mountains of stage 9 in 1996.

⬇ René Vietto's last chance to win the Tour disappeared before he got out on to the road between Vannes and St-Brieuc in 1947.

LAST CHANCE

René Vietto was an irascible man who by 1947 was a fairly old irascible man. He was French, and a good enough racer to have won the Tour, but he never did. He was unlucky before the Second World War, which then filled up his best racing years, but it really looked as if he'd win in 1947. With two days to go Vietto led by over 90 seconds, but there was a problem. The next stage was the Tour's longest ever time trial, and Vietto hated time trials. Still, he had to try, and to help him he had a silk yellow jersey made because silk slips through the air faster than wool. Just before his start an official told him he couldn't use it, he had to use the regulation one. Vietto went mad and stormed off to his hotel. The officials chased, and after a lot of pulling and pushing Vietto began the time trial. He grumbled and cursed his way through 139 kilometres (86 miles) between Vannes and St-Brieuc, losing 14 minutes and his very last chance of winning the Tour.

YOUNGEST AND OLDEST

The careers of top-class professional road race cyclists start at around 23 or 24 and usually continue until they are 33 or maybe 35. It's not unusual for a 21-year-old to race in the Tour, and riders approaching 40 have competed and still do. What is more, some at either end of the scale have achieved major Tour success. This section is devoted to them.

YOUNGEST

They say that excellence knows no age, but it's very hard for an under-23 racer to win the Tour de France. Three-week stage races favour mature racers. Stage races make tremendous demands on stamina, something that develops with age, but they are also a test of experience and clear thinking. That doesn't mean young riders cannot win the Tour, because they have. It's even been won by a teenager.

NEW KID ON THE BLOCK

Pro cycling, and especially the Tour de France, has been dominated by just a few major equipment manufacturers. Benelux and Simplex gears from France held sway after the Derailleur gear shift was first introduced in 1937. Next came domination by an Italian company, Campagnolo. It took Shimano over 30 years, from their Tour debut in the early 1970s until 2005, for a bike with their equipment to win overall. SRAM didn't take nearly as long – having first appeared on top road racers' bikes in the 2000s, SRAM won the 2009 Tour, powered by Alberto Contador's legs.

ARMSTRONG'S FIRST STAGE

Lance Armstrong was 21 when he won his first Tour stage in 1993 at Verdun, one of the youngest ever road stage winners. Jan Ullrich, Armstrong's biggest rival for the yellow jersey in years to come, was only 22 when he won the time trial stage at St-Emilion in 1997.

⬆ *Luxembourg's François Faber braved dire weather to win the 1909 Tour. Aged 22, weighing 90kg, and the first foreigner to win the Tour, Faber set a still-standing record of five consecutive stage wins.*

YOUNG GIANT

François Faber was not quite the youngest to win the Tour, although he was only 22 when he won in 1909, but he was certainly the biggest bike racer ever to succeed in this ultimate test of endurance. Faber weighed over 90 kilos, which is huge for a road race cyclist, but this was the last Tour before the race began climbing the biggest mountains, where extra weight is a huge drawback. Faber's Tour also had terrible weather, which bigger racers cope with better. It's to do with skin surface area compared to body volume. We all lose heat through our skin, and thin people have a large skin surface area in relation to their body volume. Perfect when it's hot, but bad news when it's cold.

⬆ *Jan Ullrich surprised everyone when he won the Tour de France in 1997, but it was even more of a surprise that he didn't win another Tour.*

YOUNGEST COUNTRY

No American had ridden the Tour de France until Jonathan Boyer in 1981, yet Greg LeMond became the USA's first winner in 1986, and between them LeMond and Lance Armstrong won 10 Tours in the following 20 years. No country except France has dominated in the same way. Who will be the next LeMond or Armstrong? Look out for a young racer called Taylor Phinney.

← *Henri Cornet was a teenager when he won in 1904. No other teenager has won the Tour.*

THE TEN YOUNGEST TOUR DE FRANCE WINNERS

Age	Year	Winner
19 years 11 months	1904	Henri Cornet
21 years 11 months	1935	Romain Maes
22 years 6 months	1909	François Faber
22 years 9 months	1910	Octave Lapize
22 years 9 months	1965	Felice Gimondi
22 years 9 months	1913	Philippe Thys
22 years 11 months	1983	Laurent Fignon
23 years 6 months	1957	Jacques Anquetil
23 years 7 months	1997	Jan Ullrich
23 years 9 months	1978	Bernard Hinault

YOUNGEST PASS

The Hourquette d'Ancizan pass in the Pyrenees is the latest high mountain pass to be included in the Tour route. It was first used in the 2011 Tour, when Laurent Magnel was first over the top.

FIRST OF THE FEW

Henri Cornet was a few days short of his 20th birthday when he finished fifth in the 1904 Tour de France. It was a fine result, but what he didn't know was that the organizers had evidence that the four riders in front of him had all cheated, and in different ways had cut the course. Cornet was the first of those whose overall time was above suspicion, so in their minds he was the true winner, but they didn't dare say so for fear of partisan fans rioting. The true result wasn't announced for several months, until passions surrounding the race had died down a little. Cornet never won the Tour again, and his career was cut short by heart problems. He remains the youngest ever winner.

THE TOUR BABY

The "Benjamin du Tour" is French for the baby of the Tour, or in other words the youngest rider in the race. In 2011 it was the 21-year-old Frenchman Anthony Delaplace. Britain's Geraint Thomas was the Benjamin du Tour in 2007.

→ *"Benjamin du Tour" Geraint Thomas in time trial action during the 2007 Tour.*

OLDEST

The Tour de France tests skills in every facet of road cycling, many of which develop over time in those who take part. Naturally this tends to favour age and experience. Old pro racers say you have to ride a Tour before you know the demands it makes, and although some special talents have won at their first attempt, generally that's true. Within limits the Tour favours older and more experienced riders, but among them there have been some exceptional personalities who have pushed the envelope of how athletes are expected to perform as they age.

↗ *Jens Voigt's character has animated the Tour de France for a good few years, and there's no sign that he's slowing down yet.*

↑ *The longest time gap between victories belongs to Italy's Gino Bartali, but he lost many opportunities to win because of the Second World War.*

WAR HERO

Gino Bartali, an Italian who won the Tour de France before the Second World War in 1938, aged 24, and after it in 1948 at 34, lost his best years to the conflict, so one can only guess how many Tours he would have won but for the fighting. Bartali was a national hero when war broke out, and he used his status to work against the Germans by helping the Assisi movement transport forged documents to help Jews escape arrest. Bartali used the cover of his training rides to collect the papers from forgers and carry them to safe houses. The Italian authorities knew what was going on but didn't dare arrest Bartali until the Germans forced them to. He was interrogated by them and beaten, but he didn't give anyone away. Bartali was even more active after that and helped transport Jews out of Italy to safety in Switzerland.

THE HARDEST-WORKING MAN IN CYCLING

Jens Voigt of Germany was the oldest man in the 2011 Tour at 39. He is a legend in pro racing: seemingly indestructible, always attacking, superstrong and with a never-say-die spirit that endears him both to fellow pro racers and to fans all over the world. He's also one of the most quoted cyclists. You can even buy a Jens Voigt T-shirt with the slogan "Shut Up Legs", which is what he shouts when he's in one of his famous lone breakaways and his legs begin to complain.

VETERAN STAGE WINNER

Pino Cerami was the king of the late bloomers. He had a long racing career, but most of it was spent racing as a good team man in support of better racers. Then, in 1960, at the age of 38 and in a team with no particular leader, Cerami won two of the biggest single-day races in the world: the Paris–Roubaix and the Flèche Wallonne. That kick-started Cerami's career as a big winner, and he won more races, including stage 9 of the 1963 Tour de France, his only Tour stage win. He was 41 and Cerami is still the oldest winner of a Tour stage.

↑ *41-year-old Pino Cerami becomes the oldest rider ever to win a stage as he crosses the line at the end of the Bordeaux to Pau stage in 1963.*

THE ETERNAL SECOND

Raymond Poulidor started 14 Tours, finished 12, and took three second places and five thirds. His last time on the podium was 1976 when he was 40, and he is still the oldest rider to place in the top three of the Tour de France. He is very popular in France, more popular than riders who won the Tour. Journalists called him "The Eternal Second", and the name has stuck, even though Joop Zoetemelk finished second six times and Poulidor was more often third than runner-up. "Eternal Third" doesn't have the same ring, though.

THE TEN OLDEST TOUR DE FRANCE WINNERS

Age	Date	Winner
36 years 4 months	1922	Firmin Lambot
34 years 6 months	1923	Henri Pélissier
34 years 6 months	2011	Cadel Evans
34 years 0 months	1948	Gino Bartali
33 years 10 months	2005	Lance Armstrong
33 years 10 months	1926	Lucien Buysse
33 years 7 months	1980	Joop Zoetemelk
33 years 4 months	1919	Firmin Lambot
33 years 4 months	1921	Léon Scieur
32 years 10 months	1952	Fausto Coppi

↑ *Raymond Poulidor (centre) on his way to podium number eight in 1976, thus becoming the oldest racer ever to finish a Tour de France in the first three.*

THE OLDEST WINNER

Firmin Lambot of Belgium was 35 when he won his second Tour de France in 1935. He is still the oldest racer ever to win the Tour. Closest to Lambot is the Frenchman Henri Pélissier (1923), who was 34 years and 181 days old when he won, and then comes the Australian Cadel Evans, who won the 2011 Tour aged 34 years and 170 days.

OLDEST MOUNTAIN

The Col du Tourmalet was included for the first time in 1910 on the day the Tour first climbed over the highest Pyrenean passes. Since then the climb has been included in the Tour 70 times, more than any other, and has featured in 50 Tours since 1947.

RADIO DAYS

The record for the oldest team to take part in the Tour was set in 2011 by Radio Shack, whose average age was 33.16 years. The previous oldies were Alessio-Bianchi, who had an average of 33.13 in 2004.

➔ *Proving the old adage that "old 'uns can still be good 'uns", Radio Shack in 2011.*

ICONIC TEAMS

One man wins the Tour de France, but it is incredibly difficult to win a modern Tour without the support of a good team. And, like individuals, there have been teams that stood out above the rest. Whether through their dominance, tactical cleverness or even their ability to shepherd a sprinter to the finish of a Tour stage, these are the iconic teams of the Tour de France.

The Peugeot-BP-Michelin team line up before the start of the 1966 Tour. The only racer not in their iconic checkerboard black-and-white kit is Tom Simpson (third right) who's wearing the rainbow jersey of world champion.

ICONIC TEAMS

The Tour started out as a race for individuals, but as cycling became more sophisticated as a sport, teamwork grew in importance. A modern Tour is like a three-week chess game, with teams placing their players on an ever-changing board of stages so that they can help their leader get to Paris first. Even the strongest racer would find it difficult to win the Tour without a very strong team.

COMMERCE VERSUS COUNTRY

The first Tour teams were sponsored by bicycle manufacturers. These works teams tried to get the best racers, no matter where from, to race in their colours. Some teams, probably because they paid better wages, were better at this than others, which saw one or two teams begin to dominate the Tour. Henri Desgrange didn't like the idea of a business concern becoming bigger than the Tour, so in 1930 he changed the rules and said only national teams could ride. But that caused problems because the sponsors who picked up the bill for teams to race the rest of the pro calendar were being deprived of publicity during its biggest race. The sponsors' names were stitched on to their riders' national kit, but it didn't have the same impact as carefully thought-out company colours. The Tour returned to trade teams in 1962, tried national teams again in 1967 and 1968, but then reverted once more. Since 1969 it has been trade teams only.

VIVE LA FRANCE!

Turning to national teams virtually gave the Tour de France to French riders. They had strength in depth spread throughout the trade teams before 1930, so when they banded together in national colours they were the major players for most of the next decade. French riders won six of the next ten Tours.

WHO SPONSORS?

Although in the early Tours team sponsors were all bike manufacturers, and the growth of bike use over the last few years has seen a return of bike businesses to the Tour, most sponsors are manufacturers of products that appeal to a mass market. So, the Tour has seen the racers' jerseys dominated by the makers of cars and soft drinks – and of harder ones before they were banned from sponsoring most sports – and by coffee makers, confectioners, bakers, insurance companies and banks.

ITALIAN STALLIONS

The 1940s saw the emergence of Italy as the great cycling nation. Gino Bartali won the 1938 Tour and won again in 1948. Then Fausto Coppi led Bartali into Paris to score a Tour one-two, but he had beaten his compatriot by almost half an hour. Coppi was similarly dominant in 1952, causing a cycling journalist to write that a stopwatch wasn't needed to time Coppi's victory margin, it could be done with a church clock.

← Fausto Coppi led the Italian team during the late 1940s and early 1950s, winning the Tour twice.

MONEY TALKS

France often had four regions plus the national team in the race, but they didn't band together – quite the opposite in fact. When it looked as if Henri Anglade, racing for the Centre-Midi team, would win in 1959, the French national team conspired to work for the Spanish racer Federico Bahamontes, who did win. It was nothing to do with pride, but all to do with money. The French national racers all had the same commercial agent, Daniel Dousset, who negotiated their team contracts and other money deals. Bahamontes too was on Dousset's books, while Anglade was signed to Dousset's big rival, Roger Piel.

B TEAMS

Up until the 1980s cycling was predominantly a European sport. This meant that, in the days of national teams, those of France, Belgium, Italy, Holland, Germany, Spain and later Great Britain, plus a mixed team representing smaller European nations, each with nine or ten racers, would have made only a small field. Also a lot of outstanding riders from big cycling countries wouldn't have been able to race in the Tour. So the organizers invited teams from the French regions, and asked some other countries to enter national B teams. When Roger Walkowiak won in 1956 he was racing for the Nord-Est-Centre French regional team.

⬇ *The Alcyon team take a photo break during a pre-stage discussion during the 1928 Tour.*

⬆ *Sylvère Maes storms up the Col d'Iseran in 1939 on his way to winning the Tour and claiming the King of the Mountains prize too.*

HOW MUCH?

Sponsoring a modern Tour de France team is expensive. The cost varies according to the riders' wages and the level of back-up, but it can take anything between two and ten million euros to put a team on the road for one year. The commitment stretches far beyond the Tour de France, which is one race among many; the pro cycling season runs from January to late October and visits five continents, although the majority of races are in Europe.

THE KINGFISHERS

The dominant team of the early Tours was that of Alcyon, a bike, motorbike and car manufacturer. The company was named after the French word for kingfisher, and the team raced in kingfisher blue and on kingfisher blue bikes. Their riders, François Faber, Gustave Garrigou, Octave Lapize and Maurice De Waele, all won the Tour. In fact it was De Waele's win in 1929 that finally set Henri Desgrange against trade teams. De Waele was ill for the last three stages and his team virtually carried him to Paris, causing Desgrange to complain in *L'Auto*: "My race has been won by a corpse."

They never won the Tour, but Anquetil won... Tours in... haël colours. The... happened... explains how pro cycling teams are... The team is owned by a person, often the manager or a holding company, and it is they who attract the sponsors. The people behind the St Raphaël team found Ford motors as their next sponsor, then Bic pens, and the team continued into the 1970s and beyond.

⬇ *Feisty Spaniard José Manuel Fuente, nicknamed "Tarangu", embodied the spirit of the Kas team.*

⬆ *Jaques Anquetil (centre) won three Tours for St Raphaël in the 1960s, ensuring his team would attract another sponsor when the drinks company pulled out.*

CYCLES PEUGEOT

This company is the longest-serving sponsor in cycling, their patronage running from the first Tours until the late 1980s, when they were the Z-Peugeot team. Peugeot pulled its name from the team in 1990, but the same staff and managers continued under the Z banner, and won the Tour twice with Greg LeMond. The team then took the name Gan Assurances and later that of the French bank Crédit Agricole, but the most iconic Peugeot team ran from 1963 until Z took over. They raced in white, with a black-and-white checkerboard band just below the chest. When the team was called Peugeot-BP, their top man Bernard Thévenet won the 1975 and 1977 Tours.

THE RED GUARD

Teams are often built around one rider, and that rider demands absolute dedication. Such teams will execute their tactics with iron discipline, earning respect from but not necessarily popularity with their fellow racers. One such team was the Flandria squad of Rik Van Looy, who is the only cyclist ever to win every single-day Classic. They raced in red and earned the name Red Guard for the way they set up races, including Tour de France stages, for their talented boss to win.

TARANGU

They never won the Tour, but the Spanish racers of the Kas team were such superb climbers that they constantly worried the men who did. Their attacking spirit was personified by José Manuel Fuente, a tiny, feisty man from Asturias known to local fans as Tarangu. The word doesn't have a direct English translation, but it describes someone who would die rather than be conquered and admit another's superiority. When Eddy Merckx was at his best and his rivals were at a loss as to how to beat him, Fuente could be relied on to attack, and sometimes he had Merckx in real trouble.

↑ *La Vie Claire was cycling's first super-team, where money brought together some of the best racers in one squad and gave them the best back-up.*

REVOLUTION

The 1980s were times of revolution in cycling: bikes were changing, as was clothing, and the way and the amount racers were paid. The top men of the Tour always did well, and some of them retired very wealthy men, but up until the eighties it was necessary for some Tour racers to work at another job during the winter. That changed with the first million-dollar contract given to Greg LeMond by Bernard Tapie, a French businessman who created a super-team under the brand name of a company he owned, La Vie Claire. The team started in 1984, with Bernard Hinault as the leader, and having already won the Tour four times he couldn't have been getting paid less than LeMond. Still, it was the American's contract that was big news when he joined La Vie Claire to race beside Hinault in 1985. Hinault won the Tour that year, and LeMond won in 1986.

SKY'S THE LIMIT

Team Sky is showing the way teams should be run now. From its Formula One-style team bus to its rider-centric policy of making their racers responsible for tactical decisions, right through their no-stone-unturned approach to the best preparation possible, this is a team for the 21st century. They have only raced two Tours. The first was for learning, but they made a big impact during their second. Team Sky and others such as Garmin-Barracuda are establishing the blueprint for future team success.

BANKING ON INDURAIN

The Spanish bank Banesto backed Miguel Indurain to five consecutive Tour wins – he was the first to achieve that run of success. And in doing so their management evolved a template for winning the Tour that, although refined by subsequent winners, has remained essentially the same. Indurain won his first Tours when it was still possible to win the Giro, or Tour of Italy, in the same year, but as the fight to win both these races intensified, Indurain had to focus only on the Tour. So did his team. Riders could try their luck in other races, but in the Tour they were totally committed to Indurain.

THE POSTAL TRAIN

When Johan Bruyneel took over as manager of the US Postal team in 1999 he adopted Banesto's Tour-winning template and refined it further. He worked with Lance Armstrong, the team's leader, on a one-to-one basis to create an impregnable Tour racer, and he did so by focusing on the controllable in sport, which is training, rather than the uncontrollable – racing. Bruyneel also recruited racers who were good enough to rival Armstrong to work for him. The results were plain to see in the crucial mountain stages of the Tour, when US Postal's talented climbers would ride in line at the front of the race and set a brutal pace, which literally burned off all but the very best of Armstrong's rivals, leaving him to take care of them later.

➔ *The US Postal team train gets to work, with their driver, Lance Armstrong, directing things from behind in the yellow jersey.*

ABOUT THE BIKES

Bikes may not have developed quite as much as motor vehicles over the 100-plus years of the Tour de France, but they are not far off. Like racing cars, modern bikes are built from the most advanced materials, are subject to wind tunnel testing, and have been refined so much that to compare them with the first Tour machines would be like comparing a modern racing car with a Model T Ford.

Team cars carry enough spare bikes to cover any eventuality and enough spares to make on-the-road repairs.

ABOUT THE BIKES

The first Tour riders competed on what today would seem the most rudimentary bikes. They were made from steel tubes, welded together, and had steel handlebars, a leather saddle, very basic brakes, wooden wheel rims and balloon-like tyres. But just as motor sport helped the advance of cars, the demands of the Tour de France pushed the advance of bikes until they became the ultra-light, multi-geared, silent-running machines of today. In doing so, the Tour de France helped develop the bikes that we all ride and are a delight to use.

GEARING UP

The gearing on a bike is a function of the size of the chainring, which is the bit the pedals drive, and the sprocket, which is on the rear wheel hub and is turned by a chain that also runs around the chainring. The first Tour bikes had two gears, but no mechanical way of shifting between them. Instead they had two sprockets, of different sizes, one on either side of the rear hub. When the rider wanted to change gear he had to stop, dismount, undo the rear wheel, take it out of the frame, turn it around and replace it in the frame so the other sprocket engaged with the chain, then tighten up the rear wheel nuts and off he went.

⬇ *Racers, such as Gustave Garrigou, did everything themselves. Even if a spectator held his bike while he worked on it, he would get a time penalty.*

⬆ *Everyone raced on a bike supplied by the Tour in 1930. After the Brest to Vannes stage, Georges Laloup wished he could have used his own machine.*

YELLOW BIKES

When Desgrange banned trade teams in 1930 he made all the racers ride the same bikes too. The Tour had 150 bikes specially made, all painted yellow, and with no manufacturer's name on them. The Tour also had to pay the racers' hotel bills, because not surprisingly the bike manufacturers who sponsored them for the rest of the year were unwilling to do so. The race needed extra money to fund this, so Desgrange invented the publicity caravan, which offered the opportunity for any business to have a vehicle drive directly in front of the race carrying any advertising they wanted. The caravan grew and today comprises hundreds of vehicles that follow the Tour.

MENDING PUNCTURES

Another burden racers had to endure in the early Tours was the rule that said they had to finish on the bike on which they started. If it broke they had to repair it; there could be no outside help. This meant that not only did they have to carry spare tyres and change them if they punctured, but if they ran out of spares they had to mend their own punctures. This wasn't easy because they used tubular tyres, meaning that a canvas carcass with a tread on it was sewn around an inner tube, then the whole thing stuck to a wheel rim with glue. The punctured tyre had to be prised off the rim, the stitching unpicked to reveal the inner tube, and then it could be mended. After that the racer had to sew up the tyre and put it back on the rim before he could get going.

THE BLACKSMITH'S ARMS

When the forks in Eugène Christophe's bike broke while he was descending the Col du Tourmalet in 1913, he jogged ten kilometres, carrying his bike, to a blacksmith's in Sainte-Marie-de-Campan at the foot of the climb. Once there he used the forge to heat a metal tube to join the forks together, but he had to ask the blacksmith's boy to operate the bellows, because he couldn't do that and work the metal at the same time. He was delayed for hours, losing any chance of winning the race, but watching officials still gave him an extra time penalty for getting outside help.

➡ *Eugène Christophe negotiates a tricky mountain pass the year before his catastrophic equipment failure in the Pyrénées.*

LITTLE CHANGES

By the 1940s Tour racers were riding bikes made of special lightweight steel, which had aluminium parts and ten gears. Little changed then for several decades; bikes got slightly lighter, gear ratios increased to 12, and tyres improved slightly. Big changes came in the 1980s after track cyclists discovered that improving air-flow over themselves and their bikes helped them break world records that had looked beyond their reach.

THE SOFT ROUTE

It wasn't long into the 20th century before a way of shifting the chain between multiple sprockets on the same side of the rear hub was invented, but Henri Desgranges considered such contraptions suitable only for pleasure riders and tourists. The Tour was a hard race for hard men, and shifting gear while in the saddle was for softies, so Desgrange didn't let the professional Tour racers use them until 1937. However, there was another kind of racer in those early Tours called "touriste-routiers". They were independent racers, or adventurers who paid to ride the Tour, and they were allowed to use Derailleur gearshifts. A touriste-routier called Joanny Panel was the first racer to use such a gearshift mechanism in 1912.

EVIDENCE OF MISFORTUNE

Soon after the First World War the race rules were relaxed slightly. Riders were allowed to take replacement parts from a spares van that followed the Tour, but only if the part they replaced was damaged beyond repair, and they had to carry it to the finish to prove it. Léon Scieur was leading the 1921 Tour when, on the penultimate stage, his rear wheel collapsed. He got a spare from the van, but to avoid an extra time penalty from the judges he had to carry his broken wheel on his back for 300 kilometres to the end of the stage. The wheel sprocket dug into Scieur's back so deeply that the 1921 Tour winner had a star-shaped scar there for the rest of his life.

⬅ *Once spare tyres were allowed, a rider, such as Léon Scieur, would carry them looped around their shoulders to use should they puncture instead of repairing the old one.*

WHEEL CHANGES

If a rider suffers a puncture in a modern Tour, he drops back through the peloton, raising his arm to draw attention, and the first car following, which has the race director in it, tells his team by radio that he has punctured. A mechanic sits on the back seat of every team car with a front and back wheel, and he jumps out to help when the rider stops. By the time the mechanic reaches him the rider has removed the punctured wheel and is holding his bike. The mechanic fits the replacement wheel, the rider mounts up and gets a running shove to help him back up to speed. If the problem is more serious the mechanic uses a spare bike from the roof of the team car to get his man going again.

← *Manuel Quinziato of Liquigas punctured on stage 8 in 2008. He held up the wheel in question, so the team mechanic knew what needed to be replaced before he got to him.*

RIDE BY WIRE

Aerodynamic adaptations have found their way on to the bikes used on normal stages. Most Tour racers ride carbon fibre frames with tubes shaped to slip through the air. Their wheels are carbon fibre too, often with deep section rims and flat spokes to score an aerodynamic advantage. Their rear wheels have ten or 11 sprockets, combined with two chainrings to create 20 or 22 gear ratios. Gearshifts are still made by cable, but some bikes have electronic shift systems, and all are precise – a single click of a lever or switch effecting a single, precise gearshift. The transmission is still driven by a chain, but one so flexible that it causes very little friction. Some riders race on tubular tyres, but they are far lighter, thinner and more dependable than the ones used in early Tours.

KEEPING A LOW PROFILE

When Francesco Moser beat Eddy Merckx's world hour record in 1984 he did it on a radical bike. It had solid disc wheels to smooth air-flow, rather than spokes that churn it up. A lot of the bike's frontal area was cut by having the top tube slope down almost to the top of the forks; and it had cow-horn handlebars, because the tops of traditional handlebars weren't needed for a constant paced effort on a flat track against the clock. Moser's bike cut wind resistance to a minimum, and that is a cyclist's biggest enemy in a time trial. It was called a low-profile bike, and it wasn't long before low-profiles with gears and brakes were being used for Tour time trials.

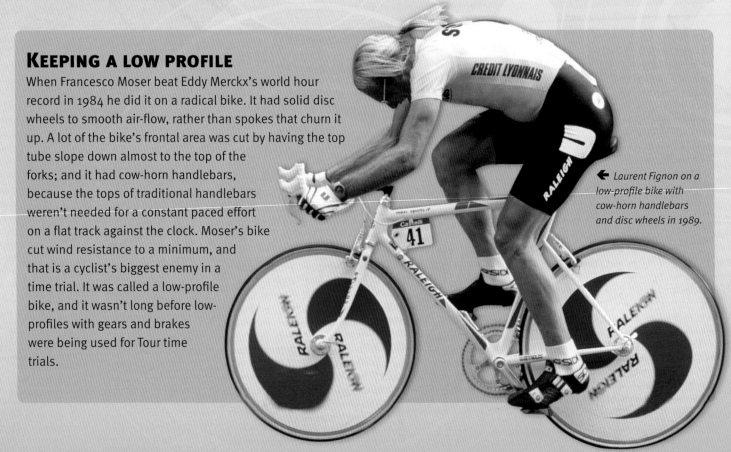

← *Laurent Fignon on a low-profile bike with cow-horn handlebars and disc wheels in 1989.*

↑ *Bikes are now as light as the rules permit. As they can no longer reduce weight, manufacturers are trying to make them more aerodynamic and one way is to cut down the number of spokes in wheels like this Astana team bike.*

FUTURE BIKES

The body that runs cycle racing, the UCI, have imposed a minimum weight limit on bikes of 6.8 kilograms. This is a contentious safety measure, because many manufacturers say they can build lighter bikes that are safe. In fact some do, and you can buy them, but the racers sponsored by those manufacturers have weight added to their bikes to bring them in line with regulations. There are also rules about frame shape and riding position, which could make them more aerodynamic, and bikes are checked for compliance throughout the Tour. As for the next major developments, electric gearshifts will probably become standard in the Tour. We may also see disc brakes, which would be a safety step because rim brakes can heat rims and cause tyre blowouts. Disc brakes are not affected by wet and are also fractionally easier to use.

BRITISH TOUR WINNERS

Joop Zoetemelk won the 1980 Tour de France on a Raleigh bike designed and built in their special development unit near Nottingham. It was Raleigh's only Tour win, although they supplied bikes to Tour racers throughout the eighties, among them Laurent Fignon of France when he finished second to Greg LeMond in 1989. But Raleigh isn't the only British Tour-winning bike. The Spanish racer Luis Ocana was a great bike innovator, and he used an experimental ultra-light titanium bike for some of the mountain stages when he won the 1973 Tour. The titanium frame was built by a Birmingham-based company called Speedwell.

ON THE FLY REPAIR

Tour racers are marvellous at handling their bikes, and their mechanics are fearless. It's not unusual to see running repairs being made at over 50 kph as a mechanic leans precariously out of the team car while the rider casually steers an inch-perfect course.

↓ *Tour leader Alberto Contador gets something adjusted on his bike during a stage in 2010.*

TIME MACHINES

Modern Tour time trial machines are the pinnacle of bike technology. Equipment is debuted at every Tour that trickles down to the shops too. Racers go for deep section front wheels and rear disc wheels as the best compromise between good handling and aerodynamics. Low-profile bikes have gone, replaced by aerodynamic handlebars with extensions so that racers can adopt a ski-tuck position. They wear tear-drop helmets and special suits to smooth air-flow over and around their bodies. Many top time triallists spend time in a wind tunnel to get their positions absolutely right on their time trial bikes, and they spend hours training on them so they can operate with ease on race day.

MISCELLANEOUS RECORDS

The Tour de France is so big that it's full of facts and figures that are difficult to categorize. So are some of the incidents, facts ancillary to the race, and the rare occasions on which the event has been hit by tragedy. This section is for them, for everything from the numbers that make up the Tour to the four occasions when racers died during the race.

Before the Tour de France begins various events are staged in the city hosting Le Grand Départ and in the centenary of the Tour in 2003, Paris was treated to a history lesson on wheels. Antonin Magne and André Leducq won four out of the five Tours between 1930 and 1934.

MISCELLANEOUS RECORDS

The Tour de France is the biggest annual sporting event in the world, which fact on its own generates some formidable records, but the whole thing is on the move for three weeks every year, which is an incredible feat of logistics. It also has the biggest live audience, and the largest media audience of any annual sports event, so in a way we all play a part in the story of the Tour.

STRIKES

The riders have protested on a few occasions by getting off their bikes, most notably at Valence d'Agen in 1978 when they dismounted and walked across the line to protest at having three short stages in one day. They also protested by walking the first part of a stage in 1966, after drugs tests were first introduced. The race has been stopped on a few occasions by workers involved in industrial action, although such occasions have never caused much disruption and are good-natured. In days gone by, cycling was known as the people's sport in Europe, and pro racers shared a fraternity with manual workers.

⬇ *Ivan Basso (near) and a T-Mobile rider go strike-breaking on a grass verge, rounding French workers who were protesting by blocking the road.*

⬆ *The agony of France's Ronan Pensec valiantly, but vainly, trying to defend the yellow jersey in 1990 was broadcast at close range.*

TV COVERAGE

Action from the 2011 Tour de France was broadcast by 100 TV channels to 190 countries, 60 of which received live transmission. The filming is done by one company who sell their feed to the others. Cameramen mounted on motorbikes record most of the action, with others in helicopters adding different angles, while static cameras get the finish. The commentators from each channel are allocated space at the stage finishes, where they work from TV monitors.

CROWD COVER

It's impossible to say exactly how many people watch the Tour de France along its whole route. Nobody needs a ticket, so there's no way of counting spectators, but to take an example, the police estimate that 500,000 stood on Alpe d'Huez to watch the 2004 time trial, which is a crowd density of 32 people per metre. The Tour organizers reckon that between 12 and 15 million stand by the road every year to watch at some point during the Tour. A survey they conducted also reveals that 70 per cent of spectators are male, 80 per cent are French and the average time they spend by the roadside is a staggering six hours.

Publicity Caravan stats

- It is 20 kilometres long.
- It comprises 160 colourful and decorated vehicles.
- Around 600 people are in or on them.
- Thirty-three brands are represented.
- The caravan gives 16 million gifts away.
- Twelve members of the republican guard and four traffic motorcyclists police it.
- Three medical cars also follow the race at the head of the caravan.
- Each advertiser pays between €200,000 and €500,000 to be part of it, the price depending on the number of vehicles they want and the area of road they take up.

➜ *A tired and emotional Abdel-Khader Zaaf was tended to by spectators at the roadside near Nîmes until the race ambulance arrived.*

Giro-Tour double

Seven riders have won the two biggest Grand Tours, the Tours of Italy (the Giro or Giro d'Italia) and France in the same year:

Rider	Times	Years
Eddy Merckx	3	1970, 1972, 1974
Fausto Coppi	2	1949, 1952
Bernard Hinault	2	1982, 1985
Miguel Indurain	2	1992, 1993
Jacques Anquetil	1	1964
Stephen Roche	1	1987
Marco Pantani	1	1998

Wrong direction

During the 1950 Tour, 15 kilometres from the end of stage 12 from Perpignan to Nîmes, the Algerian racer Abdel-Khader Zaaf was in the lead but began to weave all over the road. He collapsed and dragged himself to the side, where he passed out. He recovered consciousness minutes later, got back on his bike but, in a confused state, began riding in the opposite direction. Then the race ambulance arrived and Zaaf was stopped and placed in it. All sorts of accounts have entered Tour history, including that Zaaf had drunk some wine after raiding a cafe in the heat; but he was a Muslim, so that is probably untrue. It's more likely that he suffered from heat stress due to dehydration – the racers never drank enough water in those days.

The caravan

When Henri Desgrange banned commercial sponsored teams, and the bikes they raced on, from the Tour in 1930, he needed to find a way to pay for the board of the riders from invited national teams, and for the Tour-owned yellow bikes they all had to race on. He came up with the publicity caravan, inviting companies to deck out vehicles with their logos and precede the race. The caravan grew, and even after trade teams came back in 1969 it continued. Now the publicity caravan precedes the Tour for its whole route. It travels along the route of the stage a couple of hours before the Tour goes by, taking around 45 minutes for to pass. People working on the caravan throw cheap free gifts to the crowd, and in a 2011 survey 35 per cent of spectators said they had come primarily to see the caravan pass.

← *Yes it can be rather cheesy, sorry; but the Tour de France publicity caravan is an integral and fascinating part of the whole show.*

RACER DEATHS

Four racers have died during the Tour de France. Adolphe Hélière of France drowned while swimming in the Mediterranean on a rest day in 1910. Spanish racer Francisco Cepeda crashed on the descent of the Col du Galibier in 1935 and died in hospital as a result of the head injuries he sustained. In 1967 the first British yellow jersey, Tom Simpson, collapsed and died from heat exhaustion, and traces of amphetamine drugs were found in his body. Finally, in 1995 Fabio Casartelli, the 1992 Olympic road race champion, crashed on the descent of the Col de Portet d'Aspet, collided with a concrete block and was killed instantly.

← *Fabio Casartelli's beautiful memorial stone on the west side of the Col de Portet d'Aspet. It is a sundial which highlights three dates: his birth, Olympic gold medal and death.*

OTHER ACCIDENTS

In the days before live TV, radio commentary used to be done by journalists mounted as pillion passengers on motorbikes. In 1957 Alex Virot and his pilot René Wagner crashed down a ravine near Ax-les-Thermes and were killed. In 1958 André Darrigade, the top sprinter of his day, collided with a race official, Constant Wouters, who was standing too close to the track as the riders sprinted past, and Wouters died after the impact. The worst Tour de France accident occurred away from the race in 1964, when a supply truck collided with a bridge, killing 20 people.

THE PODIUM

The day before each stage, part of a team of riggers assemble the Tour village at the start, while the rest travel to the next stage town to set up the finish, which includes an inflatable podium, where the winners of each stage and the different jersey wearers are presented each day. Eight podium girls work on this, two to present the stage winner and two each for the yellow, polka-dot, green and white jerseys. Love has blossomed on the podium: Tour racers Christophe Moreau and George Hincapie married podium girls. Five times Tour winner Bernard Hinault oversees everything that goes on, ensuring that riders don't miss their cue and that local dignitaries and sponsors, who also make appearances, are well looked after.

THE MEDIA

Seventy radio stations, 400 newspapers and press agencies and 70 websites covered the 2011 race, sending 2,300 journalists from 35 different countries. The Tour's own website www.letour.fr had 14 million unique visitors during the three weeks of the race.

→ *The Tour de France's media centre is a multi-lingual hive of activity.*

EATING TO WIN

Depending on the severity of the stage, riders eat between 6,000 and 10,000 calories per day. They start drinking water as soon as they wake, because dehydration has enormous impact on performance. Breakfast starts with a fruit drink with electrolytes, particularly potassium, which plays an important role in the body and is lost easily through sweating. Then come cereals, some bread and pasta and some protein such as eggs or cheese. Protein is very important for Tour riders, because it provides the building blocks for muscle recovery. Protein is also taken in the form of whey powders. Riders continue drinking between breakfast and the start, and will sip electrolyte drinks on very hot days. During stages they will drink up to one bottle per hour and eat sports bars, rice cakes, ordinary cakes and energy gels.

↑ *Tour riders need constant refuelling as they are on the road. They will drink up to a bottle every hour and snack on a variety of energy foods.*

MEALS ON WHEELS

The racers start each stage with two bottles of liquid to drink carried on their bikes, and they put food in special pockets in their racing tops. This is enough for about two to three hours, and during that time they can also get extra bottles from their team support vehicles or from some of the motorbike marshals. They all get extra supplies from a feed station on the route. Some staff from each team drive ahead to these and stand in the road handing the bags called musettes to their men as they ride past. The bags contain bottles of liquid, energy bars, gels and/or cakes. The racers transfer these from the bags to their pockets and throw away the bags, which then become Tour souvenirs for the roadside spectators.

TOUR PARTICIPATION RECORDS

Rank	Rider	Country	Starts	Finishes	Between	Best result
1	Joop Zoetemelk	Holland	16	16	1970–86	1st
2	George Hincape	USA	16	15	1996–2011	14th
3	Lucien van Impe	Belgium	15	15	1969–85	1st
4	Viatcheslav Ekimov	Russia	15	15	1990–2006	18th
5	Guy Nulens	Belgium	15	13	1980–94	22nd
6	Christophe Moreau	France	15	11	1996–2010	4th
7	André Darrigade	France	14	13	1953–66	16th
8	Erik Zabel	Germany	14	13	1994–2008	43rd
9	Raymond Poulidor	France	14	12	1962–76	2nd
10	Sean Kelly	Ireland	14	12	1978–92	4th

LONG ARM OF THE LAW

The race has its own police force, part of the Gendarmerie Nationale, which liaises with local forces on all matters of road closure, safety and routing. Together the local officers and the Gendarmerie police the race and ensure its smooth passage through France and, in some years, into and out of other countries.

➔ *Closing down the roads of France allowing the Tour de France to pass is a tough job and it only succeeds because of an intense and prolonged police operation.*

PART 2
THE GREAT CYCLING NATIONS

The subject of this chapter is the nations who have played a part, big or small, in the history of the Tour de France, some of which have a bigger part to play in the future. Inevitably France and its closest neighbours have supplied the greatest number of winners and riders, but now other countries are writing their chapters of the Tour.

A modern Tour is a truly international race. Whereas the 78 riders who started in 1903 were from just five European countries, the 200 who lined up in 2011 represented 26 different nations and all five continents.

As interest in road racing in general – and the Tour de France in particular – has spread around the world, so has interest in taking part. The Tour de France peloton today is made up by a band of brave men from all of the world's continents.

FRANCE

France has had the biggest influence on the Tour de France. It has the highest number of winners, and French racers feature at the top end of nearly every list of statistics you can think of. But the French role is much bigger than a collection of numbers. The Tour de France is huge today, truly international both in participation and in the audience it attracts, but it is still solidly French. The closest comparison is with Wimbledon in tennis, an event that is part of a global tour but is still uniquely British. The Tour de France is and forever will be French.

France inevitably leaves its mark on the visual aspect of the Tour, especially on the final day when it goes along the streets of Paris, but the race's spirit is still uniquely French too.

FRANCE

France has supplied more Tour winners than any other country. The first hat-trick of successive Tour wins was by a Frenchman: Louison Bobet in 1953, 1954 and 1955. The first five-time winner was French: Jacques Anquetil in 1957, 1961, 1962, 1963 and 1964. Two out of the four men who won five Tours each are French: Anquetil and Bernard Hinault. Hinault spent 79 days in the yellow jersey, the third highest total ever, and his 28 stage wins rank him number two behind Eddy Merckx. Frenchman Charles Pélissier is one of three riders who won eight stages, the most in a single Tour. Another Frenchman, Richard Virenque, won the most King of the Mountains titles with seven. France dominates Tour de France statistics from almost every angle you look at them.

FRENCH TOUR WINNERS

Rank	Rider	Wins	Years
1	**Bernard Hinault**	5	1978, 1979, 1981, 1982, 1985
=	**Jacques Anquetil**	5	1957, 1961, 1962, 1963, 1964
3	**Louison Bobet**	3	1953, 1954, 1955
4	**Lucien Petit-Breton**	2	1907, 1908
=	**André Leducq**	2	1930, 1932
=	**Antonin Magne**	2	1931, 1934
=	**Bernard Thévenet**	2	1975, 1977
=	**Laurent Fignon**	2	1983, 1984
9	**Maurice Garin**	1	1903
=	**Henri Cornet**	1	1904
=	**Louis Trousselier**	1	1905
=	**René Pottier**	1	1906
=	**Octave Lapize**	1	1910
=	**Gustave Garrigou**	1	1911
=	**Henri Pélissier**	1	1923
=	**Georges Speicher**	1	1933
=	**Roger Lapébie**	1	1937
=	**Jean Robic**	1	1947
=	**Roger Walkowiak**	1	1956
=	**Lucien Aimar**	1	1966
=	**Roger Pingeon**	1	1967

↗ *The Tour de France has been part of the French way of life for more than a century.*

HEART AND SOUL

Even though France hasn't produced a winner of the Tour de France since 1985, the heart and soul of the race are French. The international nature of today's Tour makes this all the more remarkable. Its sponsors, like the riders, are from all over the world. An American won seven out of the last 13 Tours, an Australian won in 2011. In recent years even French stage victories have been quite scarce, but the Tour's heart and soul remain French. So much that even when it visits other countries they become France for the day. Much of the credit for this belongs to its race directors, who have all been French. Either by dictating to or working with sponsors, they have brought continuity to and preserved the essential Frenchness of the Tour de France.

THE DIRECTORS

Henri Desgrange 1903–36
Jacques Goddet 1936–88
Félix Lévitan 1947–87
Jean-Pierre Carenso 1989

Jean-Marie Leblanc 1980–2005
Christian Prudhomme 2006–present

Goddet was a fine journalist with a great command of language who continued writing while he ran the Tour. He was an extrovert character – wearing a safari outfit, complete with pith helmet, when the Tour was in the south – but he wasn't as good with money as he was with words. That's why the race owners appointed a joint director, Félix Lévitan, to work with him and keep an eye on the bottom line. Jean-Pierre Carenso had some big ideas but not the right background, being neither a racer nor a journalist. Jean-Marie Leblanc was both, a reasonable pro who rode the Tour twice before working as a journalist. Christian Prudhomme was a journalist too. Today he presides over a race that is modern and has moved with the times, but has always done so with regard to its past. He and Leblanc led the Tour through the years it was worst affected by doping.

THE RASCAL

There has usually been a certain dignity about the French winners, from the serious Antonin Magne to the aloof Jacques Anquetil. One man who doesn't quite fit the mould is Roger Lapébie. He won in 1937, mainly because the race leader, Sylvère Maes, abandoned the race close to the finish because of what he saw as some very biased decisions by race judges. Crowd participation also saw Lapébie pushed up mountains, while Maes found himself delayed on one occasion by closed level crossing gates when no train was due through. Lapébie even bragged about the outside help he got, saying it proved how popular he was. However, Lapébie was wronged too when his bike was sabotaged and he crashed. The Tour is no picnic now, but it was a rough old race in those days.

➔ *Home rider Roger Lapébie smiled through the controversy, the assistance of local spectators and the sabotage to win the 1937 Tour de France.*

RICHARD VIRENQUE

Everyone likes to win, good athletes want to win, but the best *need* to win. That's why drugs are a threat to sport, and why if left unchecked they will run rife. You can talk about moral fibre and just saying no for as long as you like, but humans are capable of adjusting morals to suit, and it has to be said that there was a time in professional cycling when drugs were accepted. That didn't mean everybody doped, because they didn't, but the pro collective, the peloton, wasn't overly offended if somebody did. Richard Virenque walked into that world when he turned pro, and he was ready, willing and able. In pro racer's slang, doped riders were "chaudières", meaning heaters. An old pro in Virenque's first team predicted, before he even knew him well, "You will be one of the hottest heaters in cycling." And so it proved: Virenque was the biggest name involved in the 1998 Festina scandal, when it was revealed that the team had an institutional system of doping. It was a shame, because Virenque was a talented, gutsy racer who won seven King of the Mountains titles among other things, but he ruined his reputation with doping.

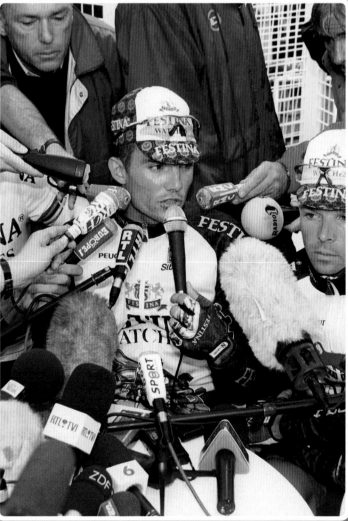

← *Richard Virenque was a talented cyclist who succumbed to the temptation of doping.*

THE MIRACLE OF BONSECOURS

Jean Robic won the 1947 Tour with a well-timed attack on the last stage. It happened on a hill that climbs out of Rouen called Bonsecours. Robic attacked when the yellow jersey, Pierre Brambilla, was boxed in. Brambilla chased, but couldn't quite close the gap and exhausted himself trying to do so. Robic then romped away, helped by another racer, Edouard Fachtleitner. Robic was a short, stocky man with a battered-looking face who came from Brittany, a fact that led one journalist to call him a goblin from the Breton bogs. He was incredibly accident prone, and it's said that he broke every bone in his body at least once in his life.

← *Jean Robic riding through the pain barrier, his wrist strapped up as a result of one of the many injuries he suffered.*

THE LANGUAGE OF CYCLING

Many French words are used as cycle racing terms in the English-speaking world, although oddly some of them are not used in French to describe the same things. Frequently used French words include *bidon*, meaning drinks bottle; *échelon*, the riders' formation in a crosswind; *domestique*, a team rider who races to support the team leader; *flamme rouge*, the red square hung over the road with one kilometre to go; *prime*, an interim prize awarded at a point during a stage; *finale*, the part of the stage from five kilometres out to the line; *col*, a mountain pass; *soigneurs*, team staff who look after the riders between stages; and *rouleur*, a racer capable of riding hard over a variety of terrain, often on his own.

L'EQUIPE

The offices of *L'Auto*, the magazine that created the Tour de France, were closed by the Allies when they freed Paris at the end of the Second World War. Although Jacques Goddet worked for *L'Auto*, he was allowed to set up another magazine in offices across the street. His new publication was a daily sports newspaper and he called it *L'Equipe*. They organized the first post-war Tours with another paper, *Le Parisien*, but the race's finances were precarious until *L'Equipe* was taken over by the Amaury publishing and media concern in 1965. This became ASO, who are now one of the biggest sports organizers in the world with brands like the Tour, the Dakar Rally (formerly the Paris–Dakar Rally) and the Paris Marathon.

ANQUETIL'S RIGHT-HAND MAN

Jean Stablinski had the most traumatic childhood. During the Second World War, when he was ten years old, he witnessed his Polish father, who was a coal miner, being shot by German troops outside their home in the north of France. Jean was the eldest of five children, and in order to keep their company-owned home his mother had to promise that her eldest son would work down the pit as soon as he was 14. He learned to play the accordion and supplemented his mine income by playing at Polish clubs, which he rode to and from on an old bike. He was strong and fast, so he started racing just across the border in Belgium, where prizes were cash. Stablinski eventually became a pro, winning five stages in the Tour, and his tough work ethic made him the perfect team-mate for Jacques Anquetil. "Jacques was so laid back he would go to sleep on some stages. I don't know how many times I hauled his backside from the back to the front of the race," he once said.

↑ *Jean Stablinski, in the red white and blue colours of the French national champion, rarely left Jacques Anquetil's (in yellow) side during the 1960s.*

THE FRENCH CAV

André Darrigade is the best French road sprinter of all time. He was the Mark Cavendish of his age, so lightning fast that he won 22 stages in a Tour career that lasted from 1953 until 1964. In the days before the prologue time trial, Darrigade made a speciality of winning the first stage, which brought him five yellow jerseys – he wore yellow for 16 days in total. Darrigade was involved in a fatal accident in the Parc de Princes stadium in 1958, when an official trying to take a photograph walked on to the track in front of sprinting riders and totally underestimated the speed at which they were travelling towards him.

➜ *André Darrigade (right, alongside Ireland's Shay Elliott) won the opening stage of the 1958 Tour, so was in yellow from Ghent to Dunkerque.*

JOIE DE VIVRE

Georges Speicher was a natural. He couldn't even ride a bike until he landed a delivery job in Paris when he was 19. He started racing the following year and turned pro three years later, in 1932, when he made his Tour de France debut and finished in tenth place. Speicher won the Tour in 1933, and in doing so earned enough money to indulge a passion for enjoying himself. He already had a love for Paris night clubs: later that year, after hearing he hadn't made the final cut for the French team for the world road race championships, which were held in France, he hit the clubs. On the eve of the race, a team member fell ill, so the selectors searched the clubs to drag Speicher out and sober him up for the race. Next day he won the world title. Even the best cannot keep that kind of life up. Speicher won four stages when finishing 11th in the 1934 Tour, but only one in 1935, on his way sixth overall. He started the next three Tours but failed to complete any of them.

⬇ *The slog of the Tour de France is a long way from the glamour of Paris night life, but Georges Speicher enjoyed both, especially in 1933 when he won the Tour and the world road race title.*

TOURISTES-ROUTIERS

As well as the top commercial and then national teams, until 1938 the Tour was open to anyone who could support himself. These riders were called touriste-routiers, and they ranged from people who were having a laugh and hardly lasted the first stage, to some very good racers. Bike shop owners often rode because doing so was good publicity. In 1907 a French nobleman, Baron Pepin, raced in the Tour, paying two good pros to help him. One touriste-routier, Julien Deloffre, was quite good and finished in the top 20 four times. However, he never had enough cash to pay for his hotels, so when he finished a stage he would perform an acrobatic act for the crowd and then pass his hat around for donations.

TOMMY V

Although there has been no French winner of the Tour since Bernard Hinault in 1985, French cyclists have animated the race with their willingness to attack. A good example is Jacky Durand, who during the 1990s spent more kilometres ahead of the peloton, either on his own or in breakaway groups, than he did riding with it. The French hero of the last decade is Thomas Voeckler. His attacking spirit has seen him spend two long spells in the yellow jersey, the second of which, in 2011, brought him quite close to winning.

← *Thomas Voeckler's showmanship nearly brought him overall victory in the 2011 Tour de France.*

THE LAST SHALL BE FIRST

Pierre Matignon must have been lulling everyone into a false sense of security in 1969. He'd been a solid last for much of the race, when he saw a chance on stage 20. He got a big lead, but the stage was a prestigious one because it finished on top of the super-tough Puy de Dôme climb. Eddy Merckx and the other top place riders began to chase, but Matignon gritted his teeth and held on, weaving from side to side up the final part of the climb to collapse exhausted over the finish line. He only raced one other Tour, when he finished 75th overall in 1972.

RELUCTANT CHAMPION

Roger Pingeon considered stopping cycling altogether because he was so disappointed with his results. He seemed to lack confidence although he had loads of talent and a good appreciation of tactics, while he also put a lot of faith in nature cures and maintaining a very strict diet. But then he won the 1967 Tour, after reading the race perfectly, and his confidence rose. In 1969 he won the Tour of Spain and was second to Eddy Merckx in the Tour de France, which considering Merckx's domination of the era was the same as winning a Tour for mortals.

← *Talented and diffident Roger Pingeon had to win the Tour – in 1967 – before he fully believed in himself. He nearly repeated the feat in 1969, when only the legendary Eddy Merckx beat him.*

FIGHTER PILOT

Octave Lapize won the first stage that crossed the Pyrenees in 1910, and went on to win that Tour. He volunteered the moment war broke out and became one of the world's first fighter pilots. He was shot down and killed over Verdun in 1917. There is a memorial to Lapize on top of the Col du Tourmalet.

➔ *Octave Lapize, struggling between Lyon and Grenoble in 1910, is one of 21 Frenchmen who have won the Tour de France a combined 36 times between them.*

HAPPY HOLIDAY

One of the reasons for the enduring success of the Tour de France is that it runs during the country's traditional summer break, which centres on Bastille Day, when France celebrates becoming a republic. Bastille Day, 14 July, is huge, a real national celebration, and winning a stage on Bastille Day is something every French bike racer dreams of.

ASSUMED NAME

Lucien Petit-Breton was born Lucien Mazan in Brittany, but emigrated to Argentina with his parents when he was quite young. He started bike racing in and around Buenos Aires, but didn't tell his parents because they were well off and saw cycling as something peasant boys or factory workers did. The first time he raced he wanted to use the name Breton, but there was already a Breton in the race, so the organizer put him down as Petit-Breton. The name stuck and when Mazan finished his national service he stayed in France to race, eventually becoming a pro and riding the 1905 Tour. He was fifth in that, fourth in 1906 and won the Tour in 1907 and 1908. He was killed during the First World War.

◄ *Petit-Breton (right) in 1907, don't take his yellow jersey as evidence of its existence that year, these old photographs were often coloured in much later.*

THE REST OF EUROPE

The Tour de France never was only about the French. Even in the first Tour there were riders from other European countries, and their numbers grew steadily. France's immediate neighbours provided the core of the field for the first 50 years, but after that there was a slow growth in representation from further afield, especially after the Berlin Wall fell in late eighties. Now there are nine other European countries that have supplied a winner, some of which have won several times.

The French started writing the story of the Tour de France, but other Europeans have made their mark too. Italian star Alessandro Petacchi won the first stage of the 2010 Tour – coincidentally keeping the cross-European theme alive – from Rotterdam in the Netherlands to Brussels in Belgium.

BELGIUM

For a tiny country, whose longest axis is the length of a big bike ride, Belgium has had an inordinate impact on world cycling, and on the Tour de France. Belgians have won the Tour 18 times, more than any other nation except France. Cycling in Belgium, or more particularly the region of Flanders, forms part of the national identity.

BELGIAN TOUR WINNERS

Rank	Rider	Wins	Years
1	**Eddy Merckx**	5	1969, 1970, 1971, 1972, 1974
2	**Philippe Thys**	3	1913, 1914, 1920
3	**Firmin Lambot**	2	1919, 1922
=	**Sylvère Maes**	2	1936, 1939
5	**Odile Defraye**	1	1912
=	**Léon Scieur**	1	1921
=	**Lucien Buysse**	1	1926
=	**Maurice de Waele**	1	1929
=	**Roman Maes**	1	1935
=	**Lucien van Impe**	1	1976

↑ *Eddy Merckx's hunger for victory was insatiable and his success in road racing included everything from one-day classics to grand tours.*

THE CANNIBAL

The greatest that ever lived. For once the hyperbole rings true – Eddy Merckx's career record towers over that of every other great cycling champion. Even Lance Armstrong, who won two more Tours de France than Merckx, freely acknowledges that his obsession with the Tour cannot compare with Merckx's year-round brilliance and appetite for racing. Flemish born but raised in a French-speaking suburb of Brussels, this truest of bilingual Belgians won 445 races in a 13-year career. Apart from his five Tour wins he also won the Tour of Italy five times, the world road race championship three times and no fewer than 32 of the great one-day classics. Not for nothing was he nicknamed "The Cannibal".

FIRST FOREIGN TOUR

In 1954 the Tour de France had its first foreign start in its 51-year history. The 1954 Tour was counter-clockwise (Pyrenees first, then the Alps) and started in Amsterdam with the first stage finishing in Beveren, Belgium. The Tour's inaugural foreign start was won by Wout Wagtmans (Holland).

THE "BELGIAN BULLET"

Sylvère Maes won the last Tour de France before the outbreak of the Second World War. The 1939 Tour was boycotted by Germany and Italy, and Spain did not attend after the civil war, but Maes, who had already won the Tour in 1936, overcame an ailing René Vietto in the Pyrenees and took the yellow jersey after impressive riding over the Col d'Izoard and winning the first ever Tour mountain time trial up the Col d'Iseran. Maes's winning time set a new record average speed of 31.9 kph, just under 20 mph. Maes was the owner of a cafe in his native Flanders which he named Tourmalet, after the great Pyrenean climb.

← *Sylvère Maes approaching the summit of the Col d'Iseran in 1939. His ability as a climber, whether in the Pyrenees or here in the Alps, helped him to win the 1939 Tour, just as it had in 1936.*

LUCIEN VAN IMPE

A climber won the 1976 Tour. Lucien van Impe profited from the absence of a fading Merckx, and the illness which did for Bernard Thévenet in the Pyrenees. Van Impe climbed into the yellow jersey after stage 9 from Divonne-les-Bains to L'Alpe-d'Huez. He lost it to Frenchman Raymond Delisle a couple of days later, but benefited from an attack on stage 14 by 1973 Tour winner Luis Ocana of Spain on the road to St-Lary-Soulan, grabbing the opportunity to leave close challenger Joop Zoetemelk behind and retake the yellow jersey. Van Impe held the jersey to Paris and shared the podium with another Belgian, Freddy Maertens, who in his first Tour won eight stages and the green jersey thanks to a ballistic sprint and solo power in short time trials.

➡ *Lucien van Impe climbing in the polka dot jersey with Frenchmen Robert Alban on his right and Bernard Hinault on his left.*

ROARING TWENTIES

Belgium dominated the 1920 Tour, with 12 stage wins out of 15. It also provided the overall winner in Philippe Thys, who became the first rider to win the Tour three times after his victories in the last two pre-war races in 1913 and 1914. Belgium was confirmed as the new cycling superpower, filling the first seven places overall and controlling the race through the Pyrenees and Alps. The only non-Belgian stage winner was Henri Pelissier of France, who, like his brother Francis, was vocal in his dislike of the Tour's harshness and of its autocratic patron Desgrange. Henri Pelissier was a potential Tour winner but he had to wait another three years, while Belgians Léon Scieur, in 1921, and Firmin Lambot, in 1922, continued to crush the French opposition.

FIRST YELLOW MAN

In 1919, the year of the creation of the yellow jersey, Firmin Lambot of Belgium was the first rider to win in Paris wearing the famous garment. He is one of 18 Belgian riders to have won the Tour de France.

MILLSTONE OF SUCCESS

The country's cycling history, with all those great racers and glorious victories, is a source of national pride in Belgium, but it places a huge weight of expectation on their young bike racers. Cycling matters to Belgian people and to the Belgian media, a fact that has resulted in a succession of "new Eddy Merckxes" who crumbled under the mantle. Meanwhile, no Belgian has won the Tour de France since 1976. This is due partly to the globalization of the sport – France hasn't had a victory since 1985, while Americans have won ten Tours – and partly to pressure. Jurgen van den Broeck was fourth in the 2010 Tour. Will he be the next Belgian Tour de France winner, or will he go the way of all those other "new Eddy Merckxes"? Belgium awaits!

⬅ *A country expects ... Jurgen van den Broeck was fourth in 2010, his best result yet, but will Belgium's high expectations weigh him down?*

STAGE GIVE-AWAY

Freddy Maertens won eight stages of the 1976 Tour, making him joint record holder with Charles Pélissier and Eddy Merckx. He won two stages in 1978 and five in 1981, and he was the green jersey winner in 1976, 1978 and 1981. At his best Maertens was amazing, so good that he says he didn't fully contest one stage sprint in 1976, because the eventual winner of it had told him his team's sponsor was threatening to pull out if they didn't win a stage. If Maertens had won he'd have set an absolute record of nine stage wins in one Tour, like his record of 13 in one Tour of Spain. Maertens was young, perhaps too kind and trusting for his own good. Soon after 1976 he lost a lot of money through bad investments made on his behalf by people he trusted, and his life and career slowly spun out of control.

← *Freddy Maertens must have regrets about his racing career, but they don't show. He still works in cycling at the Tour of Flanders museum in Oudenaarde, Belgium.*

YELLOW JERSEY CAFE

It was traditional in Europe for retired racers to open a cafe if they'd earned enough money from cycling. Double Tour winner Sylvère Maes opened one in his home town, and his namesake Romain Maes, the Tour winner in 1935, opened one in Brussels, calling it the Yellow Jersey.

SAMSON

There have been Belgians in the Tour since day one. One of them, Julian Lootens, lined up for the first Tour under the name "Samson". He finished seventh overall in Paris, one place behind countryman Marcel Kerf.

COBBLED CLASSICS

There are a number of races held each spring in Belgium and northern France called the Cobbled Classics. They are the speciality of Belgian bike racers, who have a long and proud tradition of winning them, and because the sport is so big in Belgium every few years the Tour de France includes a stage over some of the same roads. They are often crucial, and just as often are a big headache for Tour contenders who aren't usually good at this type of racing. For one thing, riding over rough surfaces favours heavier riders, and Tour contenders tend to be good climbers, so of a much lighter build. It's also crucial to be at the front of the race, which lighter riders again find difficult on flat, rough terrain. The last cobbled stage was in 2010, when Andy Schleck was looked after throughout the whole stage by his team-mate, Fabian Cancellara, who has won several of the Cobbled Classics. All Schleck had to do was follow Cancellara, who paced, cajoled and pushed him through the stage to gain a minute and a half on Alberto Contador.

→ *Fabian Cancellara leads Andy Schleck across the treacherous cobblestones to take time from Alberto Contador in the 2010 Tour.*

TOMMEKE

Tom Boonen is the darling of Belgian cycling, but that brings huge pressure and responsibility because the sport is such a big deal in the country, especially in Flanders, and Boonen is Flemish. He's good at the races Belgians love, the Cobbled Classics, and he's won six stages in the Tour de France, plus the green jersey in 2007. He's still only 31, but the last few seasons have been difficult for Boonen, who moved to Monaco for a time to escape the interest of Belgian fans when they started following their beloved Tommeke on training runs in their cars. Boonen tested positive for cocaine in 2008 and was barred from competing in the Tour. The same thing happened in 2009, but that time he went to court and won the right to compete in the Tour.

➜ *Tom Boonen was good enough to wear the yellow jersey in the 2006 Tour, but will he be good enough to wear it again?*

THE KERMESSE

One of the reasons why Belgians have made such a big mark on international cycling is the kind of races they grow up on. The kermesse started out as a religious festival in Flanders and northern France, but it slowly became a village fair and holiday. Once bike racing took hold, races became part of the day's events, but they were held on a short lap of about ten kilometres, using the town or village's main street and a few of the surrounding roads. Young racers would do five laps, juniors and amateurs a few more, and the pros would do up to 20 laps. The thing is, there was a cash prize on the finish line every lap, plus cash for the race winner and down the field, which extended down to 30th in pro races, so there was always something to fight for. This racing bred the tough, fast racers that Flanders is famous for, and that over the years have made a much bigger impression on the Tour de France and on world cycling than you'd expect from a country of Belgium's size.

VAN IMPE II

Belgium has waited many years for a climber like Lucien van Impe, but now they might have one. Jelle Vanendert rode his first Tour in 2011 and won the prestigious stage to Plateau-de-Beille. He was second on the equally big stage to Luz-Ardiden, and both stages are mountain-top finishes. The future looks very bright for Vanendert.

➜ *Jelle Vanendert after winning the Tour stage to Plateau-de-Beille in 2011. He looks likely to be one of the Tour's top climbers in the coming years.*

HOME FROM HOME

The 2012 Tour de France will set off from Parc d'Avroy, in the heart of Liège. No fewer than 37 Belgian towns or cities have hosted starts or finishes since the Tour first came to France's northern neighbour as a gesture of international goodwill when the race resumed in 1947 following the hiatus of the Second World War.

SCANDINAVIA

The Scandinavians didn't have much of a cycling road race programme at home until well into the second half of the twentieth century, which is when they began competing in the Tour. Since then, however, and especially recently, their presence has grown and they make up a significant part of the Tour today. They will play an even bigger role in the years to come.

← *Magnus Backstedt in time trial action in Liège at the start of the 2004 Tour.*

SCANDINAVIAN TOUR WINNER

Bjarne Riis (Denmark)   1 win   1996

VIKING INVASION

It started with the Danes. Hans Andresen, Eluf Dalgaard, Kay-Allan Olsen and Fritz Ravn lined up as part of a team called the Internationals in the 1958 Tour de France. By coincidence this was the British racer Brian Robinson's fourth Tour, and he was in the International team too. Denmark, like Britain, had little road race history until the 1960s, aside from time trials, but the Danes, again like the British, were a force in track racing. It was a track world and Olympic champion, Mogens Frey, who took the first Danish Tour stage win in 1970.

SWEDISH STAGE

The only Swede to win a Tour de France stage also holds the Swedish record of seven participations. His name is Magnus Backstedt and he won his stage in 1998. His last Tour was in 2008, but he still races for a British team and lives in Wales.

GREAT DANE

Bjarne Riis is Scandinavia's only Tour winner. The Dane, who now manages the Saxo Bank team, won in 1996. Riis was a member of the German T-Mobile team, and when a number of team-mates from Riis's era admitted many years later they had doped in the Tour de France, Riis confessed he had too. It was the era of EPO, a hormone that boosts the oxygen-carrying capacity of blood and so boosts performance in any endurance event. There was no effective test in the mid-1990s to detect it, but there is now. In fact the rules and testing for drugs are so tight in cycling, and in particular in the Tour de France, that it leads the way in the fight against drugs in sport.

← *Denmark's Bjarne Riis is still the only Scandinavian Tour winner, even though he subsequently admitted to having taken the blood doping substance EPO in 1996.*

NORWEGIAN YELLOW

The first Norwegian in the Tour was Knud Knudsen in 1975. The record number of participations for Norway goes to Thor Hushovd with ten. Hushovd is the only Norwegian to have worn the yellow jersey, which he's done three times in 2004, 2006 and 2011. Hushovd, who was world road race champion in 2010, has won the green jersey twice (2005, 2009) and has won ten stages.

➜ *Norway's Thor Hushovd has made a huge impression on the Tour, not just for his excellence as a racer but for his dignity and sense of fair play.*

THE FLYING PETTERSONS

The first Swedish racer to take part in the Tour was Goran Karlsson in 1960. He didn't finish. It was another decade before another Swede rode the Tour, but he had a huge impact. Four brothers, Tomas, Sture, Erik and Gosta Petterson, were the world team time trial champions from 1967 to 1969, and they won an Olympic silver medal in 1968. The team time trial championships were only for amateurs and teams of four, and with Sweden having no pro racing the brothers didn't turn pro until late in their careers. When they did, the eldest two, Erik and Gosta, both rode the Tour, and Gosta, who was 30 by then, finished third in the 1970 Tour de France. He was the first Scandinavian to make it to the Tour podium.

EVERY DAG HAS ITS DAY

That was what the TV commentator Phil Liggett announced when Dag-Otto Lauritzen won a mountains stage to Luz-Ardiden in 1987. Lauritzen was a tough racer who had been a paratrooper. He took up cycling after it was recommended to him as rehabilitation for a broken leg. He rode eight Tours and still works on the race with Norwegian TV.

NORTHERN STAR

Big things are being predicted for Norway's Edvald Boasson-Hagen, even that he might win the Tour one day. He's 24 years old but has ridden two Tours, taking two stage victories in 2011. Boasson-Hagen rides for Team Sky, often sharing a room with Geraint Thomas, the man responsible for feeding the Norwegian's newly acquired Welsh Cake habit.

← *Edvald Boasson-Hagen, a Welsh Cake-eating Norwegian, might win the Tour one day.*

GERMANY

One hundred and sixty-five Germans have taken part in the Tour, and they have been coming to the race almost from the beginning. The first German Tour competitors were Joseph Fischer and Ludwig Bartlemann in 1903. Bartlemann didn't make it all the way through, but Fischer finished 15th overall. Political upheaval within Europe affected German participation, and no East Germans could compete from just after the Second World War until the end of Communism. Still, the country has played a big part in the Tour de France and continues to do so.

GERMAN TOUR WINNER

Jan Ullrich	1 win	1997

↑ *Karl-Heinz Kunde races out of an ice tunnel during the 1966 Tour in the yellow jersey.*

RUDI ALTIG

One of the best all-round cyclists Germany has ever produced, Rudi Altig won Classics, a world title and the green jersey in the 1962 Tour de France. He also won seven Tour stages, the Tour of Spain overall, and two world track titles. He was very talented but a little too heavily built for the high mountains. Always outspoken, Altig now works as a TV commentator on the Tour de France and other races, where his pithy comments are entertaining, although the racers on the receiving end of them don't always appreciate his candour.

↓ *Rudi Altig sports a natty line in headgear during a 1960s Tour de France. One of Germany's greatest cyclists, his weakness was the high mountains.*

THE SHORTEST YELLOW JERSEY

Karl-Heinz Kunde was tiny, standing just 1 metre 59 and weighing 50 kilos. He was a very good cyclo-cross racer who rode the Tour five times. His best year was 1966, when he wore the yellow jersey for five days and finished ninth overall. Jacques Anquetil called him the Microbe.

FALL OF THE WALL

Germany was divided after the Second World War into east and west. East Germany was under communist rule and part of the Soviet Bloc, while West Germany had free elections and was part of Western Europe. These distinctions had an impact on sport, because the communist countries would not allow their sports people to compete in professional sport or against professionals. Instead their focus was the Olympic Games, which until 1996 were only for amateurs, and sports that were supposed to be amateur, like athletics, or who had an amateur category, as cycling did. By the end of the 1980s the amateur–professional boundaries had become blurred, while at the same time the countries of the Soviet Bloc were going through a period of reform. East and West Germany finally became one free country in 1990, which allowed East German cyclists, who had been a major force in world amateur cycling, to turn pro and start riding the Tour de France.

Jan the man

Jan Ullrich was born in Rostock, in the former East Germany, and was trained in their system, which was tough and very effective. Ullrich was a super athlete, extremely powerful and with great powers of recovery, but he seemed to have problems reading a race and lacked the killer instinct that many successful sports people have. He also found it difficult to ignore the trappings of success and focus on the long-term training needed to be the very best, even if an individual is super talented. He won the Tour de France in 1997 when he was 23, made a mistake the following year and came second, but still looked good enough to win many more. Then Lance Armstrong came along. He never read a race wrong; he was more dedicated than Ullrich, and he had the killer instinct in spades. Even Amstrong's manager, Johan Bruyneel, says that Ullrich was the more talented athlete, but talent isn't always enough.

↑ *Jan Ullrich certainly had the talent to win more than the one Tour de France he took in 1997,, but he didn't have the drive of Lance Armstrong.*

Potential winner

Erich Bautz only rode two Tours but in his second, in 1937, he won a stage and was ninth overall, having spent five days in the yellow jersey. What's more, Bautz beat no less a racer than Gino Bartali to win his stage, and Bartali won the Tour the following year. Bautz didn't ride that race because of tensions in Europe, and of course he couldn't ride during the war as there was no Tour de France. After the conflict, travel was difficult for Germans, and Bautz was restricted to racing at home for the rest of his career.

Green record

Erik Zabel holds the German record for Tour participation with 14 starts and 12 finishes. He also holds the Tour record of six victories in the green jersey competition, and he won 12 stages. He wore the yellow jersey twice as well. Zabel was a sprinter, not the fastest but very durable, which meant his sprint was as good on the last day of the Tour as it was on the first, and that he didn't have a problem, as some sprinters do, with lasting three weeks and getting through the mountain stages. He's a former East German from East Berlin, and for several years was a sprint coach/adviser for Mark Cavendish in the HTC-Columbia team.

The devil

Have you seen the guy dressed as the devil who gets in a camera shot somewhere on every stage of the Tour de France, often by running alongside the riders waving his trident towards the top of a climb? His name is Dieter Senft and he's German. He's been doing his devil stunt on the Tour since 1993, at first to publicize the unusual bikes he invents, but now he is sponsored by various businesses on the lookout for publicity. Senft also attends the Tour of Italy every year, as well as other sporting events. He is credited in the *Guinness Book of Records* as having made the world's biggest mobile guitar.

← *Dieter Senft celebrated the Tour de France's 100th birthday in 2003 in his own unique way.*

GREAT BRITAIN AND IRELAND

British and Irish cyclists didn't start competing regularly in the Tour de France until the 1950s and '60s, but when they did they made an immediate impact. Their level of participation has fluctuated over the years. An Irish rider has won the Tour, which no Briton has done yet. Both countries have a strong presence in the Tour today, so with luck it's just a matter of time before a Briton wins and there is another Irish winner.

IRISH TOUR WINNER

Stephen Roche   1 win   1987

↑ *Brian Robinson was the first English-speaker to win a Tour stage, when he won for Great Britain in 1958.*

LABOURS OF HERCULES

In 1937 British racers Bill Burl and Charles Holland took part in the Tour de France, but cycling in Britain was very insular until the mid-fifties, and nobody else took part. Then a bike company called Hercules hatched an ambitious plan to ride the 1955 Tour. They signed up the best British road racers, based themselves in France and started to race there in preparation for the Tour. Great Britain was invited to send a team, and the selectors picked half of the Hercules team and some riders from other British race teams. They were outclassed, except for Brian Robinson, who finished 29th, while Tony Hoar, who was last, at least fought through to the end.

EARLY DAYS

The Hercules team folded at the end of 1955, but Robinson stayed in France, kept racing and rode the 1956 Tour with a mixed-nations team that included Charly Gaul. Robinson finished 14th, just one place behind Gaul, and he made enough of an impression to gain a regular place in a European trade-sponsored team. Robinson became the first British stage winner in 1958, and he won another in 1959.

KELLY AND ROCHE

Between them Sean Kelly and Stephen Roche won nearly every big bike race in the world. Together they were a phenomenon, and individually they complemented each other. Kelly was a good sprinter, a Tour stage winner and a Classics winner; Roche was superb at time trials and a great stage racer. He was at his best in 1987 when he won cycling's triple crown, the Tour of Italy, Tour of France and the world road race title in one year, something only Eddy Merckx has done. Ireland had some lean years after Kelly and Roche, but they are a force once more in the shape of Roche's son Nicholas, who has raced in several Tours with a best position of 22nd in 2010, and Nicholas's cousin, Dan Martin, who has yet to make his Tour debut but is a very good climber.

PROGRESS

More British riders, and a few Irish, followed Robinson to France and began to make their names in European pro racing. In 1962 Tom Simpson took the Tour de France yellow jersey for a day in the Pyrenees before finishing sixth overall. The following year the Irish racer Shay Elliott won a stage and led the Tour for three days. Progress was halted when Tom Simpson died in the 1967 Tour. It was left to Barry Hoban to fly the British flag in the Tour through the late sixties and early seventies. He did it well, though, winning eight stages.

← *Tom Simpson established a British presence in the Tour de France in the 1960s.*

THE FOREIGN LEGION

The 1980s saw a British and Irish revival. Robert Millar became the first British racer to win one of the Tour jerseys when he became King of the Mountains in 1984. He finished fourth overall in that race, a performance only equalled by Bradley Wiggins in 2009. Millar also won three stages. More British racers followed Millar and found places in Tour de France teams. Sean Yates finished nine Tours out of 12 starts, second to Barry Hoban's 11 finishes out of 12, and in 1988 Yates became the first British rider to win a Tour de France time trial.

SORRY, DON'T SPEAK THE LINGO

No, that's not an Englishman abroad, it's a reference to Michael Wright, who won three Tour stages for Great Britain but hardly spoke a word of English. He had an English father and a Belgian mother, and although he was born in Bishop's Stortford, they moved to the French-speaking part of Belgium shortly after and he grew up speaking French.

SPEED KING

Winning the prologue time trial is a big deal. It guarantees the yellow jersey, sometimes for several days, so it also guarantees lots of exposure, which in turn means that anyone capable of winning it is hot property among the teams. Britain's Chris Boardman is the Tour's best ever prologue racer, winning three and spending a total of five days in the yellow jersey.

↑ *Robert Millar (polka-dot jersey) finished fourth in 1984, the best overall finish by a British rider until Bradley Wiggins matched the feat in 2009.*

MILLAR TIME

David Millar won three Tour stages between 2000 and 2003 and wore the yellow jersey for three days in 2000. He's still racing in the Tour, the elder statesman of the new wave of British Tour racers. Millar has been through the mill and was caught up in the doping arms race of the early twenty-first century, but having served his suspension and come to terms with his mistakes he's taken up a strident anti-doping stance.

SKY'S THE LIMIT

Three British trade-backed teams have ridden the Tour de France since the early initiative of Hercules. Raleigh started a project in the 1970s with a group of British racers, but by the time the team was good enough to take on the Tour there was only one British rider left in it. They won, though, in 1980 with Joop Zoetemelk of Holland. A company called ANC put a team in the 1987 Tour, but it was hopelessly underfunded and only three riders reached Paris, powered by their own bravery and their manager's maxed-out credit card. Now, however, there's Team Sky. They are one of the most highly funded teams in world cycling. They include the top British Tour racers, Mark Cavendish and Bradley Wiggins, and they are staffed by people committed to a Briton winning the Tour de France. Bradley Wiggins came fourth in 2009, had a difficult 2010 Tour, which was Sky's first, and crashed out when looking very good in 2011. The 2012 Tour route really suits Wiggins and he has a tremendous chance of success. If he doesn't do it, Geraint Thomas and Peter Kennaugh are names to watch for the future.

↑ *Will Team Sky deliver the long-awaited British victory in the Tour de France? With Bradley Wiggins, fourth in 2009, there must be a chance.*

ITALY

Italy is one of the great road cycling nations along with France and Belgium. Riders from each of these countries have won every major professional race in the world, often many times. Yet only six Italians have won the Tour de France, although three of those won it twice. Belgium has won 18 Tours with 11 racers, Spain 13 with seven, while two US riders have won ten Tours. The reason for Italy's relatively poor showing is that, when it first started, the Tour was just another race and Italy had some well established events, so very few Italians rode the first Tours. Then, when the Tour showed that the concept of stage racing worked, Italy copied it by creating the Tour of Italy in 1909, and the Giro became the focus of Italian bike racing for a long time. It still is to a certain extent, which is why every Italian Tour de France winner except one has won the Tour of Italy too.

ITALIAN TOUR WINNERS

Rank	Rider	Wins	Years
1	**Ottavio Bottecchia**	2	1924, 1925
=	**Gino Bartali**	2	1938, 1948
=	**Fausto Coppi**	2	1949, 1952
4	**Gastone Nencini**	1	1960
=	**Felice Gimondi**	1	1965
=	**Marco Pantani**	1	1998

↑ *Ottavio Bottecchia escaped from poverty on his bike, but his life ended in mysterious circumstances at the age of 32 in June 1927.*

MURDER MYSTERY

The first time Italians entered the Tour in numbers was 1908, and their best rider, Luigi Ganna, finished fifth. Next year he won the first Tour of Italy, and the Italian presence in the Tour slowly grew until Ottavio Bottecchia won in 1924 and 1925. He was very poor and only took up bike racing when he discovered a talent for it in a bike-mounted branch of the Italian army. Bottecchia could hardly read or write when he rode his first Tour, and he only knew three French phrases: no bananas, lots of coffee and thank you. He was an amazing racer who sang snatches of opera while winning stages by many minutes, but he fell ill after a Pyrenean stage in 1926 that ran through a terrible storm – and he never raced again. One day, while he was trying to rebuild his strength, Bottecchia was found dead on the road close to his bike. The assumption was that it was an accident, although a number of question marks remained. Then, many years later, two men made separate deathbed confessions to having murdered Bottecchia. One said it was a Mafia hit; the other was the farmer near to whose land Bottecchia's body was found, who said he'd found the cyclist stealing grapes and hit him over the head with a rock.

↑ *Fausto Coppi , one of three two-time Tour de France winners from his country, is still the greatest Italian Tour racer.*

TAKING THE FIGHT TO LANCE

Such was the strength of Lance Armstrong and his team, and so total their domination of the Tour de France, that his rivals looked impotent at times. On their best days his team would exhaust the peloton by setting an unbearable pace. Then Armstrong would roll up his sleeves and administer the coup de grâce. Only one rider, a young Italian, could live with Armstrong at his best, and that was Ivan Basso. In the 2004 Tour he even beat Armstrong to win a stage in the Pyrenees. However, Basso was involved in a doping case known as *Operacion Puerto*, and received a suspension from racing. He's back now and won the 2010 Giro, but he hasn't yet made the impression he did in 2004.

➜ *On his day Lance Armstrong could shake anyone off his wheel, but he couldn't always do it to Ivan Basso, who beat the American on the 2004 stage to La Mongie. Basso would finish that Tour third overall.*

KEEPING EDDY HONEST

Felice Gimondi won the Tour at his first attempt in 1965. He was a new pro, 24 years old, and although an opportunist move got him the yellow jersey, Gimondi took more time out of the field while defending it. He won the Tour of Italy in 1967, 1969 and 1976 and the Tour of Spain in 1968, becoming one of only five racers who have won all three Grand Tours. Gimondi had similar qualities to Eddy Merckx in that he could win any kind of race, from Grand Tours to single-day Classics. Had there been no Eddy Merckx, Gimondi might have been one of the top three racers of all time. Merckx says that the Italian was his strongest rival. It's true too that on some occasions when they went head to head at the height of their powers, Gimondi beat Merckx.

IL PIRATA

Thirty-three years passed between Felice Gimondi's Tour win and the next Italian victory in 1998, the country's longest wait since the Tour began. That just underlines how important the Tour of Italy is, because in the same period Italians won their own Tour, the Giro d'Italia, 15 times. Before the 1998 Tour, the eventual winner Marco Pantani didn't think he stood a chance, because he'd already won the Giro that year. Then Jan Ullrich, who was in the yellow jersey, made a mistake on a stage that really suited Pantani. The Italian was a magical climber and he attacked on the Col de Galibier, quickly leaving Ullrich behind. Ullrich had a reasonable lead, so there was no need to panic: a strong chase on the other side of the climb and in the valley could limit Pantani's gains. Except it was freezing cold; Pantani slowed at the top of the Galibier to put a waterproof on, and Ullrich didn't. The German froze on the descent, and his muscles couldn't produce the power he needed in the valley and up the final climb to Les Deux-Alpes. Pantani was a mountain genius, which makes it all the more tragic that his life spiralled out of control until he died from a cocaine overdose in 2004.

⬅ *Mountain specialist Marco Pantani attacked race leader Jan Ullrich on the Col de Galibier, a brilliant move that won him the 1998 Tour de France.*

TRAGEDY ON THE PORTET D'ASPET

The 1992 Olympic road race champion Fabio Casartelli crashed on the descent of the Portet d'Aspet in 1995 and died. Casartelli was on a particularly steep part of the climb when he fell, so he was travelling very fast. He slid across the road and his head hit a concrete bollard positioned to stop cars crashing over the edge. There is a beautiful memorial stone close to where this happened. It's sculpted in marble from Casartelli's home region in Italy and was designed with precision. At the exact time on the date when he died the sun illuminates a small hole at the base of the sculpture. When it does it lights up three dates: the day Casartelli was born, the day he won Olympic gold and the day he died.

THE LION KING

Italian bike fans like calling their heroes lions, and their great sprinter Mario Cipollini was known as the "Lion King". Cipollini won 12 Tour stages between 1992 and 2004 and spent six days in the yellow jersey, but he never once finished the Tour de France. Cipollini couldn't climb mountains, or he wasn't motivated enough to suffer through them and get to Paris – some pointed to the fact that he got through the Giro, which is just as tough. The Tour organizer at the time, Jean-Marie Leblanc, took this as Cipollini not respecting The Tour de France. His disregard for the rules about wearing approved team kit also upset the Tour organizers, and his team weren't invited to the Tour from 2001 until 2003, even though Cipollini was world champion in 2003.

⬇ *Popular with fans, not so with Tour de France organizers, nevertheless Mario Cipollini played a big part in the way the race looks today.*

⬆ *Gastone Nencini, in the yellow jersey, won the 1960 Tour by climbing well and descending fearlessly.*

THE LION OF MUGELLO

Gastone Nencini was a strong racer, not only a good climber but also reputed to have been one of the best at going downhill. Raphaël Géminiani raced against Nencini and he says, "The only way you would try to follow Nencini down a mountain was if you wanted to die." To prove Géminiani's point, Roger Rivière was following Nencini when he ran off the road on the descent of the Col de Perjuret and plunged into a ravine, breaking his back. Nicknamed the "Lion of Mugello", Nencini won the 1960 Tour, after winning the Tour of Italy in 1957.

ITALIAN STAGES

The Tour frequently crosses into Italy, especially during stages in the Alps. A stage of the 2011 Tour finished at Pinerolo in Italy, and Team Sky's Norwegian racer, Edvald Boasson-Hagen, won it after a fantastic descent into the town. Next day's stage started in Pinerolo too, from where the riders climbed the Colle del Agnello, the summit of which is the border with France. At 2,744 metres it was the highest point of the 2011 Tour, and Maxim Iglinsky of Kazakhstan crossed the summit first.

CRAZY HEART

Franco Bitossi must be the only man who ever had a heart attack during a race and carried on to finish it. In fact it happened a few times during his career. He had a cardiac arrhythmia which could strike at any time. It meant he had to stop in the road to wait for his heart to slow down to normal levels before he could go on. This probably cost Bitossi some victories, but he had a brilliant career nevertheless. He was another racer who concentrated on the Tour of Italy, but he won the points classification in the 1968 Tour de France, the only year that a red, not green, jersey denoted the leader. Bitossi also won the first ever combined classification that year, and he finished eighth overall.

➔ *Even a heart attack couldn't stop Franco Bitossi.*

RELUCTANT LEADER

Fausto Coppi was a brilliant racer but sometimes a complex person. He was at his very best in the 1952 Tour, having already won the Tour of Italy, but when the races started he didn't seem interested in winning. This began to worry Andrea Carrea, Coppi's team-mate and most faithful *gregario* – the Italian equivalent of a domestique. Things came to a head on stage 9, when a breakaway – containing some good riders – gained a big lead, though Coppi seemed unconcerned. Carrea began to nag him, saying he should try to catch the break, but Coppi said, "If you're so worried, you go with it." Carrea did, and the break gained so much time that he took the yellow jersey. He should have been happy, but instead he was in a panic, worrying about what Coppi would say. Carrea wouldn't even go to the podium until he'd apologized to his leader, who just laughed and told him to enjoy the moment. Next day Coppi went on the attack, won the first ever stage to L'Alpe-d'Huez, and then proceeded to crush everybody in the Tour to win by 28 minutes.

IN HIS ELLI-MENT

Alberto Elli is the Italian record holder for Tour de France participations with 11 finishes from 11 starts. He had a wonderful symmetry to his Tour career too, competing every year from 1990 to 2000. His best place was seventh in 1994, and he wore the yellow jersey for four days in 2000.

ROUGH TREATMENT

There was an Italian in the first Tour, Rodolfo Muller, who finished fifth overall. The great Italian champion of the era, Giovanni Gerbi was less successful. He raced the 1904 and 1906 Tour, but didn't finish either. In 1904 he was set upon by spectators and so badly beaten he couldn't continue, and in 1906 he fell ill and abandoned the race.

⬅ *Andrea Carrea (light jersey), between Gino Bartali (left) and Fausto Coppi (far right) was interned in Buchenwald during the Second World War. No wonder he only wanted to ride his bike and serve others afterwards.*

LUXEMBOURG

Belgium is the country most renowned for punching above its weight in terms of the effect it has had on the Tour de France in relation to the size of its population, but with four winners, and two brothers who are potential champions in 2012, Luxembourg's half a million people have a Tour de France past and present to be proud of.

LUXEMBOURG TOUR WINNERS

Rank	Rider	Wins	Years
1	**Nicolas Frantz**	2	1927, 1928
2	**François Faber**	1	1929
=	**Charly Gaul**	1	1958
=	**Andy Schleck**	1	2010

LADY'S BIKE

Nicolas Frantz was an elegant, extremely talented racer who won the Tour twice, in 1927 and 1928, finished in the top five in all the other races from 1924 to 1929, and won 20 stages in six Tours. He was the first Tour de France specialist, taking part in few races other than the Tour. In 1928 he finished the stage to Charleville on a lady's bike. His bike broke irrepairably on a level crossing 100 kilometres from the end of the stage. The team mechanic said they should travel to the nearest Alcyon bike supplier to get a new one; the team manager, however, saw a woman spectator with a bike, so he asked to borrow it. The bike had mudguards, a saddle bag and a bell, but Frantz pedalled it to a 27 kph average to finish the stage 37 minutes behind the winner Marcel Hulot. His overall lead of 75 minutes was cut to 47 minutes, but he still became the second racer of only four all time to lead the Tour from start to finish.

↑ *François Faber was the biggest ever winner of the Tour de France, in terms of physical size at any rate.*

GIANT WINNER

François Faber was huge for a Tour de France winner. Miguel Indurain gets described as a giant, and at 80 kilos he was heavy, in comparison with the Tour average of 72, and climbers like Marco Pantani who weighed 58 kilos when in top form. But François Faber was 1.86 metres tall and weighed 91 kilos. He won the 1909 Tour, the last before the inclusion of stages in the Pyrenees (1910) and the Alps (1911), but there were still a few significant slopes for Faber to haul himself over. He was called the "Giant of Colombes", and his stature might have been an advantage in 1909, because the Tour that year was blighted by terrible weather. Lightly built racers suffer in the cold because their body volume, which is where heat is produced, is small compared with the surface area of their skin, where heat is lost.

PROLOGUE

In 2002 the Tour de France prologue was held in the streets of the city of Luxembourg, and Lance Armstrong won. There was a race around the Duchy for stage 1, which Rubens Bertogliati won, taking the yellow jersey from Armstrong.

← *Nicolas Frantz – the only Luxembourg rider to win the Tour de France on two occasions – let nothing stop him on the Tour and, in 1928, that included breaking his bike.*

FULL HOUSE

Charly Gaul is Luxembourg's most successful Tour racer. As well as his one overall win, he achieved three King of the Mountains titles and nine stage wins, both of which are Luxembourg records. He also finished seven out of the ten Tours he started, so is the national Tour record holder for participation too.

➜ *Charly Gaul is the most famous Luxembourg cyclist ever, with a host of honours to his name in the Tour de France and other races.*

FIRST NATIONAL TEAM

Before 1936, Tour participants from Luxembourg were either part of trade-sponsored teams or touriste-routiers. When national teams were introduced they continued as touriste-routiers until 1936, when a combined Luxembourg and Spanish team rode the Tour. They made a big impression too. Mathias Clemens won stage 3 and Arsène Mersch took the yellow jersey for a day. Mersch won the final stage and Pierre Clemens finished fourth overall, with Mersch fifth and Mathias Clemens seventh.

THE KIRCHENS

There must be something about families and cycling in Luxembourg. As well as their father being a pro, the Schlecks' grandfather, Gustave, was a racer too, although he didn't ride the Tour. However, Kim Kirchen, who won Tour stages in 2007 and 2008, has the most impressive cycling lineage. His father, Elmy Kirchen, was a good amateur racer, but his grandfather, Jim, and great-uncle, Jean, both raced in the Tour. Jean Kirchen was fifth overall in the 1948 and 1950 Tours.

THE BROTHERS

Frank and Andy Schleck are two of the best Tour racers of the present generation. Andy has won the Tour white jersey three times and finished second overall three times, but his 2010 runner-up spot was boosted to first place when Alberto Contador was stripped of the victory in 2012. He is a fantastic climber but has been let down by his poor time trial ability in the past. His elder brother Frank has three top five finishes in the Tour, and he was third in 2011 to Andy's second, making them the only brothers ever to have stood together on the Tour podium in Paris. They aren't the only cyclists in their family either; their father, Jonny, was a pro and completed six out of the eight Tours he rode.

➜ *Some feel brotherly love might have held back Frank (left) and Andy Schleck, but Andy was awarded the 2010 Tour after Alberto Contador (yellow, middle) was stripped of the title in 2012.*

THE NETHERLANDS

The land of the bicycle should produce good bike racers, and the Netherlands has had two Tour winners and loads of success in stages. What's surprising, for the flattest country in Europe, is that several great Dutch climbers have made their names in the mountains of the Tour de France. In fact their success on one particular climb, the Alpe d'Huez, sees an exodus of Dutch bike fans to the Alpine resort each year, some of whom camp up there for days in anticipation of the race coming through.

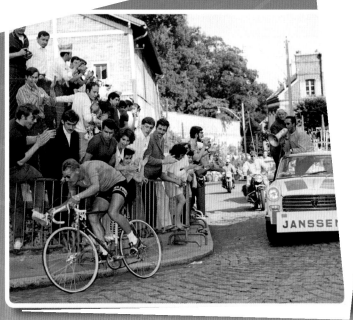

↑ *Jan Janssen used his Classics-winning speed to great effect in the time trial on the final day of the 1968 Tour, taking the stage and the Tour.*

DUTCH TOUR WINNERS

Rank	Rider	Wins	Year
1	**Jan Janssen**	1	1968
=	**Joop Zoetemelk**	1	1980

THE JOKER

Gerben Karstens was a great sprinter who won six Tour stages between 1966 and 1976, when he won the big sprint stage on the Champs-Elysées. He also wore the yellow jersey in 1974. He was equally famous for his sense of humour and for the tricks he played. He once faked a crash and was rolling on the floor in agony while photographers snapped away. Then he stood up, took a bow and pedalled off. There was plenty more like that, and Karstens was popular with the public – and with his fellow riders, except for one occasion. He attacked very early in a stage, before anyone was expecting it, but immediately stopped and hid in a village as the race went through. Everybody saw him go, but no one in the race saw him stop. As the peloton sped past, thinking he was ahead, Karstens got back on his bike and rejoined the field. It was quite some time before race officials figured out what had happened and told the peloton, who had been furiously chasing Karstens, or so they believed. He was killing himself laughing, but not many of the racers thought it was funny.

FIRST DUTCH WINNER

The first Dutch Tour winner was Jan Janssen in 1968. Janssen was a great all-round racer who won Classics as well as stage races. He was slightly lucky to win, because going into the final time trial the race was being led by Belgium's Herman van Springel, who was a better time triallist. Another Belgian time trial specialist, Ferdinand Bracke, was also close to the yellow jersey. However, they both let the occasion get to them and Janssen beat them to win the stage and take the Tour by 54 seconds, which was then the closest ever margin. Janssen was the first rider ever to win the Tour wearing spectacles.

RECORD MAN

The other Dutch winner of the Tour was Joop Zoetemelk in 1980. Some say he won because Bernard Hinault was forced out with a knee injury, but Zoetemelk points out that part of the ability of a Grand Tour racer is having the strength to last three weeks. And he should know, because Zoetemelk holds the world record for the number of Tours de France completed with 16. He was also second six times, another record, and fourth three times, giving him ten top-four placings.

← *Sixteen finishes from 16 starts makes Joop Zoetemelk the most durable man in Tour de France history.*

POLKA-DOT TWINS

They called Steven Rooks and Gert-Jan Theunisse the Dutch twins, not because they looked identical, although they were both tall, slim and had long blond hair, but because they were both great climbers and both won the King of the Mountains title, Rooks in 1988 and Theunisse the following year. They were team-mates and close friends, at least within cycling, although they had different characters. Rooks is laid back, very Dutch, but Theunisse is incredibly intense. He trained extremely hard when he was a pro, and still does, riding his mountain bike for up to ten hours a day. In 1997 Theunisse was hit by a car, and it was feared he would be left a paraplegic. But he taught himself to walk again and, within six months, was back riding. Later he suffered a heart attack, but even that didn't stop him. He still has physical problems and is classified as 13 per cent disabled. Rooks carried on riding too, and although he's 51 he achieved a high place in the 2011 Etape du Tour, which is a Tour de France stage for all-comers.

↓ *Inseparable when they race, Gert Jan Theunisse and Stephen Rooks (polka dot – Pedro Delgado is in yellow) are very different people with very similar talents.*

↑ *Wim van Est was the first Dutchman to enjoy regular success in the Tour, being the first to wear yellow, but he is also known for crash on the Col d'Aubisque in 1951.*

IRON WIM

As well as leading the 1951 Tour, until he crashed down the side of the Col d'Aubisque and had to abandon, Wim van Est won three stages and wore the yellow jersey on three occasions. It was the first time a Dutchman had worn the yellow jersey, and there's a stone on the Aubisque marking where Van Est fell that reads: "There in that ravine is the beginning of Dutch Tour de France history."

THE WRITER

Peter Winnen won two stages on the Alpe d'Huez as well as another mountains stage between 1981 and 1983, when he was third overall in the Tour. He took a degree in fine art after he stopped racing and is now a serious Dutch journalist, although he also writes about cycling. His books are best-sellers in Holland.

DUTCH DEBUT

The first official team from Holland took part in the 1936 Tour. The team was Albert and Antoon van Schendel, Theo Middelkamp and Albert Gijzen. They made an impression and Middelkamp became the first Dutch rider to win a stage. He won another in 1938.

DURABLE NATION

Six Dutch riders have completed ten or more Tours: Zoetemelk, Janssen, Gerrie Knetemann, Henk Lubberding, Michael Boogerd and Erik Dekker, winning 35 stages between them. The Dutch record for stage wins is shared by Zoetemelk, Knetemann, Jan Raas and Jean-Paul Van Poppel with ten each.

SPAIN

Spain's contribution to the Tour is huge because Spanish riders excel where the Tour is decided, in the high mountains. Not all the great Spanish mountain climbers have won the Tour, but they have provided some of the best moments in its history by attacking where the race is most dramatic. A Spaniard on the attack, dancing up into the clouds with the rest of the field struggling to stay in contention, is one of the enduring images of the Tour de France.

SPANISH TOUR WINNERS

Rank	Rider	Wins	Years
1	Miguel Indurain	5	1991, 1992, 1993, 1994, 1995
2	Alberto Contador	2	2007, 2009
3	Federico Bahamontes	1	1959
=	Luis Ocana	1	1973
=	Pedro Delgado	1	1988
=	Oscar Pereira	1	2006
=	Carlos Sastre	1	2008

↑ *San Sebastian, in the Basque region of Spain, hosted the Grand Départ in 1992. Spaniard Miguel Indurain won the opening stage – and later the Tour.*

SPANISH STARTS

The Tour visits Spain quite a lot. Pyrenean stages drop into the country from time to time, and a few have started and finished there. Spain hosted the Grand Départ in 1992, when the race set out from San Sebastian. That was to honour the previous year's Tour winner, Spain's Miguel Indurain, who replied by winning the prologue before pedalling to his second successive Tour victory.

THE WATCHMAKER OF AVILA

Julio Jimenez was the archetypal Spanish climber. It was all he could do. He didn't descend well, he was a poor time triallist, and he wasn't very good at single-day races, but show him a stretch of road winding up a mountain and he was in his element. Jimenez was prematurely bald, looked ten years older than he was, was a little bit pale and very thin. He even looked slightly at odds with his bike, until he went uphill. Then he flew. Vin Denson, a British racer who rode the Tour at the same time as Jimenez, used to marvel at where the Spaniard's strength came from: "He didn't have any muscles, it was like he fluttered his eyelids and, hey presto, he was gone." Denson wasn't a great climber, so he probably never saw Jimenez after his initial attack, but the Spaniard's style was quite unusual. He didn't spin the pedals at a high cadence as Charly Gaul did, or as modern racers do now, but used quite a high gear and was constantly in and out of his saddle. Jimenez won five Tour stages, the King of the Mountains title in 1965 and 1967, and he was second overall in the 1967 Tour. He was apprenticed to a watchmaker in Avila before he turned pro.

← *His style was unusual but Julio Jimenez was a great climber with an eye for spectacular lone breakaways. It brought him a handful of Tour de France stage victories and two King of the Mountains titles.*

MERCKX BEATER

Luis Ocana didn't just beat Eddy Merckx in the 1971 Tour, he took him apart. On a stage in the Alps that finished at altitude in Orcières-Merlette, Ocana took eight minutes out of Merckx. The Belgian started winning time back next day, and Ocana eventually crashed out of the Tour while still in yellow, but he was still over seven minutes ahead of Merckx. The Belgian's Tour record might have been very different if Ocana hadn't crashed. The Spaniard won the 1973 Tour, almost unopposed with Merckx choosing to do the Tour of Spain and Tour of Italy double that year. Ocana was a class act, and Merckx certainly respected him, although Ocana was never as strong after 1973. Merckx was, but the two didn't speak much until they stopped racing. Ocana started producing his own Armagnac in France, but in 1994, with his business and his health failing, Ocana took his own life.

PERICO

Pedro Delgado was not as flashily talented as Luis Ocana, but he was more than the one-trick climbing ponies that Bahamontes and Jimenez were. Ocana learned his racing in France when he moved with his family as a child, and by the time Delgado started riding, Spanish racing had changed. Modern Spanish racing is fast, and fast races breed riders who don't just rely on climbing talent to win. Delgado (Perico to his fans) was a strong time triallist, as well as a good climber, and used both strengths to take a controversial Tour win in 1988. It was controversial because after one stage only, he tested positive for probenicid in what was a slightly strange test result. Probenicid has no direct benefit for athletes, but can be used as a masking agent for steroids, but arguments are moot because it wasn't on the Tour's list of banned substances.

TAIL-END CARLOS

There was one climb left in the 2008 Tour. Cadel Evans led, but three riders were close to him overall: Frank and Andy Schleck and Carlos Sastre, all from the same team. They were going to attack in turn on the Alpe d'Huez and Evans would have to chase, at least that was the plan. What happened was that Carlos Sastre attacked first and nobody could bring him back. Evans chased but made no impression, the Schlecks couldn't chase because Sastre was their team-mate, and that would have been a professional no-no. Sastre was inspired and in the length of the Alpe gained enough time to win the Tour.

➡️ *Another Spanish mountains specialist, Carlos Sastre won the 2008 Tour de France on the final climb of the race.*

OSCAR'S AWARD

Oscar Pereiro would admit he's not the most talented Tour winner ever. In 2006 he got in an early break which put him in the yellow jersey, and although he lost the lead to Floyd Landis, the American was stripped of his title after the Tour for breaches of the rules on testosterone, so Pereiro won the 2006 Tour.

⬅️ *In 2006 Oscar Pereiro was the fifth Spaniard to win the Tour. Spanish riders won nine of the 20 Tours between 1991 and 2010.*

SPANISH FLEA

Spain was among the countries that fielded a team when the Tour de France changed to national squads in 1930. Vicente Trueba was their best finisher that year, in 36th position, and in 1933 he was third overall and won the first King of the Mountains title. Trueba was called the "Spanish Flea" by the French press. He set the scene for Spanish participation, with a number of great climbers following in his tracks. Jesus Lorono won the mountains title in 1953. Compatriot Federico Bahamontes won the following year, and he won it five more times out of the next eight Tours. In 1959 Bahamontes became Spain's first Tour de France winner.

SWITZERLAND

Swiss riders have competed in the Tour de France ever since it began. Two of the Tour's most highly respected winners are Swiss, and Swiss riders have featured throughout the Tour's history. They are a real force today, and with the route of the 2012 Tour favouring time triallists who can climb, one Swiss racer, Fabian Cancellara, could be a contender if Andy Schleck chooses to focus on the Giro d'Italia instead of *La Grande Boucle*.

SWISS TOUR WINNERS

Rank	Rider	Wins	Year
1	**Ferdinand Kubler**	1	1950
=	**Hugo Koblet**	1	1951

↑ *Ferdi Kubler suffering during an attack on Mont Ventoux during the 1955 Tour.*

THE WINNERS

The 1950 and 1951 Tours were won by Ferdinand Kubler and Hugo Koblet. Both were larger than life characters, but for very different reasons. Kubler was loud, proud and as strong as a horse. He won Classics and was world champion, as well as winning big stage races. He raced in a frenzy of attacks that succeeded or failed but never had any regard to tactics. It wasn't a pretty sight either: Kubler in full flight was a tangle of jutting elbows, with contorted face and a lolling tongue. Hugo Koblet was entirely different: totally classy, effortless and immaculate. He attacked when it was right to do so and looked as though he was pedalling in a different world from the rest. He even kept a comb and a sponge in his back pocket so he could spruce himself up while on the bike. Kubler is 92 now, the oldest surviving Tour winner. Hugo Koblet is another of cycling's suicides, having driven his car into a tree in 1964 at the age of 39.

MISSING IN ACTION

Some Tour racers are very highly strung. They live on their nerves, and whereas most of them will ride through fire once the race gets started, before a race begins they can be put off by the slightest thing. The 1982 Tour began in Basle in Switzerland, and Jean-Marie Grezet was in good form, so a lot was expected of him – maybe too much. He went for a warm-up ride before the prologue and didn't return. For their race numbers team leaders are given those with the figure 1 in them, so that's 1 for the previous year's winner, 11 for the leader of the next team, 21 for the next and so on down the teams. It's said that Grezet was upset because Beat Breu was given the 1 in his Cilo-Aufina team, and it shattered his confidence.

→ *The style of Fabian Cancellara – one of the top time triallists of his generation*

FAB 1

Fabian Cancellara is one of the best time triallists in the Tour. He's a multiple world champion and the reigning Olympic champion too. He's won six Tour stages, including two time trials and three prologues. He has not featured very high in the overall classification of the Tour yet, but there are those, including 1987 Tour winner Stephen Roche, who think Cancellara could be a Tour contender if he focused on the overall. He'd need to do what Bradley Wiggins did and change his body slightly, losing some upper body muscle, but the Swiss rider could be a contender in 2012. The route suits him.

➔ *He won two stages in the Tour, but if Beat Breu had concentrated on road racing and given up cyclo cross, he might have had an even better record.*

POLYGLOT

Tony Rominger was born in Denmark but grew up in and raced for Switzerland. He was a bit unlucky with timing, both of the Tour de France and his career. When Rominger first became a pro racer he won things at the beginning and end of each year, but he suffered from pollen allergies during high summer. By the time he sorted that out, Miguel Indurain was at his best. Rominger tried in vain to beat the Spaniard; but the closest he got to him was second place in 1994, when he won three stages and the King of the Mountains title. Rominger is a true European who speaks seven languages.

EGG-SHAPED

Oscar Egg has to be the best name in cycling. The Swiss racer rode two Tours, winning two stages in 1914. He was a very good track racer, and between 1912 and 1914 he raised the most prestigious record in track racing, the hour record, from 41.522 to 44.247 kilometres.

PASSAGE DU GOIS

This slippery strip of concrete, which is submerged daily by the tide, connects the Ile de Noirmoutier and Beauvoir-sur-Mer. The Passage du Gois was used on stage 2 of the 1999 Tour de France and may have cost Alex Zulle, the Swiss rider, a Tour de France victory. Zulle crashed, Lance Armstrong didn't; Zulle lost six minutes all in one go, and Armstrong won the Tour from him by seven.

STAND-UP

Beat Breu won two mountain stages in 1982, when he finished sixth overall in the Tour. He was a talented climber, but he was also very good at cyclo-cross, so he raced summer and winter and never was as successful in the Tour de France again. He always had a dry sense of humour and a good sense of the ridiculous too, which is why, when his career ended, Breu tried something not many ex-professional sports people do. He invested in a couple of businesses, and also launched himself into a career as a stand-up comic. He landed a few TV appearances, but you are unlikely to see him at your local comedy club as he soon opted for a more conventional retirement.

SWISS RECORD

Erich Maechler holds the Swiss Tour participation record with nine finishes from ten starts. He also led the Tour for seven days in 1987, the year that his team-mate Stephen Roche won the Tour.

➔ *French fans called the stylish Swiss cyclist, Hugo Koblet the Pedalleur du Charme, and you can see why. He won the Tour in 1951, carrying a comb and a sponge, just so he could look his best at any time.*

OTHER EUROPEAN COUNTRIES

Since Eastern Europe gained more political freedom, a big wave of talented cyclists has washed into the Tour de France. Poland was the first country to become liberal, and Poles were the first Eastern Europeans in the Tour. But more followed, and now two of the Tour's regular teams come from countries which used to be behind the Iron Curtain. No East European except Jan Ulrich has won yet, but it's only a matter of time.

↑ *Joachim Agostinho was a tough fighter who made a name for himself, and Portugal, in the Tour de France.*

AUSTRIA FIRST

Some European countries were never Communist but are either very small or had their own bike racing and didn't mix much with the rest of Europe. Austria falls into the last category. Max Bulla won three stages of the Tour, wore the yellow jersey for a day and finished 15th overall in 1931. After him Austrians have been a bit thin on the ground, although Adolf Christian finished third in the 1957 Tour, the best placing ever by an Austrian after Bernard Kohl lost his 2008 third place because of a doping offence.

NEVER RETURNED

Romania and Yugoslavia entered teams in the 1936 Tour, but none of their riders finished and the countries didn't return. Individual Yugoslav riders rode the Tour as part of pro teams during the 1980s, and there are some from the countries into which Yugoslavia was split who ride today, but no Romanian ever rode again.

PORTUGUESE MAN-OF-WAR

Portugal has its own bike racing scene, but quite a few of its riders have taken part in the Tour. Alves Barbosa was the first Portuguese Tour racer in 1956, but the best Portuguese Tour rider started his journey in 1969. He was an ex-soldier called Joachim Agostinho, and he finished 12 Tours out of 13 starts, winning four stages and twice achieving his best overall placing of third, in 1978 and 1979. Agostinho finished in the top ten in all but four of the Tours he took part in. One of his stage wins was on the Alpe d'Huez.

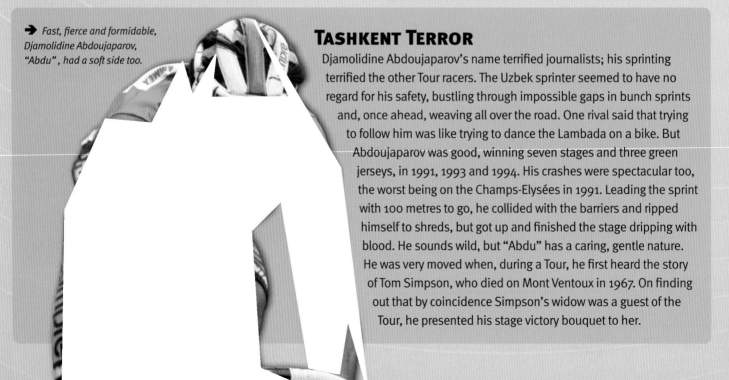

→ *Fast, fierce and formidable, Djamolidine Abdoujaparov, "Abdu", had a soft side too.*

TASHKENT TERROR

Djamolidine Abdoujaparov's name terrified journalists; his sprinting terrified the other Tour racers. The Uzbek sprinter seemed to have no regard for his safety, bustling through impossible gaps in bunch sprints and, once ahead, weaving all over the road. One rival said that trying to follow him was like trying to dance the Lambada on a bike. But Abdoujaparov was good, winning seven stages and three green jerseys, in 1991, 1993 and 1994. His crashes were spectacular too, the worst being on the Champs-Elysées in 1991. Leading the sprint with 100 metres to go, he collided with the barriers and ripped himself to shreds, but got up and finished the stage dripping with blood. He sounds wild, but "Abdu" has a caring, gentle nature. He was very moved when, during a Tour, he first heard the story of Tom Simpson, who died on Mont Ventoux in 1967. On finding out that by coincidence Simpson's widow was a guest of the Tour, he presented his stage victory bouquet to her.

EASTERN PROMISE

The Astana team have won the Tour de France, although not with an East European racer. Astana is the capital of Kazakhstan, and the city backs the team that won the 2009 Tour with Alberto Contador. It was set up as a vehicle for Alexandre Vinokourov to win the Tour. He was the best of a number of strong Kazakh racers who entered pro cycling during the 2000s. However, he was found guilty of blood doping during the 2007 Tour and suspended, while Astana were also thrown out of the Tour and weren't invited in 2008. Vinokourov returned to racing but suffered a very bad leg break during the 2011 Tour. The other East European team is Katusha, the Russian global cycling project. This is a well funded team backed by some big Russian businesses, but has yet to make an impression on the Tour, although its riders have won other major races.

↑ *The Kazakhstan-based Astana team is presented to the public before the start of the 2009 Tour de France.*

FOR THE FUTURE

Roman Kreuziger of the Czech Republic was a top ten finisher in the 2009 and 2010 Tours, and he was the best young rider and finished sixth overall in the 2011 Tour of Italy. He is 25 and a good all-rounder. It's possible that he may develop into a Tour contender. The Slovak twins Peter and Martin Velits and fellow countryman Peter Sagan are worth watching for the future too.

CIPOLLINI OF THE NORTH

Jaan Kirsipuu comes from Estonia. He was a good sprinter who won four stages and had six days in the yellow jersey between 1993 and 2005. Unfortunately Kirsipuu was a bit like Mario Cipollini, a very fast but specialized racer who couldn't make it over the Tour's mountains. He started 12 Tours, but like the "Lion King" he didn't finish a single one.

GRAND TOUR WINNER

Russian rider Denis Menchov is the best East European stage racer. He won the Tour of Spain in 2005 and 2007, and the Tour of Italy in 2009. He was promoted to second in the 2010 Tour de France (after Alberto Contador was stripped of his win), having previously won the white jersey and a stage in the 2003 Tour. He is a strong but not flashy rider who has been nicknamed "The Assassin" because he lets long races come to him rather than go on the attack. His consistency kills off the opposition one by one.

← *There is no doubting that Russian cyclist Denis Menchov is one of the great modern Grand Tour racers, but the question remains: "Is he good enough to actually win the Tour de France?"*

THE REST OF THE WORLD

From the early days of the Tour a few intrepid bike racers have travelled thousands of miles to take part in it, but in the 1980s the pull of the Tour began to attract many more. Their numbers grew slowly but steadily until the last decade, when there was huge growth in riders from all over the world. The Tour de France is now a truly global sports spectacle.

Lance Armstrong in yellow. Because of his personal story and the way he sparked and spread interest in the event around the globe, for many people, this is the image of the Tour de France.

AUSTRALIA

Australia was part of the Tour de France long before Britain and America. The first Australian entrants, Don Kirkham and Ivor Munroe, rode the Tour in 1914, finishing 17th and 24th. Australia even had a racer strong enough to win in the 1920s, although the rules prevented him from showing it. It's no surprise then that an Australian won the 2011 Tour; it's more of a surprise that they didn't win before.

AUSTRALIAN TOUR WINNER

Cadel Evans	1 win	2011

↑ *Sir Hubert Oppenheim ploughs a lonely furrow on the roads of Europe.*

SKIPPY

Phil Anderson won the Commonwealth road title in 1978 in Edmonton, Canada, then moved to Paris in 1979. There he gained a place in the ACBB cycling club, which was set up as a feeder for the Peugeot pro team. Anderson gained a contract with Peugeot for 1980 and rode his first Tour the following year. There weren't any other Australians in that Tour, so the press christened Anderson "Skippy", after the programme about a kangaroo that could communicate with humans that was on French TV at the time. Anderson did well and was told to support the team's leader for as long as he could in an important stage that finished on Pla d'Adet in the Pyrenees. He thought the best way to do it was stay at the front and let the leader follow him, but when there was a big attack, Anderson went with it and the leader couldn't, so Anderson got the yellow jersey. He only wore it for a day, but it was the first for Australia. Next year Anderson led the Peugeot team in the Tour, and he had the yellow jersey for nine days before finishing fifth.

➡ *Phil Anderson was a real force of nature who blazed a trail in the Tour for other Australian racers to follow.*

OPPY

Sir Hubert Opperman was a cabinet minister in Australia and High Commissioner to Malta, but before entering politics he was an Australian sporting hero. By far the best cyclist of his generation, Oppy, as he was affectionately known, inspired the *Melbourne Herald* to launch a campaign to send him to ride in the 1928 Tour. The idea was that Opperman, three other Australians, and a New Zealander, would go to Europe, race and train there, then race in the Tour. Opperman soon proved his ability with third place in the Paris–Brussels race, but he was far better than his team-mates. That was a big problem, because 15 of the 28 stages of that Tour were team time trials, and they had to take on ten-man teams. Opperman finished 18th, which got him a place in a top French team, and he won some big races for them, including the Paris–Brest–Paris. He rode the Tour again in 1931 but fell ill when he was lying sixth overall and dropped to 12th.

STUEY

Stuart O'Grady holds the Australian Tour participation record jointly with Phil Anderson, both having finished 13 Tours. O'Grady has also won two stages and has worn the yellow jersey for nine days. He's 38 and still racing in the Tour. In 2012 he will join the Green Edge team, who are aiming to be the first Australian-registered team to ride the Tour. Everybody in cycling knows O'Grady simply as Stuey. He typifies Aussie cyclists: tough, fast, independent, and he never stops smiling.

ROBBIE'S DOZEN

After starting his cycling life as a BMX racer, which is where he gets his sprinter's reflexes from, Robbie McEwen has become one of the best sprinters in the Tour de France over the last decade. He has raced 12 Tours, and has won 12 stages and the green jersey three times, in 2002, 2004 and 2005. McEwen will be a Green Edge rider in 2012.

➜ *Robbie McEwen(in green) takes out another intermediate sprint. Stuart O'Grady (left) is in the yellow and green Australian national champion's kit.*

TRACK RACERS

Track racing was more popular than road in Australia until well into the 1980s. The country did well in the Olympic Games, and a lot of their top track racers travelled to Europe to ride the winter six-day track races. Some stayed for the summer and raced on the road as well. That's how a track sprinter, Russell Mockridge, ended up riding the 1955 Tour, and in a way it was the same for another talented track racer, Don Allen, in 1974 and 1975. But by then road racing was growing in Australia, and some good road riders gained places in big amateur teams in France that were really just schools for pros who wanted to ride the Tour de France.

THE ALCHEMIST

Anderson was followed into the Tour by Allan Peiper, who rode five Tours between 1984 and 1992. Then, during the second half of the nineties, the number of Australian Tour racers grew dramatically. Peiper became a team manager later and worked with Cadel Evans when he raced for a Belgian team. Evans was a great mountain biker but had to learn some of the arts of a road stage racer from scratch, particularly how to ride time trials – which are now one of Evans's strengths.

SPIKY CHARACTER

Australia's first Tour winner, Cadel Evans has earned a bit of a reputation for being difficult, especially within the media. He isn't glib or silver tongued. He's not a great source of wry quips after a stage, and he gets very nervous before important days in the Tour. Sometimes he doesn't handle the hassle of the Tour well, particularly the media scrum that a contender attracts. But Evans wears his heart on his sleeve; he's nervous and sometimes short-tempered because he is ambitious and wants to win. He's defensive in interviews because he's quite shy. He's very intelligent, very tough and extremely talented, and he thoroughly deserved his victory in 2011. He's also very honest, and there's not been a hint of scandal or an accusing finger pointed at Evans throughout his career.

⬆ *July 2011, and Cadel Evans is just a couple of laps of the Champs Elysées away from becoming the first Australian to win the Tour de France.*

COLOMBIA

Colombia has a long tradition of bike racing, so it was only natural for men who raced and trained in the heights of the Andes to look at the mountains of the Tour de France and think, "I can win that." They came in droves from the 1980s onwards, and over 50 Colombians have taken part in the Tour. They haven't won yet, but their climbers have made a huge impression on the Tour.

COLOMBIAN TOUR STAGE WINNERS

Rank	Name	Wins	Years
1	**Luis Herrera**	3	1984, 1985 (2)
=	**Santiago Botero**	3	2000, 2002 (2)
3	**Fabio Parra**	2	1985, 1988
4	**Félix Cardenas**	1	2001
=	**Chepe González**	1	1996
=	**Oliverio Rincon**	1	1993
=	**Nelson Rodríguez Serna**	1	1994
=	**Mauricio Soler**	1	2007

↑ *Lucho Herrera climbs in the polka dot jersey, a king of the mountains at home in his realm.*

COLOMBIA'S FINEST

The two best Colombian Tour de France riders were Luis Herrera and Fabio Parra. Herrera, nicknamed "Lucho", was one of the best climbers ever, and won the King of the Mountains title in 1985 and 1987, but he was never good enough in a time trial to win the Tour. Fabio Parra was good enough. He was third in 1988, the only Colombian ever to get on the Tour podium. The duo were key members of the Colombian pro team sponsored by Cafe de Colombia that took part in several Tours in the 1980s. Herrera holds the Colombian record for Tour participation with seven completed, and Parra is now a politician.

KIDNAP

King of the Mountains in 2000, fourth overall in 2002, and winner of three stages, Santiago Botero was Colombia's best racer of the last decade. Cycling has lost ground in Colombia to football, and life hasn't been easy for any sports people there. A number of former Tour racers have disappeared, and Lucho Herrera was kidnapped and ransomed in 2000. Botero had a doubly difficult time, because even before his earnings from cycling, his family were rich. He was such a target for kidnap that, when he trained in Colombia, he could only use a short stretch of straight open road. There he would ride up and down, followed by armed security men in an open Jeep, until he'd completed the distance needed for that training session.

MONDIALIZATION

The early 1980s saw an economic downturn in Europe and the number of sponsors in cycling fell. This forced the Tour de France to throw its doors open to some of the top amateur nations in the world in 1983. The move was called the mondialization of cycling, from the French word monde, meaning world. Colombia was the only country to take up the challenge. Cycling was at its height in Colombia then, so over 40 journalists travelled with the team and Colombian radio broadcast live commentary from the Tour. And even though it was the middle of the night many thousands listened in. Patrochinio Jimenez spent five days in the polka-dot jersey and Edgar Corredor finished 16th overall, but most of the team were exhausted by the fast racing on flat terrain before they reached the mountains. Lessons had been learned, though.

← *Santiago Botero was a good all-rounder who challenged for the Tour during the early 2000s.*

THE FLYING PAPER BOY

Oliviero Rincon won the stage to Pal, a ski station above Andorra, in 1993. It was his only stage win, but he dominated what was a marathon day in the mountains with seven huge climbs spread over 231 kilometres that took over seven hours to ride. When asked where he got his strength from, Rincon said it was from delivering newspapers as a boy in the hills around his mountain home – on a bike that weighed 40 kilos when fully loaded.

↑ *Mauricio Soler reminds everyone of the Colombian climbers of old, though his recent injuries might prevent him ever racing again.*

VICTOR HUGO

Victor Hugo Pena, who was named after the French author, is the only Colombian to wear the yellow jersey in the Tour de France. It happened in 2003 when Pena was part of Lance Armstrong's US Postal team. He was a modern type of Colombian racer, being quite adept at fast races on flat routes as well as a good climber, and was the highest placed of the US Postal riders before they won the team time trial on stage 4. He wore the jersey for four days, until the first day in the mountains.

BLAST FROM THE PAST

When Mauricio Soler made his Tour debut it was like going back in time. Many were reminded of the great Fausto Coppi, for two reasons. First, the tall Colombian looks like Coppi, even down to his style on a bike. Second, Soler too is a gifted climber. He won the stage that climbed the Galibier, and he won the King of the Mountains title. Since then Soler has been plagued by illness and injury, apart from a brief window of form when he was fourth in the 2009 Tour of Italy. He looked good in 2011 when he won a stage of the Tour of Switzerland, but a few days later he suffered a terrible high-speed crash on a mountain descent. He suffered a fractured skull and brain injury and was put into an induced coma. Soler has since been brought round, but has cognitive difficulties and it's not known if he will make a full recovery.

COCHISE

Ironically the first Colombian to ride the Tour got his place in a European team because of his ability on the flat. He had won all of Colombia's top road races, but Martin Rodriguez, who sometimes used Cochise as his Christian name because he admired the Apache chief, was also a very good track racer. He came to international notice by competing for Colombia in the world championships, and was offered a place in Felice Gimondi's team. Rodriguez raced in the Tour of Italy, where he won two stages, and he rode the 1975 Tour de France, finishing 27th overall.

← *Victor Hugo Pena leads the 2003 Tour de France, the tough all-rounder is the only Colombian ever to do so.*

UNITED STATES

No nation other than France has made such a big impression on the Tour de France in the short time the United States has. The first American took part in the Tour in 1981, whereas the first Australian appeared in 1914, the first Briton in 1937 and the first Irishman in 1956. Australia took its first win in 2011, Britain has yet to win, Ireland has one winner, but Americans have won ten Tours de France. That's a big impression.

AMERICAN TOUR DE FRANCE WINNERS

Rank	Name	Wins	Years
1	**Lance Armstrong**	7	1999, 2000, 2001, 2002, 2003, 2004, 2005
2	**Greg LeMond**	3	1986, 1989, 1990

⬆ *Jonathan Boyer, the American pioneer, in action in the 1983 Tour, when he finished a more than respectable 12th overall.*

TYLER FARRAR

Farrar is a sprinter and is growing into a rival for Mark Cavendish. He has occasionally got the better of Cavendish too, and he's getting faster. Farrar races for another American Tour team, Garmin-Cervelo, which is run by Jonathan Vaughters, a promising Tour rider in his day and one of the keenest brains in pro cycling. If they passed out degrees in the subject, Vaughters would have his masters and be teaching it by now.

THE YANKS ARE COMING

The first American Tour rider was Jonathan Boyer. He came as a loner to Europe, made his way through European amateur cycling, became slightly Frenchified, to the extent of calling himself Jacques Boyer at times, and won a place in Bernard Hinault's team on merit. He finished 32nd in his debut Tour and rode four more after 1981, with a best position of 12th overall in 1983.

⬆ *7-Eleven in action during the team time trial in 1986. The first North American to wear the yellow jersey, Alex Stieda, is at the back of the pack.*

7-ELEVEN

Greg LeMond followed Boyer to a pro contract, again ploughing a lone furrow – but a better-funded and very talented furrow. Then two things happened in 1984 that paved the way for more American bike racers to join Boyer and LeMond in Europe. One was LeMond taking third place in the 1984 Tour; the other was the huge success American racers had in the 1984 Los Angeles Olympics. That happened partly because the strong East European cycling nations boycotted the games, but it allowed Jim Ochowicz, a former cyclist and speed-skater, to attract an American sponsor to back a team for the Tour de France. He was pushing on an open door, as the Tour wanted exposure in the US, so once 7-Eleven proved they could cut it in Europe, they were invited to the Tour in 1986. On their first road stage a Canadian called Alex Stieda took the yellow jersey for the team, the first North American to wear it.

HTC-COLUMBIA

This team was created by an American businessman, Bob Stapleton, who took over the German T-Mobile squad and walked into a drugs storm. He wasn't told any of this when he took over, quite naturally when you think about it, but it transpired that widespread doping had been going on in T-Mobile in the past. The revelations, however, didn't dent Stapleton's faith that certain members of the team staff who had been there a long time had reformed and could contribute to his vision of drugs-free cycling. And, luckily, a slow change occurred in the peloton's attitude to doping during the same period. Stapleton was able, like many other managers at the time, to get his riders to buy into a clean racing policy, and at the same time he created one of the most successful teams in cycling history. As HTC-Columbia, the team will always be remembered for the high-speed lead-out train they created to launch Mark Cavendish to so many stage victories in the Tour de France and numerous other races.

NEXT BIG THING

Who are America's future Tour de France stars? Taylor Phinney – the son of the first American to win a stage in the Tour, Davis Phinney (in 1986) – is seen as a potential Tour winner. He's only 21 and hasn't ridden the Tour yet, but could make his debut in 2012. He turned pro in 2011, having won junior and senior world titles, and looks particularly impressive on the track, where he is brilliant at the individual pursuit. That event was Bradley Wiggins's speciality, and Phinney, whose mother Connie Carpenter was 1984 Olympic road race champion, is of a similar build to Wiggins. If he can make the same physical changes as Wiggins, Phinney could win the Tour. He has the genetic potential.

↑ *Andy Hampsten racing for the French, La Vie Claire team in 1986 when he won the Tour of Switzerland.*

STARS AND STRIPES EXPLOSION

In 1986 a huge revolution took place in European pro cycling and in the Tour de France. Greg LeMond won the Tour. Andy Hampsten had won the Tour of Switzerland just before it. And 7-Eleven got half of their team to Paris. They even took a stage on the way with their sprinter, Davis Phinney. From such an auspicious beginning it was inevitable that 7-Eleven went from strength to strength when Motorola took over as team sponsors. When they pulled out, US Postal stepped in, and by then Lance Armstrong, who had made a big impression when he started racing for Motorola in 1992, was a very different Lance Armstrong, one ready to take on the Tour and win it. The rest, as they say, is history.

GORGEOUS GEORGE

New Yorker George Hincapie holds the American record for Tour participations. With 15 finishes (out of 16 starts), he stands a chance of beating Joop Zoetemelk's all-time record of 16 (out of 16). Hincapie is 38, but having played an important part in Cadel Evans's 2011 victory the American is giving no sign of being about to stop. Evans's win was the ninth time Hincapie has been in the Tour-winning team, and that's not a coincidence. He is one of the strongest and most tactically aware super-domestiques in the business. Hincapie has won four stages in the Tour, as well as three big single-day races, and was American road race champion three times. A tall, good-looking chap, he is sometimes referred to as Gorgeous George within the peloton.

← *George Hincapie riding the prologue time trial around the streets of Monaco in 2009.*

OTHER COUNTRIES AROUND THE WORLD

French colonial connections with North Africa meant that a few Moroccan and Algerian riders took part in the Tour from the late 1930s until the mid-fifties. Both countries have quite a history in cycling and used to host big pro races at one time. Tunisia also had a bike race scene through connections with Italy, and a Tunisian racer Ali Neffati rode the 1913 and 1914 Tours. However, except for Australia, the United States and Colombia it's only quite recently and only in small numbers that riders from more distant countries have taken part.

⬆ *Raúl Alcalá won his first Tour de France stage in a time trial at Eprinal in 1990.*

JAPAN

Kisso Kawamuro rode the 1926 and 1927 Tours but abandoned on the first stage of each. Track cycling is huge in Japan and revolves around betting on a sprint event called the Keirin, but the country doesn't have much tradition in road racing. Fumiyuki Beppu and Yukiya Arashiro both finished the 2009 Tour. The Japanese cycle component company Shimano have won many Tours, the first with Lance Armstrong in 1999.

⬇ *Yukiya Arashiro celebrates completing his first Tour de France on the Champs Elysées in 2009.*

RAÚL ALCALÁ

A number of South Americans other than Colombians have ridden the Tour. The most successful is Mexico's Raúl Alcalá, who was best young rider in 1987, finished in the top ten overall twice, and in 1989 won a stage that finished on the Spa-Francorchamps motor race circuit. He went on to win a second stage, a time trial to Epinal, the following year. Mauro Ribiero of Brazil also won a stage in 1991, riding for a French team. Three other Brazilians have followed him into the Tour, with Maurillo Fischer finishing the two Tours he started in 2007 and 2008.

MAPLE LEAF FOREVER

Apart from Australia, the United States and Colombia, of the countries outside Europe Canada has had the biggest impact in the Tour. It was a Canadian, Alex Stieda, who in 1986 was the first North American to wear the yellow jersey. Then Steve Bauer from Niagara Falls had two long stints in yellow and finished fourth overall in the 1988 Tour. Ryder Hesjedal flies the maple leaf flag in the Tour today. He was promoted to sixth overall in the 2010 Tour after Alberto Contador's disqualification.

AFRICAN-BORN STAGE WINNER

The best ever Tour rider from North Africa was Marcel Molines from the then French-governed city of Algiers. In 1950 he became the first African-born racer to win a stage in the Tour. It was incredibly hot on the road between Perpignan and Nîmes that day, so hot that the peloton stopped to have dip in the Mediterranean — except for Molines, who was used to such heat and carried on to win.

→ *New Zealander Julian Dean in a Tour de France time trial on the penultimate day of the 2010 Tour. A notable sprinter, he has completed seven Tours but has yet to actually win a stage.*

KIWI POWER

Harry Watson was the first New Zealander to ride the Tour when he raced alongside Australia's Hubert Opperman in 1928 and finished in 28th place. Opperman finished 18th. Seven others have ridden, one of the best being Julian Dean, who has a very special role in teams. He's a powerful rider with a good long sprint. Riders like Dean are often well paid to be the last lead-out man for top sprinters. Dean has performed this role for Mark Cavendish and more recently his rival, Tyler Farrar. It takes a special kind of rider who can ride very smoothly at almost Cavendish speed, and be tough enough to stand others doing the same job from other teams leaning on them to push them out of place. In 2010, while trying to lead out Farrar, Dean clashed with Mark Cavendish's last lead-out Mark Renshaw. Dean was leaning on Renshaw with his shoulders, trying to edge him from his position on the road. It's claimed that Renshaw then head-butted him, but it was more of a sideways lean of the head which Renshaw says was to resist Dean. What is amazing is that it all took place while they were riding at well over 40 mph and no one was put in danger. Nevertheless, Renshaw was thrown out of the Tour.

SUPER CLIMBER

Four Venezuelan riders have ridden the Tour, but the most exciting of them, José Rujano, didn't reach the finish of the only Tour he started. Why is Rujano exciting? Because he is an amazing climber. He weighs just 48 kilos, and when he made his European pro debut in 2005 he won two stages and the mountains title of the Tour of Italy. That landed Rujano a big contract to start the 2006 Tour de France, but he didn't settle in well with his team. Rujano is often homesick and tries to limit his time in Europe, living and training in Venezuela instead. His tactic hasn't worked in terms of results, but such is Rujano's potential that he always gets a place and a good contract in a pro team.

SOUTH AFRICA

Two riders from South Africa have competed in the Tour, and they both made an impression. Jon-Lee Augustyn is a climber. He's only ridden one Tour, in 2008, but he won the Souvenir Henri Desgrange prize for leading the race over its highest climb. In 2008 that was the highest road climb in France, the Cime de la Bonette. Augustyn tried to preserve his lead by throwing caution to the wind on the descent, but overshot a corner and went off the road. He slid for some distance down a black scree slope, and then had to drag himself back up the way he'd just fallen before resuming the race on a replacement bike from the team car. He carried on to finish five minutes down on the stage. Another South African, Robbie Hunter, has finished three Tours out of eight started, winning one stage in 2007. He's a good sprinter – not the best in a bunch finish, but a threat if he gets into a breakaway group. Hunter was racing for the Barloworld team when he won his stage. They were the first African-based team to take part in the Tour de France.

↑ *Robbie Hunter wins the first Tour de France stage for South Africa, at Montpellier in 2007.*

PART 3
THE LEGENDARY RIDERS

The Tour de France is the people's race, a sporting event that visits their towns and villages and uses their roads. Every rider becomes a mini-legend somewhere along the way. Of course, some are known around the world, even transcending their sport. But what makes a Tour de France legend? Is it a matter of winning once, or more often? No, it's not about winning; it's about the stories they create on the Tour. The deeds are recounted in bars and cafés, and celebrated in print or on the air. Winning doesn't make a legend, it's the way that victory – or defeat – is achieved.

For many cycling fans Lance Armstrong (left, alongside two-time winner Alberto Contador) is the greatest ever Tour de France rider. But supporters of Gino Bartali, Eddie Merckx, Jacques Anquetil, to name but three, would beg to differ.

JACQUES ANQUETIL

Jacques Anquetil was the iconoclast of the Tour de France. Pro cyclists live by a strict code, taking no liberties regarding diet and rest, as the sport is too hard for that – but Anquetil took no notice of such constraints. He lived by his own code, but was still the most dominant Tour racer of his generation and one of the sport's all-time greats. He was the first man to win five Tours, and if he set out to win a race he was almost impossible to beat.

TOUR RECORD

Name:	Jacques Anquetil
Nationality:	French
Born:	8 January 1934
Died:	18 November 1987
Tour career span:	1957–66
Tours contested:	8
Stage wins:	15
Tour wins:	5 (1957, 1961, 1962, 1963, 1964)

← *Anquetil combined huge natural ability with a capacity to suffer on a bike that made him invincible in the Tour.*

↑ *Anquetil depended on his wife Janine. She drove him to races, negotiated with race promoters and even gave interviews on his behalf. Then he left her.*

WHIRLWIND ROMANCE

Janine was the wife of Anquetil's doctor, but Jacques fell in love with her. She was older than him, blonde and very glamorous. Their romance could have been lifted from a French film. In spring 1958, unable to be apart from Janine, Anquetil left his pre-season training camp, flew to Normandy and went to his doctor's house in the middle of the night. He explained how he felt and Janine left with him straight away, wearing pyjamas and a fur coat. They drove to Paris, where she bought new clothes as soon as the shops opened, and they married later that year.

SCANDAL

Once they married, Janine was constantly by Anquetil's side. Although wives were discouraged from attending races in the male-dominated cycling world of the fifties and sixties, an exception was made for Janine. She was so much part of French pro racing that riders from the era say that she could walk into where the racers were changing and no one thought anything about it. It was a huge shock, a few years after he stopped racing, when Anquetil left Janine to live with his adopted son's wife, and it was also revealed that he'd had a child of his own with Janine's daughter.

PRODIGY

Anquetil was so good that he turned professional at 19. Teenage pros are rare now, but were unheard of in the 1950s. But Anquetil didn't just take part in pro races, he won them. The Grand Prix des Nations time trial was a huge race. The world time trial championships did not exist in those days, but the "Nations" was regarded as the unofficial title race. Anquetil caused a sensation when he won in 1953.

NEVER DRINK CHEAP CHAMPAGNE

That was the advice Anquetil gave to a journalist whose magazine was collecting some pro training tips. He liked a drink and he liked a party – he even went to one on a Tour de France rest day. Racers ride their bikes on rest days to keep their legs turning, then they lounge about to save their strength. On the rest day in Andorra during the 1964 Tour, Anquetil didn't ride his bike; instead he went to a reception at a radio station. Anquetil drank plenty of champagne and was the life and soul of the party, so much so that next day he felt terrible. His legs hurt and he was dropped on the first climb. He even talked about dropping out of the Tour, but his manager told him that if he was going to drop out he should do it from the front, so Anquetil rallied and caught everyone up. He felt better by then and went on to race well, gaining more time on his nearest rivals.

↗ *Never afraid of controversy, never taking the expected line, Anquetil wrote his own rules, even down to what he ate and drank.*

STRAWBERRY FIELDS

Anquetil was born in Normandy, the son of a market gardener who specialized in growing strawberries. When he started racing as a teenager, Jacques was lent two bikes by a local cycle dealer who also ran a cycling club, but once he started in the engineering job that he had qualified for Anquetil couldn't join the club's important Thursday afternoon training session, so his father said he could work for him and have every Thursday afternoon off, provided he won his third amateur race, which Anquetil duly did.

THE RIVALS

In a time of transition for France, Anquetil's rivalry with Raymond Poulidor seemed to symbolize the nation's divisions. In the 1960s France was still an agricultural country, but a lot of modern, city-based technological industries were growing rapidly. There was a huge contrast between modern and old France, where the cities represented the modern and the countryside the old ways. Anquetil fans were modernists, maybe because the efficient way he raced appealed to them, as did his glamorous lifestyle. In contrast Poulidor was liked by people who worked on the land. They were said to have identified with the bad luck that was seen to visit Poulidor more often than Anquetil. It was an illusion: Anquetil was a better racer than Poulidor, both in terms of tactics and sheer ability. On a personal level, they didn't get on together when they raced but became friends after they stopped. Anquetil died of stomach cancer in 1987, and the story goes that when Poulidor visited him shortly before his death, Anquetil said to him, "It looks like you are to be second again, my friend."

TIME MACHINE

Anquetil's obvious strength was that he was almost unbeatable in a time trial. His famous team manager Raphaël Géminiani said that Anquetil was the combination of a computer, a still and a jet engine, meaning that he always spread his energy equally around any given time trial course, that he could drip-feed energy to his legs in just the right amount to complete the course at maximum speed for the distance, and that those legs possessed jet-pack power. He used the time trials in the Tour de France to gain time on his rivals, then defended rather than attacked in the mountains.

← *The master of time at work; Anquetil held his upper body rigid, as low as possible and sat rock solid in the saddle. All are crucial in riding a time trial.*

LANCE ARMSTRONG

Lance Armstrong is the greatest Tour de France racer ever. He won seven times, two more than anyone else. He rewrote the book on how to prepare for and race the Tour. He cemented the profile of the race in North America, while it was raised in many other countries by the story of how he won after nearly dying of cancer. Armstrong is the Tour de France's first world superstar. Whether he is the best bike racer to have won the Tour is another matter, and whether history will see the story of Lance Armstrong as we do today is also a matter for conjecture.

TOUR RECORD

Name:	Lance Armstrong
Nationality:	American
Born:	18 September 1971
Tour career span:	1993–2010
Tours contested:	13
Stage wins:	25
Tour wins:	7 (1999, 2000, 2001, 2002, 2003, 2004, 2005)

➔ *Armstrong revolutionized the Tour, polarized opinion and pulverized the opposition.*

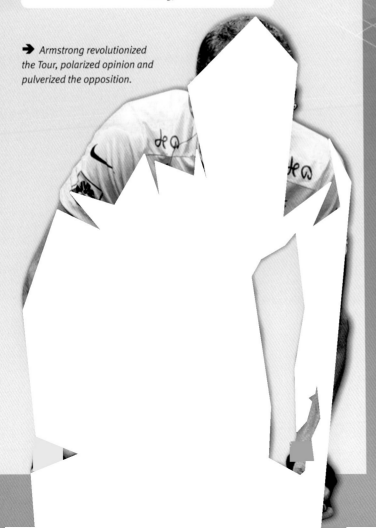

LANCE WHO?

Armstrong was born Lance Gunderson in 1971. He has never met his real father, and isn't close to his stepfather, from whom he took his name. In high school he found athletic expression in triathlon. He got into the sport because he swam well and was a good runner, but triathlon showed he was a fantastic cyclist. Armstrong was groomed for the 1992 Olympics, but bad tactics meant he fared poorly in Barcelona. Within weeks of turning pro, with a big team of experienced racers behind him, he blossomed and, in his first full pro year, he was world road race champion and, at just 21, one of the youngest ever to win the title.

⬆ *A true sporting phenomenon, at 16 Armstrong was already one of the top triathletes in the US, competing and winning against adult professional racers.*

CONTROVERSY

No one who is into cycling is ambivalent about Armstrong. He is controversial. He always said that the Tour was not a popularity contest, but when he raced Armstrong seemed to relish a fight, either with words off the bike or with his legs on it. The controversy has continued. During his career Armstrong successfully fielded accusations of doping, but they have followed him into retirement and his career is under scrutiny once more. What will be revealed? No one knows, but he was still an incredibly effective racer with a huge character, and for a generation all over the world he is still the face of the Tour de France.

CANCER

Armstrong built on his 1993 world title, quickly becoming one of the best single-day racers in the world, although his build, with a swimmer's heavy shoulders, limited his ability in the mountains that are such a feature of races like the Tour de France. He was also very young for a Tour racer. He won stages but didn't feature overall. Then in 1996 Armstrong began to struggle in races, and he also had some significant health problems that he hadn't revealed to anyone. When he eventually sought medical advice he was diagnosed with testicular cancer, which had spread to his brain and lungs. There was a significant chance that Armstrong would die. He was operated on and underwent chemotherapy, opting for the most painful kind as he was promised it would damage his athletic potential the least. Not only was Armstrong determined to live, he was determined to race again.

THE COMEBACK

Armstrong says that when he got back on his bike for the first time a lady on a shopping bike rode past him. He built back slowly, and after a hesitant return to competition it was obvious that Armstrong was different. Cancer and chemo had wasted his body, but when he started training again his legs responded while his upper body stayed skinny. Armstrong was now the right shape to be a Tour racer.

COMEBACK 2

Armstrong stopped racing after winning the 2005 Tour de France. He had more to give athletically, but as Johan Bruyneel put it at the time: "The situation had changed, we had to win the Tour; second was failure. I wanted Lance to go out winning, not be beaten, that would have spoiled the story." Free from cycling, Armstrong played to his celebrity status for a while, but he grew bored. He had kept fit by running marathons, but then he did the Leadville 100, a 100-mile mountain bike race at altitude in Colorado, which he really trained for, and he says: "I realized how much I missed the single-mindedness of real training, and once the race started I wanted that kind of competition back in my life." Armstrong announced his comeback to pro cycling, and in 2009 he finished third in the Tour de France, another unprecedented achievement in the history of the race.

↑ *Bruyneel and Armstrong do a lap of honour with the US Postal team after the 2004 Tour de France.*

JOHAN SVENGALI

Johan Bruyneel, who had just stopped racing when Armstrong came back from cancer, is an excellent talent spotter. He had not been the best racer during his career, but he had learned to watch others carefully in order to spot weakness and time his attacks. That meant he understood strength when he saw it, and he saw it in Armstrong. When Bruyneel became manager of Armstrong's team, he told the American that he could win the Tour de France, but only if he prepared the way Bruyneel said. "I had come up with a way to win the Tour, the way I would have gone about doing it if I had the talent and the opportunity. The plan was to focus entirely on the Tour, and to train in a controlled manner on the route as much as possible, rather than doing lots of races, which used to be the way to prepare."

DEAD ELVIS

One of Armstrong's greatest weapons was his mastery of the psychological side of race tactics. He developed a look, what the American author Dan Coyle described as his Dead Elvis Stare. Whether he was struggling or on top of his game, Armstrong kept the same fixed look. It made him seem impenetrable and very frustrating to race against, while he seemed to be able to read the body language of his rivals perfectly.

← *Armstrong on comeback No.2 in 2009; he had the same stare, same winner-takes-all attitude but, unfortunately, just a little less firepower.*

FEDERICO BAHAMONTES

Federico Bahamontes was one of the great climbers of the Tour de France, one who had the ability to attack on the steepest and longest climbs and hold off the entire peloton all day. He won the King of the Mountains title six times and the Tour de France once, in 1959. He was a very nervous and quite unpredictable racer, who was so much a climbing specialist that sometimes he struggled when a stage wasn't hilly. His self-confidence level was equally uneven, which meant that although he could dominate he was just as likely to be hit by crippling self-doubt at any stage of any race.

TOUR RECORD

Name:	Federico Bahamontes
Nationality:	Spanish
Born:	9 July 1928
Tour career span:	1954–65
Tours contested:	10
King of the Mountains:	6
Stage wins:	7
Tour win:	1 (1959)

➜ Federico Bahamontes may have lacked the all-round ability to win more than one Tour de France, but he was one of the best climbers in the event's history.

MERCURIAL NATURE

It was said of Bahamontes that when he raced he could be either very good or very bad, but he was never average. His nerves often got the better of him when he felt the pressure to win. On the Col Luitel in the 1956 Tour it all got too much for Bahamontes and he stopped and threw his bike into a ravine. He wanted to abandon the race, but was talked out of it and finished the Tour fourth overall. One year later he stopped again, climbed into the broom wagon, and this time he refused to come out.

⬆ "The Eagle of Toledo" soared on the most testing of climbs, including Le Tourmalet in 1954, when he was first crowned King of the Mountains.

THE EAGLE

Born and growing up in Toledo, where he still has a bike shop, Bahamontes was christened the "Eagle of Toledo" after he first won the King of the Mountains title in 1954. He went on to win it five more times, but it wasn't so much the number of titles that Bahamontes won as the way he won them that earned him his reputation. When he attacked he would soar off into the clouds, often repeating the feat on the next climb, and the one after that. He never chased points on small hills either. The Eagle only took off for the biggest and best climbs.

ICE CREAM MAN

Because he was such a brilliant climber, Bahamontes never mastered the finer points of descending when he raced as an amateur in Spain. Consequently he was always nervous about the mountain descents on the Tour de France and preferred to follow other riders, taking their lines in and out of the corners. In his early Tours he would sometimes slow down until someone caught him after the summit. On one occasion, he even stopped and ate an ice cream on the summit of a while he waited for the next racer.

ELIMINATION

Mountain virtuoso Bahamontes never liked or became adept at the fast, close-quarter racing across rough roads that is typical of stages in Belgium and northern France. The Spaniard was so at sea on stage 2 from Brussels to St-Malo in 1960 that he was dropped by the peloton early in the stage and abandoned the race.

TALENT SPOTTER

It was Bahamontes who spotted the talent in Lucien van Impe when the young Belgian rode an amateur stage race near Toledo in 1969. Bahamontes told Van Impe he should turn professional straight away, because he would suit the climbs of the Tour de France far better than anything he'd race over as an amateur. The Spaniard even arranged for Jean Stablinski, an old racing rival who now managed a pro team, to meet Van Impe. Stablinski offered Van Impe a place in his team, and a few weeks later he started his first Tour de France.

↑ *A brittle morale saw Bahamontes abandon the Tour on more than one occasion here he waits for the train home in 1960.*

ATTACKING SPIRIT

Bahamontes would often attack on the first slopes of a mountain stage. This would animate the race, but it caused problems for those who couldn't climb. Britain's Barry Hoban remembers the stage that began in Andorra during his first Tour de France in 1964, the stage when Jacques Anquetil suffered so much after partying on the rest day. "The stage started with a huge climb out of Andorra called the Port d'Envalira, and Bahamontes attacked while we were still tightening up our toe straps. He set such a pace that we had to work like mad all through the stage. Usually, if you were in the back group you could take the final climb a bit easier because you should be nicely within the time limit, if you've done your sums right. But on this day Bahamontes was a whole mountain in front of us by the end and we had to race like mad up and down the final climb to avoid being eliminated."

TOPS ON THE TOURMALET

Thanks to his ability and the way he raced, Bahamontes still holds the record on many Tour climbs for the number of times he led the race over the top. For example, Bahamontes led over the Col du Tourmalet four times, three of them in succession between 1962 and 1964. He had a preference for the Pyrenees but was just as good in the Alps, and in 1959 he won the time trial stage up the Puy de Dôme, an extinct volcano in the Auvergne. The time trial was only 12.5 kilometres long, but Bahamontes was so fast that four riders finished outside the stage time limit, which is unheard of on such a short stage.

← *Eight years after his first King of the Mountains title, Bahamontes was first over the Col de Tourmalet in 1962, a feat he would repeat the following year and in 1964.*

GINO BARTALI

Was Gino Bartali the greatest ever Tour racer? He won in 1938, aged 24, just before the Second World War, and he won again in 1948. There were no Tours for seven years, 1940–46, a period when Bartali was at the peak of his powers. Indeed he won many big races in Italy, where the war in its early and later stages didn't impinge on life quite as much as in the rest of Europe. Bartali had his mind on other things too. He played an important part in the Assisi resistance movement that prevented thousands of Italian Jews being sent to concentration camps.

TOUR RECORD

Name:	Gino Bartali
Nationality:	Italian
Born:	18 July 1914
Died:	5 May 2000
Tour career span:	1937–53
Tours contested:	8
King of the Mountains:	2
Stage wins:	12
Tour wins:	2 (1938, 1948)

➔ *How many Tours would Bartali have won if it hadn't been for the Second World War?*

↑ *Gino Bartali was a great climber and very skilful on the descents, an attribute he used to good effect on several occasions.*

COOL CUSTOMER

It's not a tactic that is used much now, but very often in early Tours a rider would wait for one day that he felt suited him and make a giant effort to win by as big a margin as possible. In 1938 Bartali picked stage 14 that went from Digne to Briançon over the Col de Vars, the Col d'Allos and the Col d'Izoard. All of these climbs are well over 2,000 metres, and all are very steep. Bartali even waited for the last one, the Izoard, to make his move, but when he did it was one of the best moves in Tour de France history. He left the others in his group, gaining time on the ramps of the Izoard, and all the way down the other side into Briançon. The previous yellow jersey, the Belgian rider Félicien Vervaecke, finished more than 17 minutes behind him. Now Bartali had the lead, and virtually cruised to Paris.

LIFE SAVER

Bartali took the yellow jersey in the 1937 Tour, his first time in the race, but in the Alps he crashed into a fallen team-mate on a wooden bridge that crossed a mountain torrent. Bartali was hurt in the fall and couldn't breathe in the deep cold water. He was in danger of being swept away when a team-mate dived in and rescued him. Bartali carried on, his jersey covered in blood and mud. He also battled through the rest of the Alps, but was forced to retire when the race reached Marseilles.

ITALY'S SAVIOUR

Bartali started the 1948 Tour as leader of the Italian team, but he struggled at first, which was a surprise considering his success in Italy. There was trouble at home, which may have affected him; trouble that led to the leader of the Italian Communist Party, Palmiro Togliatti, being shot by a student. While he fought for his life, the Communists tried to take control of the country, and this led to the Prime Minister telephoning Bartali. He needed something to distract the people, which an Italian victory in the Tour de France would do. He told Bartali that his country needed him and, duly inspired, Bartali won the next three stages, some of the toughest in the Tour, and won the race. Peace was restored in Italy, and Bartali had done his bit to help.

Bartali was tough, strong, patriotic and very brave.

RIVALRY

Fausto Coppi was younger than Bartali, very talented and very different. Bartali looked what he was, the tough, muscular son of a manual worker who would have been good at many sports. Coppi was tall, skinny and ungainly, but his body was perfectly suited to cycling. With his long legs, barrel chest and not an ounce of fat on him, Coppi looked like a skinned cat, according to Bartali. The two men were very different in other ways too. Where Bartali was religious, Coppi managed to get himself excommunicated from the Catholic Church. Where Bartali was private, Coppi's life filled the gossip columns as well as the sports pages. Where Bartali was frugal, Coppi had a very lavish lifestyle. They clashed, but it was only because they both wanted to win, not because they represented old and new Italy. Anyway, when Bartali finished second behind Coppi in the 1949 Tour, he gracefully conceded that he'd lost to the better man.

WITHDRAWAL

During a Pyrenean stage of the 1950 Tour, Bartali broke away with the 1947 Tour winner, Jean Robic of France. While climbing the Col d'Aspin they managed to collide somehow and fell. Bartali said that some of the crowd thought he'd pushed Robic and he claimed they set on him, punching him, and that he was threatened by a man with a knife, but no one else agreed. In fact Louison Bobet, who rode past a minute or so after the fall, said that the crowd were trying to help Bartali get back on his bike. Bartali won the stage but announced that the whole Italian team were pulling out. Fiorenzo Magni held the yellow jersey, but he wouldn't speak out against the great Bartali, so the Italians left.

SMOKING GINO

Like many racers of his era, Gino Bartali smoked. Some made a secret of the fact, but Bartali always carried a pack of cigarettes with him, gave interviews while he smoked and was even known to light up during quiet parts of a Tour de France stage.

← *Fausto Coppi leads Gino Bartali on the High Alps stage from Briançon to Aosta in 1949. The rest of the field is nowhere in sight.*

LOUISON BOBET

Louison Bobet was not the first man to win three Tours de France – that was Philippe Thys – but he was the first to win three Tours in succession. He was very driven, quite highly strung and very dedicated. He made no compromises in his preparation, which he undertook with almost religious zeal. His contemporary Raphaël Géminiani said, "Louison would beat himself up for a week because he wanted a beer before drinking it, then beat himself up for another week for doing so."

TOUR RECORD

Name:	Louison Bobet
Nationality:	French
Born:	12 March 1925
Died:	13 March 1983
Tour career span:	1947–59
Tours contested:	10
King of the Mountains:	1
Stage wins:	11
Tour wins:	3 (1953, 1954, 1955)

← *Perfect training, attention to detail and absolute dedication made Louison Bobet a champion.*

↑ *Louison (right) and brother, Jean Bobet discuss tactics during the 1955 Tour.*

BAKER'S BOY

He was born in Brittany, the son of a baker in St-Méen-le-Grand. Brittany has produced more cycling champions than any other province of France, so it was a great school, and he made his Tour de France debut at 22. Bobet had a younger brother called Jean, who also loved cycling but wanted to go to university. They were very close, and when Jean graduated Louison invited him to join his racing adventure. Jean later became a journalist and is now an award-winning author.

DEFINING MOMENT

Bobet started his winning run in the 1953 Tour, the 50th anniversary race. He won in the way Bartali had, with an attack on the Col d'Izoard. That was the day he took the yellow jersey, but the following year he won on the Izoard, this time while wearing the yellow jersey. Somehow that picture, Bobet in yellow riding through the rock pinnacles towards the Izoard summit, became the thing every generation of French pro racers wanted to achieve. Only one of them has, Bernard Thévenet in 1975, but it's still as if the picture is subliminally printed on every French racing licence.

THALASSOTHERAPY

Bobet also had a good head for money and invested in a nature cure called Thalassotherapy, which is the use of seawater to revitalize the body. Inspired by a course of treatment he personally undertook following a car crash, Bobet built several centres around the French Atlantic coast.

THE COST OF WINNING

The 1955 Tour was probably the hardest Tour for Bobet to win, and he chose the hardest place to do it. Mont Ventoux in Provence has a difficult climate. It can be boiling hot or freezing cold in the summer, and Bobet chose a time when it was boiling hot. The French team, which included Jean Bobet, were brilliant, setting a hard pace to the foot of the mountain to discourage attacks. Then Louison went for it on the climb. He battled into the lead and held it all the way up the Ventoux, down the other side and to the stage finish in Avignon. The French team were jubilant in their hotel, but Jean couldn't find his brother. He eventually discovered him, lying alone in his room, the shutters closed, too exhausted even to remove his cycling shoes. Louison had won the Tour de France, but had dug so deep to do it.

➜ *Bobet, wearing the rainbow jersey of reigning world champion, suffers in the heat on Mont Ventoux in 1955.*

CAREER-ENDING INJURY

Jean and Louison were involved in a car crash in 1960 in which Louison suffered leg injuries that effectively ended his racing career. He died from cancer 23 years later, one day after his 58th birthday.

FLYING LOW

As well as winning three Tours, Bobet won a lot of races and was one of the highest-paid pros of his generation. He was very modern too and interested in technology. He took flying lessons, bought a light aircraft and sometimes used it to fly to races. Bobet's son became an airline pilot.

PRESSURE TO WIN

Bobet lived on his nerves and was never sure of his form, although his brother thinks that deep down he knew when he was ready to win. "If he acted confident I worried; he was bluffing and making up for the fact that he was unsure of his fitness. If he griped and fretted, if he said this hurts and that hurts and that he didn't feel good, it was different. Then I knew Louison was on top form; his worrying was just the way he coped with the pressure he put on himself to win."

⬇ *Bobet (left, with French football legend Raymond Kopa) took his sporting will to win into business, and he made a success of that too.*

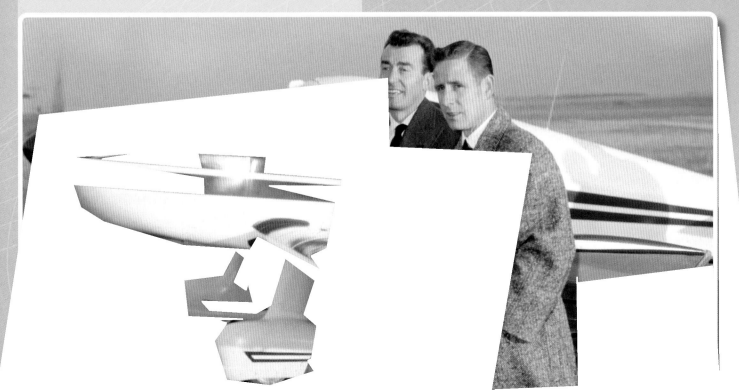

MARK CAVENDISH

Mark Cavendish is arguably the fastest sprinter in Tour de France history. By the end of the 2011 Tour he had already won 20 stages, and at the age of 26 is well on his way to beating the all-time stage win record of Eddy Merckx. Freddy Maertens is the only racer who comes near to Cavendish's dominance. The Belgian won eight stages in one Tour, and Cavendish hasn't done that. Comparisons are impossible, because Tour de France sprints are different now, but if Cavendish were to win eight stages in one Tour, his claim to the fastest man title would be beyond doubt.

TOUR RECORD

Name:	Mark Cavendish
Nationality:	British
Born:	21 May 1985
Tour career span:	2007–11
Tours contested:	5
Green jersey:	1
Stage wins:	20

← *BBC Sports Personality of the Year, an MBE, these were just two of the honours won by Cavendish in 2011. At 26, many more will come.*

PHENOMENON

No other word describes Cavendish's sprint. He can accelerate to top speed faster than anyone else, and his top speed is quicker than anyone else's. It's an unbeatable combination, and all the sprinters today agree that in a finish that suits him the racer from the Isle of Man is impossible to beat. The thing is, Cavendish is increasingly a threat when conditions don't suit him. Outside of the Tour, Cavendish has won the Milan–San Remo single-day Classic, and the World Road Race Championship, becoming the first British champion for 46 years and only the second in history. Both races were thought beyond him at one time.

⬇ *In 2011 Mark Cavendish became the first British racer to become the elite World Road Race champion in 46 years.*

EARLY YEARS

Mark was born and grew up on the Isle of Man. He trained in banking and was a competitive ballroom dancer when he was young. He was a good sprinter from the start of his cycling career, but sometimes struggled on hills. The number of races he won attracted the attention of British Cycling, the body that runs the sport in Britain. They were in the process of setting up an under-23 racing academy with lottery funding. This was a sports science-led initiative aimed at track racing. The reasoning was that funding depended on Olympic medals, and there are more medals to be won on the track than the road. It turned out that Cavendish didn't do well in the power tests that everyone had to pass to be considered, but he could beat everyone in a race. Some athletes are like that: they become super-inspired when racing but cannot achieve the same level of performance in tests. British Cycling's head coach, Shane Sutton, went out on a limb to insist that Cavendish was admitted to the academy despite his test results.

⬆ *Cavendish hit the Tour de France winning with an unprecedented four stages in his first Tour.*

TOUR DEBUT

It was nothing short of sensational: still only 22, Cavendish won four stages in his first Tour, the second highest number ever won by a British racer. He also repeated the feat of the then record holder, Barry Hoban, of winning consecutive stages. He dropped out of the Tour after two weeks to prepare for the Madison at the Beijing Olympics, where he teamed up with Wiggins again. Wiggins had already won two gold medals in Beijing, but was tired and not at his best in the Madison. Cavendish felt let down, and it put a strain on the two racers' friendship that has only recently healed. Cavendish's world road race title was won by his phenomenal ability as a sprinter, but it owed a great deal to the blistering pace that Wiggins set on the last lap of the Copenhagen race circuit, which made it impossible for anyone to attack and ensured a bunch finish.

PERSONALITY

Cavendish can appear cocky when he wins and abrasive when he doesn't. The cockiness is just realism. He is the best sprinter of his generation; he knows it, and is satisfied when victory puts that beyond doubt. The abrasiveness comes from what he says is self-loathing when he loses. He also gets angry when his team works hard from him, which sprinters' teams must, and he doesn't deliver. Away from cycling Cavendish is private and very thoughtful. Everyone who knows Mark Cavendish has a story about the first time they realized he was a remarkable individual.

TRACK TRAINING

British Cycling's academy programme involves racing on both track and road, and Cavendish's natural speed made him a great track racer. In the words of Rod Ellingworth, his coach in the academy, and the man who has played that role ever since, "Mark was fast enough to have been a track sprint specialist, especially in the 1,000 metres time trial, but he loved road racing best and when we asked him his ambitions they were always on the road." He became a world track champion first, winning Madison titles with Rob Hayles in 2005 and Bradley Wiggins in 2008, the second a few months before his Tour de France debut.

SCIENCE OF CAV

The reason he is so fast is part nature, part nurture. He is naturally an explosive athlete; he isn't tall either, which means his aerodynamic drag is low; and he has an incredible will to win. Sometimes it's that desire as much as his speed that propels Cavendish over the line first. He also rides very low when he sprints, tucks his arms in, keeps his head level with his shoulders but keeps looking forward – small things, but they combine to lower his drag factor, and since drag increases at the square of speed, reducing it is very important in a sprint.

➡ *Winning the green jersey in 2011 confirmed Cavendish as the best Tour de France sprinter of his generation. Will he be the best of all time?*

ALBERTO CONTADOR

As we enter the second decade of the 21st century this slim but elegant racer from just outside of Madrid is the best Grand Tour rider in the world. He won his first Tour at 24, and he's won twice since, although he was stripped of the 2010 race in 2012 after a protracted hearing into alleged doping. He's also won two Tours of Italy and one Tour of Spain. A true climber, he can make devastating changes of pace that hurt his rivals' legs. He is less consistent at time trials, although he rarely rides badly enough to lose a race.

TOUR RECORD

Name:	Alberto Contador
Nationality:	Spanish
Born:	2 December 1982
Tour career span:	2005–11
Tours contested:	5
White jersey:	1
Stage wins:	3
Tour wins:	2 (2007, 2009)

➡ *With two victories, Alberto Contador is the best Tour de France rider of the present generation.*

↑ *Despite his youth and inexperience, Alberto Contador showed considerable maturity to win his first Tour de France in 2007.*

COOL CUSTOMER

When he won in 2007 it was partly because the yellow jersey, Michael Rasmussen, was withdrawn from the race by his own team because of alleged breaches of the "athlete's whereabouts" system that came to light during the race. "Whereabouts" is basically to do with an athlete's availability for out-of-competition drugs tests. Suddenly Contador had a genuine chance of victory. If he produced the time trial of his life he could hold off Cadel Evans and win the Tour de France. His team manager was Britain's Sean Yates, who could not believe how in charge of himself the young Spaniard was. "He was under a world of pressure," says Yates. "The team hadn't expected to win, but they were used to it because it was effectively Lance Armstrong's old team. Now a chance came out of the blue and they wanted it – everyone was on edge except Alberto. He just got on with it, went out and raced better than he ever had and won the Tour."

RISKY SURGERY

In 2004, right at the start of his pro career, Contador fell off his bike in the Tour of Asturias and began to have convulsions. He was rushed to hospital, where it was found that he had a rare congenital defect in the blood vessels of his brain, which had ruptured. He underwent a risky operation to rectify the fault, as a result of which he has a scar running right across the top of his head from ear to ear.

CHAINGATE

Alberto Contador is no stranger to controversy. When Andy Schleck made a violent attack on the Port des Bales climb on stage 15 of the 2010 Tour, his bike chain was thrown off. Contador attacked immediately, gaining enough time, while Schleck replaced his chain and tried to mount a chase, to take the yellow jersey from the Luxembourg rider. Some said Contador had taken advantage of an opponent's bad luck, but Contador claimed he was attacking anyway and hadn't seen what happened. It could also be said that a working bike is part of the requirements for winning the Tour.

➔ *Andy Schleck, just before the infamous chaingate incident.*

STEAKGATE

After he won the 2010 Tour it was announced that Contador had failed a drugs test during the race. A sample had been sent to a lab with equipment more sensitive than the world anti-drugs agency specifies, and a tiny amount of clenbuterol (a weight-loss drug), 50 picograms per millilitre, was found. Contador immediately said that it must have come from eating contaminated meat. He was suspended, but won an appeal, best explained by his lawyer Andy Ramos: "Although the rider is responsible for what is in his body, there is a clause in the legislation that frees him of that if he can prove he was not negligent." However, UCI, cycling's governing body appealed to the Court of Arbitration for Sport and won, so Contador was banned until August 2012 and stripped of his 2010 Tour win.

BIRD FANCIER

Like many Spanish men Contador enjoys hunting in his spare time, but he also keeps and breeds canaries and finches. He is a very private person. His commercial manager who negotiates all his contracts and promotion deals is his brother; Alberto is his only client.

TOUGH GUY

When Lance Armstrong made his comeback in 2009 it put Alberto Contador in a very difficult situation. The American joined Contador's team, Astana, with the specific intention of trying to win the Tour de France. Contador had won in 2007, and in 2008 he won the Tours of Italy and Spain. However, the huge media interest in his team was suddenly all on Armstrong. And, more interestingly, you could see the dynamic change in the squad as the riders slowly gravitated towards Armstrong. As well as a champion bike racer, Armstrong is a champion at mind games. Contador was his team-mate, but would also be his biggest rival in the Tour de France. All through the 2009 race season, and right through the Tour, Contador looked isolated in his own team, and rumours came out suggesting he was. Yet it didn't seem to bother him in the slightest. He rode his own race, oblivious of Armstrong, and won with a degree of ease.

← *Contador brushed aside Lance Armstrong's return to the Tour in 2009 to win the race in a very controlled manner.*

FAUSTO COPPI

In Italy they called Fausto Coppi "Il Campionissimo", and the name struck throughout the cycling world. It means champion of champions, and Coppi is one of the very best, arguably in the top three of the sport from any era. It wasn't just the number and breadth of races Coppi won, it was the way he won them, almost always alone and often many minutes ahead of the next rider. His career was hit by bad luck and terrible injuries too, otherwise he'd have won a lot more. And he was the first cyclist to create interest in his life beyond racing, the first real celebrity of the sport as we understand that term today.

↑ Fausto Coppi alone in the Tour de France mountains in 1952, a picture of perfection.

TOUR RECORD

Name:	Fausto Coppi
Nationality:	Italian
Born:	15 September 1919
Died:	2 January 1960
Tour career span:	1949–52
Tours contested:	3
King of the Mountains:	2
Stage wins:	11
Tour wins:	2 (1949, 1952)

PIONEER

Coppi's best Tour was his second win, in 1952. He started badly and appeared distracted, but clicked into form halfway through when he won the first stage ever to climb the Alpe d'Huez. Coppi came alive next day, attacking on the first climb, the Col de la Croix-de-Fer, and riding off on his own over three more giant Alpine climbs to win at the Sestriere ski resort by over seven minutes. He won two more stages, including the first one to finish on the Puy de Dôme, to be nearly half an hour ahead of the second-placed rider in Paris, Stan Ockers of Belgium.

COMPARISONS

Eddy Merckx, who definitely has the best record of any pro bike racer, and who is probably the all-time best, put his own career in perspective when he was compared with the Italian during an interview. "How many races would Coppi have won if it hadn't been for six years of war?" he asked. Merckx lost races during his best years, and on a few occasions he lost after he had attacked and made his move for victory. With Coppi it was different. Between 1946 and 1954, according to the French journalist Pierre Chany, the Italian was never caught once he'd broken clear of the field.

← Some say that Fausto Coppi is the greatest bike racer of all time, and by any criteria he is certainly one of the top four or five.

WHITE LADY

Coppi was married when Giulia Locatelli fell in love with him. She was married to a doctor who was interested in bike racing. At first she and Coppi were friends, although even that caused some scandal. Then Coppi's brother Serse was killed by a crash during the 1951 Tour of Piedmont, and Coppi's wife Bruna begged him to give up racing. They were wealthy, he didn't need to race – but that was like asking a bird not to fly. Giulia understood and sympathized, Coppi fell for her and they began living together. In Catholic Italy in the 1950s this was huge. The police raided Coppi's house to see if the couple were sharing a bed. The Pope begged Coppi to return to his wife and refused to bless the Tour of Italy if Coppi was riding. Eventually the couple were excommunicated, but it didn't push them apart and they had a son called Faustino.

➜ *They started meeting in secret, like in this picture from a Milan night club in 1953, but soon Coppi and Giulia Locatelli's relationship made front-page news in every newspaper in Italy.*

PRISONER OF WAR

Coppi was kept out of the Second World War for as long as possible, because he was already winning big races, but even he was conscripted in 1943 and sent to Tunisia, where he was promptly caught and taken prisoner by allied forces. Rations were poor, but a bike race fan called Chiappucci recognized Coppi and shared his food with him to keep the champion's strength up. That fan later had a son called Claudio, who was raised on stories of Coppi. Claudio Chiappucci became a pro racer and won the King of the Mountains in 1991 and 1992, and in 1992 he emulated Coppi's exploit by winning alone at Sestriere.

BUTCHER'S BOY

Coppi's first job on leaving school at 12 was running errands and doing deliveries for a butcher in Novi Liguri. His immediate family were poor, but his uncle, also called Fausto, was a ship's captain, and when the young Fausto told him how much he enjoyed riding his butcher's bike and how he could beat all the other kids on it, Uncle Fausto bought him a race bike. He started racing at 14, was a semi-pro by 19, and the following year Coppi won the Tour of Italy.

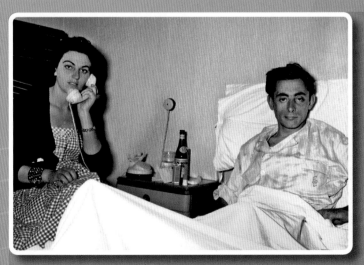

⬆ *Never the most robust racer, Coppi contracted malaria in Africa and died in January 1960 at the age of 40.*

MALARIA

Coppi carried on racing long after he should have stopped. His health was always fragile and his last few years were a shadow of his former glory. In December 1959 Coppi did some exhibition races in Africa, in what was then called Upper Volta, now Burkina Faso. Giulia wanted Coppi to stop racing, and shortly after his return he told her that he had decided to make 1960 his last season. A few days later Coppi fell ill. He was diagnosed with flu which soon developed into an intense fever and he was admitted to a clinic. Even though news reached his doctors that Raphaël Géminiani, who had been on the African trip, had suffered from malaria and been treated successfully for it, they still said Coppi had pneumonia. He died on 2 January 1960.

LAURENT FIGNON

Laurent Fignon was another prodigy, like Alberto Contador and Andy Schleck, who won his first Tour de France while also winning the young rider classification. He was a prodigious talent, and even if he was slightly lucky to win his first Tour, because Bernard Hinault wasn't there, he totally dominated his second. Fignon was aloof with the press and sometimes with the public, but he raced with a lot of heart and aggression. Injuries blighted his best years, and once he got back his form he suffered a heartbreaking defeat at the hands of Greg Lemond in the 1989 Tour, from which he never really recovered.

TOUR RECORD

Name:	Laurent Fignon
Nationality:	French
Born:	12 August 1960
Died:	31 August 2010
Tour career span:	1983–93
Tours contested:	10
Stage wins:	9
Tour wins:	2 (1983, 1984)

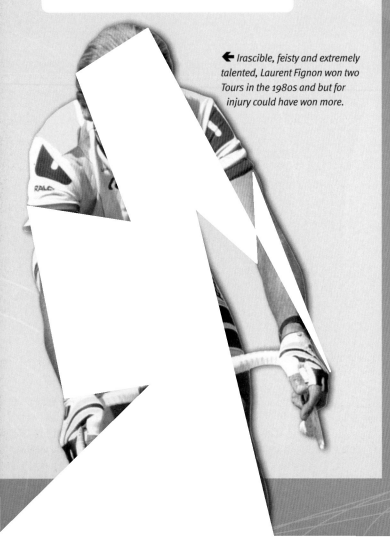

← *Irascible, feisty and extremely talented, Laurent Fignon won two Tours in the 1980s and but for injury could have won more.*

[...] the [...] be [...] ha[...] cel[...] becoming a rep[...] rout[...] y the revolutionaries took after st[...] the [...] to the King's palace but in reverse, so from Versai[...] into the heart of Paris. Fignon was a Parisian, and after an epic battle with a resurgent Greg LeMond, he was the yellow jersey for the time trial. He led the American by 50 seconds, and with only 25 kilometres to ride, Fignon couldn't lose – but he did.

↑ *Nicknamed the professor by his racing colleagues, Fignon raced with verve and intelligence to build an enviable career.*

THE PROFESSOR

Fignon had been a student before cycling became a more lucrative career option, but it was as much Fignon's steel-rimmed glasses that earned him the nickname of "Le Professeur" from his peers.

PRIX CITRON

The "prix citron", or lemon award, is an unofficial prize that journalists give to the least likeable rider in the race, and Fignon won it in 1989. To be fair he was under enormous pressure to win, as it was France's bicentenary year, and he was dogged by an American who would not give up. He was also suffering from a saddle injury that affected his style, while Lemond was using new aerodynamic advantages that no one else had. Fignon was heartbroken to lose, so it's no wonder he was a bit grumpy. For years afterwards people would ask, "Aren't you the guy who lost the Tour by eight seconds?" – and Fignon's reply was always "No, I'm the guy who won it twice."

INHERITED WIN

When Fignon turned pro in 1982, Bernard Hinault was the best cyclist in the world. Fignon joined the then four times Tour winner's team and worked hard to help Hinault win the 1983 Tour of Spain, which came before the Tour each year in those days. Fignon wasn't down to ride the Tour de France because it was thought that two Grand Tours in one year would be too much for the 22-year-old, but when Hinault pulled out before the start, Fignon was drafted in to make up the numbers. By stage 9 Fignon was second overall behind Pascal Simon, who crashed next day, breaking his collarbone. Simon continued for a while but was forced out by the pain several stages later, by which time Fignon had closed to within one minute. He then took over the lead and held it to Paris.

← *When he won in 1983 Fignon was one of the youngest racers ever to win the Tour de France.*

FAIR AND SQUARE

Even Fignon admitted that he had been lucky in 1983. If Hinault had ridden he would have spent the race working for him. Still, being close to Pascal Simon showed his ability, not least to his team and to Bernard Hinault. When Hinault left for a better contract with La Vie Claire, the Renault-Elf squad were behind Fignon from day one. He'd narrowly lost a Tour of Italy that was weighted in favour of national hero Francesco Moser, so Fignon was determined to re-establish himself in the Tour that year. Hinault was back after knee surgery, and not yet on top form, but even so he took the fight to Fignon. However, Fignon proved that the Tour was out of Hinault's reach that year. He beat him in the long time trials, and when Hinault attacked five times on the stage to the Alpe d'Huez, Fignon covered him easily. He then mounted his own attack and took three minutes from Hinault.

YOUNG AND CAREFREE

Laurent Fignon died in 2010 after a fight with cancer, but he left an indelible mark on cycling. Not just through the races he won, but through those he worked to save after his retirement, through his insightful work as a commentator on French TV and through his frank autobiography, *We were Young and Carefree*. In many ways Fignon was an old-school racer competing in a time when the sport was changing. It's one of the reasons why he lost to Greg LeMond in 1989. The difference is best summed up in his own words: "We didn't tiptoe away when the time came to light the fuse, we preferred rousing anthems to gentle lullabies." It means he never raced carefully, as modern Tour riders have to now. The race has changed almost to the point when the key to winning isn't gaining time, it's not losing any.

THE PROFESSOR'S MOUNTAIN

La Plagne is a mountain-top ski resort in the Alps that has featured four times as a stage finish of the Tour de France, and Laurent Fignon won on it twice. The first time was in 1984, when he won the Tour; the second was in 1987, when he was on his way back from injury.

↓ *Laurent Fignon acknowledges the crowd after winning the stage from Bourg d'Oisans to La Plagne in 1984.*

CHARLY GAUL

The "Angel of the Mountains" has to be one of the most evocative nicknames in sport. It was what they called Charly Gaul, not because of his angelic nature, because he didn't have one, but for the way he floated up the mountain passes of the Tour de France as if on wings. He won the Tour once, but the way he did so left a much bigger mark on the race than a single victory usually does.

TOUR RECORD

Name:	Charly Gaul
Nationality:	Luxembourgeois
Born:	8 December 1932
Died:	6 December 2005
Tour career span:	1953–63
Tours contested:	10
King of the Mountains:	3
Stage wins:	9
Tour wins:	1 (1958)

← *Charly Gaul wearing the yellow jersey in 1958; he won one Tour but that victory was one of the most beautiful in the history of the race.*

↑ *Charly Gaul (left) and Federico Bahamontes, two of the best climbers in Tour de France history, go head to head in 1956.*

KING OF THE MOUNTAINS

His first Tours de France, in 1953 and '54, were disappointing. Good climbers tend to have fragile characters, and when, in his first two years as a pro, he found he couldn't soar away from his rivals as he had done in amateur races, Gaul became depressed and abandoned a number of races. But like all successful cyclists he was tough deep down; the defeats made him train harder, and in 1956 he was King of the Mountains, having won two mountain stages, and finished third overall.

SAUSAGES

Gaul started his working life by training to be a butcher in his native Luxembourg. He had a quick temper and once, when a racing rival had upset him, he promised journalists that he was going to get out his old butcher's knives and turn the guy into sausages.

RAIN MAN

Gaul won the Tour of Italy in 1956, taking three stages including one through the Dolomites, where conditions were terrible. Rain turned to snow at the tops of the climbs, causing 57 riders to give up and stop racing. Gaul ploughed through as though it didn't exist, taking many minutes out of his nearest rivals. The day he won the Tour was cold, and again there was torrential rain. Gaul was so good that day that his performance seemed to leave a mental scar on the 1957 winner, Jacques Anquetil, who had a recurring dream in which he was following Gaul, who would then disappear only to reappear much further ahead. Anquetil would then chase him, but when he caught Gaul he saw that he was made up of millions of raindrops. Then Gaul would promptly disappear again, and the dream continued like that until Anquetil woke.

WINNER

He might have been fragile when he wasn't on form, but nobody was more confident of his abilities when he was good than Charly Gaul. When he won the Tour in 1958 he wound up Louison Bobet, whom he didn't like, by telling him when he would attack, right down to the corner he'd go on. It was on the Col Luitel, close to Grenoble. As they approached this particular hairpin bend, Gaul turned to Bobet and asked, "Are you ready, Monsieur Bobet?" And he attacked. No one got close, as Gaul pulled away through the rest of the stage to win by over 12 minutes.

RIDING STYLE

When Lance Armstrong came back from cancer to begin his run of seven Tour victories, as well as changing physically he had also developed a much faster cadence when he pedalled. He used it to devastating effect in time trials and when climbing, and sports scientists agreed that this fast cadence put less strain on leg muscles, so they did not become so fatigued and could respond better to accelerations. Charly Gaul pedalled like that 40 years before Armstrong. A rival, Raphaël Géminiani, says: "Gaul was a murderous climber, always sustaining the same fast rhythm. He was like a little machine, but with a lower gear than the rest, turning his legs at a speed that would break your heart, tick tock, tick tock, tick tock. It was constant, never faster, never slower, but constantly at a pace you found so hard to maintain. It ate into your mind, your legs and your self-confidence until it broke your will."

DECLINE

Gaul won the Tour of Italy again in 1959, and he won stages in the 1959 and 1961 Tours de France, but his powers were on the decline. He stopped racing a number of times, saying he planned to retire, but always came back. He stopped for the last time in 1965 and opened a bar in the city of Luxembourg.

RECLUSE

Gaul hated working in his bar, maybe because he had to be pleasant to customers. He sold it after six months, bought a wooden house in the forests of the Ardennes and lived as a recluse. His house didn't have running water or electricity, and when journalists tried to call on him for an interview, Gaul would chase them off, sometimes brandishing a pitchfork.

RE-EMERGENCE

Gaul suddenly abandoned life as a hermit in 1983, came out of the woods and married again. He was always a bit odd, but he worked for the Luxembourg government, organized races and raised a lot of money for cancer charities. He died in 2005.

← *Louison Bobet (in yellow cap) struggling to hold Gaul's pace in 1958.*

↑ *The Angel of the Mountains alone on the vast expanse of Mont Ventoux in 1958, the year he won the Tour.*

BERNARD HINAULT

Another candidate to be called one of cycling's greatest racers, Bernard Hinault won five Tours de France and a lot more besides. He won the Tour of Italy and Spain. He achieved the Tour of Italy and Tour of France double. He was world road race champion and he won some of the biggest single-day Classics. And he won all those races because he had a formidable blend of talent, attacking spirit and shear bloody-minded determination.

TOUR RECORD

Name:	Bernard Hinault
Nationality:	French
Born:	14 November 1954
Tour career span:	1978–86
Tours contested:	8
Green jersey:	1
King of the Mountains:	1
Stage wins:	28
Tour wins:	5 (1978, 1979, 1981, 1982, 1985)

➜ Hinault, wearing the tricolor jersey as French national champion, won five Tours de France.

↑ *Bernard Hinault could win on any terrain, he could even beat the sprinters when it came to a madcap dash for the line.*

FIRST TOUR

Hinault turned professional in 1975, when he was 20, and quickly started winning. He rode his first Tour de France in 1978, and won that. He won again in 1979, but in 1980 he showed his first and only sign of fragility. Achilles had his heel, Bernard Hinault had his knee. An injury to it caused him to drop out of the 1980 Tour when in the lead, and although he came back and won in 1981 and 1982, it went again while he was winning the 1983 Tour of Spain.

THE BADGER

Badgers are tough customers. They try to get on with things, live in big family setts, and try to keep themselves private, but get one in a corner and it will bite. Whoever thought up Hinault's nickname knew him well. He's an affable man, a Breton who loves the countryside and family life, but cycling was his corner. Racing meant war for Bernard Hinault.

KNEE SURGERY

Hinault's knee went under the knife in 1983, and after a period of recuperation he slowly built himself back to full strength. There were a lot of new training ideas coming into cycling at this time, and although Hinault was the last Patron, and in many ways the last champion of old cycling, he drew on the new thinking to get back to full fitness. One reason given for his knee problems was over-use from millions of pedal revolutions. The new thinking said that over-using certain muscles can cause skeletal misalignments, so Hinault worked to build the support muscles in his knees and back with special weight training, gymnastics, stretching and even running. He said that when he came back it would be as a complete athlete, not just as a cyclist.

HINAULT V LEMOND

One year after finishing second to Laurent Fignon while still on the comeback trail, Hinault was at full fitness for the 1985 Tour. He'd been joined in his new team by Greg LeMond, a young American who set European cycling alight by winning the world championships in 1983 and finishing third in his debut Tour in 1984. Hinault won the 1985 Tour with LeMond second, but it was rumoured that a pact had been made whereby LeMond would support Hinault in 1985, and then Hinault would support LeMond in 1986. LeMond did win in 1986 with Hinault second, but not without coming under attack from his team-mate. Hinault still says he attacked to get rid of their opponents, and LeMond still doesn't believe him.

↑ *They started out as team-mates, but Hinault and Greg LeMond became one of the greatest rivalries in cycling.*

THE LAST PATRON

Up until the mid-1980s the world of pro cycling was almost a feudal system. The top racers earned good money and the rest needed their patronage to earn as well. These men had a big say in what happened in races, in who raced for which team, and in how lucrative contracts for exhibition races called criteriums were handed out. Inevitably the best racer of his generation had most say, and he was referred to as Le Patron, or boss. That didn't mean the big races were fixed, but what it did mean was that the Patron represented the pro peloton in almost a shop steward mode. That changed when American racers and American ways entered European cycling, which was towards the end of Hinault's career. He was the last true Patron.

RACER

Bernard Hinault was a great climber and a great time triallist. He also studied cycling and was often the first to use new products, once he established they would help him race better. Hinault was one of the first to use the pedal and cleat system that all racers use now, while his rivals were still using toe clips and straps. He also helped pioneer more aerodynamic bikes, disc wheels and tear-drop helmets in time trials. Above all, though, he had a racer's mentality and a restless desire to win, so much so that even his wife said it was a good job that Hinault won a lot, because he couldn't cope with being beaten.

NO MORE BIKE

He always said he would retire at 32, and he did, even though he still had plenty left to give. And when he stopped racing, Hinault turned his back on cycling to immerse himself in farming, and he created a renowned cattle herd, showing the same drive which had won him five Tours de France. Then, once he'd done that, he got involved with the sport again, and he now works on the Tour, looking after the podium and ensuring that visitors to the race have a great experience. Also, after saying he'd never ride a bike after he retired, he does now with the same gusto he did in his youth.

← *Welcome to my world: Hinault congratulates another yellow jersey on the Tour de France podium.*

MIGUEL INDURAIN

Tour de France cyclists tend to be slim, not too tall and borderline skinny. Indeed, in 2010 an American journalist asked the question, referring to Alberto Contador and Andy Schleck, "If this is the toughest event on the planet, how come it's being led by a couple of dweebs?" Miguel Indurain is no dweeb, he's well over six feet tall, and when he raced he was as muscular as a sprinter. But cycling ability is a function of power over weight. Contador and Schleck solve that equation by being really light. Indurain solved it by having off-the-scale power.

TOUR RECORD

Name:	Miguel Indurain
Nationality:	Spanish
Born:	16 July 1964
Tour career span:	1985–96
Tours contested:	12
Stage wins:	11
Tour wins:	5 (1991, 1992, 1993, 1994, 1995)

← *Miguel Indurain was the first man to win five consecutive Tours.*

↑ *All Tour racers undergo a strict medical examination before the race; Indurain's always provoked intense media interest.*

PHYSICAL PERFECTION

Indurain had the biggest heart and lungs ever measured in sport. His heart was so huge in his racing days that it only beat 28 times per minute at rest. This meant that he could suck more oxygen from the air and pump more oxygenated blood to his muscles per heartbeat than any other racer. His muscles were big, so they could store plenty of fuel, but they were made up of the slow-burn fibres of an endurance athlete. This combination gave Indurain a huge natural engine to power his efforts. Also, it was one suited to extended efforts, like those required to gain time in Tour de France time trials and to keep it by setting a high constant pace in the mountains.

INNER FAT GUY

Even the fact that Miguel Indurain put weight on easily was a marker of his Tour de France potential. Lance Armstrong says: "Inside every skinny Tour champion there's a fat guy trying to get out." What he means is that good Tour racers need to recover overnight, and one way they do that is by having very efficient metabolisms that quickly digest and assimilate all the food they eat. Unfortunately this often means that when they aren't racing and training hard, they can get fat.

ROUGH DIAMOND

When he turned pro Indurain made little impression at first. He was strong on the flat, but terrible when it came to climbing mountains. His team manager José-Miguel Echavarri liked him, however, so he took him to a famous coach in Italy to see what he could do. The coach tested Indurain, discovered his underlying physiology, and told Echavarri that he had a champion, but he needed to stop eating cakes. Indurain is a farmer's son who was well fed at home; he was big, but some of his size was fat, and that held him back when going uphill.

TIME LORD

Time trials were where Indurain won his Tours. He was almost unbeatable, and often won by a wide margin that destroyed his rivals' morale. In 1992, for example, Indurain raced to victory in a 65-kilometre time trial in Luxembourg that beat the next placed rider, a time trial specialist, by three minutes and beat his closest yellow jersey rival, Gianni Bugno of Italy, by nearly four. Racers don't win whole Tours by that margin now, but Indurain achieved it in 65 kilometres.

➜ *Indurain's strength was in time trials. He pushed back the barriers of what was considered possible for a cyclist.*

LAST TOUR

Indurain varied the script slightly to win in 1995, attacking and taking time the day before the first time trial, then taking more against the clock. After that he settled into defence mode and never looked troubled at all. He started as odds-on favourite to win again in 1996, but that year he faced a disadvantage. In conditions that suited him, hot and dry or even hot and humid, Indurain was an impregnable human fortress without a chink of weakness. In the cold and wet it was a very different story. His muscles didn't work well; in fact, if it was very cold they retained water, which not only made Indurain heavier but prevented his body from working properly. The weather in 1996 was appalling. It rained all through the first week and into the Alps, where rain turned to snow higher up the climbs. Indurain creaked and wheezed, got slower and eventually cracked apart while climbing the Cormet de Roselend, losing all chance of victory.

FAMILY MAN

Indurain comes from Villava, a farming village not far from Pamplona. He married a local girl and now lives near his birthplace. When he raced he used to work on his father's farm during the winter, and he still enjoys walking in the countryside. For each of his victories the whole village would pile into hired buses for the long trek to Paris to see him home. Then they'd dash back to organize a huge reception for him.

➜ *Despite being a celebrity who is known and respected throughout the cycling world, Miguel Indurain is happiest in the region of Spain where he was born.*

RETIREMENT

His career was by no means over when he lost the 1996 Tour, and Indurain proved it by winning the Olympic time trial title a few weeks later in Atlanta. An Olympic gold medal is simply an impossible dream for the huge majority of sports people, even professionals, and to win one would be the high point of most careers, but the 1996 Tour had scarred Indurain. That, together with wrangles over his contract for the following season, caused him to lose his appetite for racing. In January 1997 he announced his retirement, having made history by being the first racer to win five consecutive Tours de France.

ANDRÉ LEDUCQ

He won two Tours, and it was a long time ago, but André Leducq is still fondly remembered in the cycling world for his engaging, fun-loving character, as well as for his huge strength and natural athletic ability. He was a very elegant racer for whom winning seemed to come easily. He also heralded an era of domination by French racers after a period in which Belgians and Italians had got the better of them in their country's biggest bike race.

TOUR RECORD

Name:	André Leducq
Nationality:	French
Born:	27 February 1904
Died:	18 June 1980
Tour career span:	1927–38
Tours contested:	9
Stage wins:	23
Tour wins:	2 (1930, 1932)

➜ *André Leducq was a two-time winner of the Tour de France and one of the most gifted cyclists ever to ride in the race.*

⬆ *Leducq was part of a French national team in the 1930s that provided three separate winners and was one of the strongest teams the race has seen.*

FIRST AID

After taking the yellow jersey with ease in 1930, Leducq crashed on the descent of the Galibier and was knocked out. He lay unconscious for 15 minutes, and came round to find most of the French national team standing around him. They got him going a bit, down the mountain and up a little climb out of Valloire. Then, while he was descending the Col du Telegraphe, a pedal broke on Leducq's bike and he fell again. His team-mate Marcel Bidot stopped, and when Leducq screamed that his leg was broken, Bidot lifted up his foot, pushed until Leducq's bent knee was level with his shoulder and said, "No it's not, get back on your bike."

FIRST VICTORY

After ministering to Leducq's injuries, after a fashion, Bidot got a spanner and used the pedal from a spectator's bike to mend his team leader's and get him on the road again. Leducq kept protesting, saying he couldn't continue, but Bidot told him that the yellow jersey never gives up. They made the stage finish with the help of a few more members of the French team, and Leducq went on to win the Tour.

FRENCH CONSISTENCY

Antonin Magne was third behind Leducq in 1930, with Bidot fifth and Pierre Magne sixth. Antonin Magne won in 1931 and 1934; Leducq won again in 1932, and George Speicher won in 1933.

YOUNG AGAIN

The French selectors couldn't find a place for Leducq in the national team for his last Tour in 1938, so he was put in a team called Les Cadets, which was full of young racers. Despite being 34 years old, Leducq got a new lease of life and wore the yellow jersey for two days before tying for victory on the final stage with Antonin Magne. Always up for trying new things, André Leducq died in 1980 in a diving accident at the age of 76.

➔ *André Leducq (right) rides a lap of honour with Antonin Magne after they shared a stage win, the last of both their careers, in 1938.*

NIGHT CLUBBING

Leducq was a very sociable man who was a regular customer in a number of top Paris restaurants and night clubs after he retired. As well as trying his hand at journalism and managing a cycling team, Leducq also worked at entertaining the clients of some big movers in the French bicycle business. That's how a Yorkshire-based British importer called Ron Kitching met Leducq during the 1960s. Leducq wined and dined him with a few friends, then told him it was a tradition among their group to sing a song to entertain the others. Kitching sang "On Ilkley Moor ba'tat", and at Leducq's insistence the Englishman taught him the words.

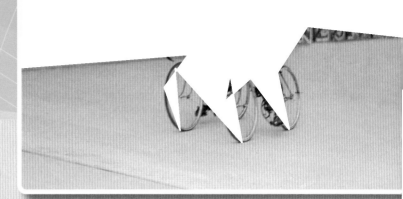

Le Numéro : 75 Centimes.   Mardi 9 Août 1932. - N° 667

LE MIROIR
DES SPORTS

DU VELO A LA PLUME
Sollicité, comme en 1930, par le "Miroir des Sports", d'écrire son récit du Tour de France, voici André Leducq, au repos de l'étape à Metz, commençant à noter pour nos lecteurs ses impressions, dont nous publions aujourd'hui le premier chapitre.

SECOND VICTORY

Leducq wasn't a great climber, but he won because he was so strong everywhere else. He could sprint, he could ride hard alone or in a group on flat and undulating stages, and he was the first Tour racer to become legendary for the way he went down mountains. It doesn't happen so much now, but in the early years of the Tour some of the best climbers were poor descenders. Leducq exploited that, and several times in his career he was distanced at the top of a big climb but caught back up with the front of the race over the other side. He won six stages as well as the yellow jersey by over 24 minutes in 1932.

WAX LYRICAL

When he was a journalist, Leducq's style of writing was in the best traditions of flowery prose that French writers still tend to use in books about cycling. Describing the riding style of Fausto Coppi in 1952, Leducq wrote: "He seems to caress rather than grip the handlebars, while his torso appears fixed to the saddle. His long legs extend to the pedals with the joints of a gazelle. At the end of each pedal stroke his ankle flexes gracefully. It's as if all the moving parts turn in oil. His long face appears like the blade of a knife as he climbs without apparent effort, like a great artist painting a watercolour."

⬅ *Leducq proved as adept with a pen as he was on a bike when he became a journalist after his racing career ended.*

GREG LEMOND

Whether Greg LeMond changed cycling or whether it was time for cycling to change is a question that's still being debated. What's certain is that Lemond was the catalyst. He introduced a lot of new ideas and he changed the way pro racers were paid. Also, by creating a wider fan base and exposure for the sport, he transformed cycling from a European to a world sport with the Tour de France right at the centre of it. But there's even more to Greg LeMond. He won the Tour three times, the second two after suffering life-threatening injuries, and he contributed to some of the most exciting and controversial moments in Tour de France history.

TOUR RECORD

Name:	Greg LeMond
Nationality:	American
Born:	26 June 1961
Tour career span:	1984–94
Tours contested:	8
White jersey:	1
Stage wins:	7
Tour wins:	3 (1986, 1989, 1990)

➜ *World champion again and winning his third Tour de France in 1990, who knows how many Tours LeMond would have won but for his accident in 1987?*

↑ *A world champion just after his 22nd birthday, Greg LeMond made his Tour debut in the rainbow jersey worn by the winner of that title in 1984.*

WORLD CHAMPION

LeMond won gold, silver and bronze medals in different events at the 1979 world junior championships in Argentina. He then did more racing in Europe, winning plenty, and turned pro for Bernard Hinault's team in 1981. He won the 1983 world professional road race championships, then took third overall in his Tour de France debut the following year. He finished second in 1985 after helping Bernard Hinault win his fifth Tour.

ALPE D'HUEZ

Agreement or not, LeMond and Hinault were head and shoulders above the rest in 1986. They broke away together on a stage that finished on the top of the Alpe d'Huez, and did so smiling all the way. A truce had been called, and as they crossed the finish line Hinault took hold of Lemond's arm and raised it in the air, while ensuring his front wheel crossed the line first. The smiles didn't last and relations between the two slowly deteriorated over the coming months.

EUROPEAN DEBUT

Born in Lakewood, California, and raised in Reno, Nevada, LeMond got into local cycling to help him train for skiing. He got into race cycling after seeing a professional race while on holiday in the Rockies. LeMond was amazed when the racers passed their family car on a mountain descent. After winning some local races and learning more about cycling, Lemond was drawn to race in Europe. He returned home with many very knowledgeable Belgian bike fans saying that they'd seen the sport's next superstar.

THE PACT

Hinault and LeMond made a pact for the Frenchman to win the 1985 Tour and the American to do the same thing the following year. At least LeMond says they did; Hinault's recollections are hazy. What happened in 1986 was fascinating. Hinault was in better form at the beginning of the Tour, and by stage 12 he led LeMond by five minutes, claiming he was attacking to draw out his and LeMond's rivals, although LeMond denies even hearing of any such plan. Hinault attacked next day, but ran out of strength towards the end of the stage. LeMond caught and dropped him, winning back a lot of time. A few days later Hinault was dropped from the front group in the Alps and LeMond took over the yellow jersey, which he kept to become the first American to win the Tour de France.

↑ *Just as adept going downhill as he was up, LeMond was also a great time triallist; he had every skill a Tour winner needs.*

TURKEY SHOOT

In April 1987 LeMond was having a short holiday from racing in America. He went hunting with a group that included his brother-in-law, who accidentally shot him. LeMond was badly hurt and lost a lot of blood, and a helicopter diverted from attending a road accident possibly saved his life. Still, 47 lead pellets, two of them close to his heart, were too dangerous to remove and would cause LeMond problems in later life.

LOST YEARS

Could Greg LeMond have won five Tours, maybe even more? He says he was capable of winning in 1985, but gave way to Hinault, so that's one. He would have been the man to beat in 1987 and 1988, as he proved when he won the next two Tours even though he wasn't as good a racer as he had been. That makes a possible six, and LeMond wouldn't have declined in the way he did without the hunting accident. It's a powerful argument.

TRI-BARS

LeMond won the 1989 Tour after a terrific battle with Laurent Fignon that came down to a time trial in the streets of Paris. It has been argued that he won because he was using a very early version of the handlebars called tri-bars, because triathletes used them, and now fitted to all time trial bikes – but the following year everyone was using them and LeMond won then too. After 1990, however, LeMond's form declined, possibly owing to the pellets in his body. He certainly had some symptoms that could be put down to the effects of lead on his muscle chemistry.

← *LeMond was a great innovator and he used every bit of the latest bike technology to beat Laurent Fignon in the final stage of the 1989 Tour and win the race by the narrowest margin ever.*

ANTONIN MAGNE

Not many legendary racers become legendary managers, but Antonin Magne did. He won the Tour de France twice then went on to help guide Louison Bobet's success and Raymond Poulidor's failure to win. In fact Poulidor may have been Magne's blind spot. They came from the same region, and Magne really admired Poulidor's strength, but then Magne's management was rooted in his own era, when strength was enough. It worked with Bobet, who was a very astute rider as well, but neither Magne nor Poulidor was tactically switched on enough to beat a racer like Jacques Anquetil. And perhaps Poulidor wasn't quite good enough anyway.

TOUR RECORD

Name:	Antonin Magne
Nationality:	French
Born:	15 January 1904
Died:	8 September 1983
Tour career span:	1927–38
Tours contested:	10
Stage wins:	9
Tour wins:	2 (1931, 1934)

⬇ *Antonin Magne won two Tours as a racer, and then helped two other Tour greats, Louison Bobet and Raymond Poulidor, as a team manager.*

⬆ *René Vietto waits for what must seem hours for a spare wheel after giving his to Magne.*

VIETTO'S SACRIFICE

A talented 20-year-old called René Vietto rode his first Tour de France in 1934 as a member of the French team. Magne was the team leader and took the yellow jersey on the second day. Vietto was a domestique in the team, but he was riding well too and up with Magne in the Pyrenees when his leader punctured. Vietto gave his wheel to Magne to replace the punctured one and lost five minutes waiting for the spares van. The next day Magne punctured again, this time with Vietto just ahead of him. Magne shouted and his young team-mate stopped in the road, turned his bike around and pedalled back to him. Vietto gave up his wheel again, then sat down on a low wall next to the road, utterly dejected. Did he know that, despite his talent, he would have more bad luck in the future, even when he led the French team, and never win the Tour de France?

FAN MAIL

The racers of Magne's era got a lot of fan mail, but on the eve of a particular stage in 1931 Antonin Magne got a very mysterious letter. Unsigned, it said that a rival, Gaston Rebry of Belgium, had written to his mother saying that he and a team-mate planned to launch a big attack next day at a particular point on the stage. The letter was postmarked from Rebry's village. Magne followed Rebry closely next day and, sure enough, the Belgian and his team-mate launched their predicted attack, which Magne was able to cover. Magne went on to win the Tour, but without that letter the story could have been different, because Rebry's breakaway gained a lot of time.

SIR ANTONIN

Magne was made a Chevalier de la Légion d'Honneur, the French equivalent of getting a knighthood, in 1962. It didn't change him; he still worried about money, and when working as a manager he wore a white coat, as they do in laboratories, to keep his clothes clean and prevent them from wearing out.

→ *Magne's services to cycling were recognized by the French state in 1962.*

WORLD CHAMPION

Magne was very good at single-day races and an excellent time triallist. He won the world road race championships in 1936 and won the Grand Prix des Nations, which was then considered as the world time trial championships in the absence of an official title race, three times from 1934 to 1936. He also won four French road race titles.

WHAT COULD GO WRONG?

When they started racing together in the French team, Magne and André Leducq were the best racers in the team and they shared a room each night, something that is still normal in the Tour de France. All the racers share; it's supposed to be good for morale. But it wasn't long before Leducq asked to be put in with somebody else. According to Leducq, when Magne wasn't moaning about the price of things he would be going on about what had gone wrong that day or what could go wrong on the next.

HOSPITAL IN A HANDCART

In 1935 Magne crashed near the bottom of the descent of the Col du Télégraphe and was too hurt to continue. He wasn't far from the local hospital, so instead of sending for the ambulance some spectators carried Magne there in a farmer's cart.

EANY MEANY ... MAGNE SAYS NO

Famously stingy with his own money, Antonin Magne was equally mean when it came to the funds of his team's sponsor when he became a team manager. Magne's most famous team was Mercier BP, and they had to race in jerseys without zipped collars because jerseys with zips cost one franc more.

→ *Famously mean, Magne would wear a white overall to protect his clothes when working as a manager.*

NO INTERVIEWS

Journalists at the time said that, as a rider and a manager, Magne was the dullest person in the world to interview. He would speak freely off the record, even if what he said was usually full of foreboding about the future or griping about bad luck in the past, but show him a notebook and he would clam up. However, those who raced in his teams say he was kind, gave good advice and was very correct in his dealings. He never let his riders get close to him, though, and always insisted they address him by the French formal "vous" and not the familiar "tu" as racers in other teams did with their managers.

EDDY MERCKX

Lance Armstrong won the most Tours, but Eddy Merckx won five as well as nearly every other big bike race in the world, some of them many times. No one has dominated cycling as Merckx did; no one had Merckx's range of abilities or the physical ability to press home his advantage year after year. Merckx has the most complete record in cycling, and he dominated the Tour from 1969 until 1974. He had the most voracious appetite for winning that the sport has ever seen, and is arguably the greatest male road racer of all time.

TOUR RECORD

Name:	Eddy Merckx
Nationality:	Belgian
Born:	17 June 1945
Tour career span:	1969–77
Tours contested:	7
Green jersey:	4
King of the Mountains:	2
Stage wins:	34
Tour wins:	5 (1969, 1970, 1971, 1972, 1974)

➜ *No rider has ever won the yellow, green and polka-dot jerseys in the same Tour de France, except for Merckx in 1969.*

LA COURSE EN TÊTE

It's a French phrase meaning "racing from the front" and it is often used to sum up Eddy Merckx. He rarely relied on tactics, but instead would go out and wring the neck of every race he could. When he won the Tour he dominated from prologue to the final stage, both of which he has won. He sums up his attitude like this: "I tried to get the yellow jersey as soon as possible. It never scared me to lead, but it scared me when I was behind. If you are behind, even a few seconds, you have to make up those seconds before you can even think about winning. I never saw the point of coming from behind." His need to dominate led one rival, Christian Raymond of France, to call Merckx "The Cannibal" in an interview; it was a throwaway line but it stuck, and Merckx has been "The Cannibal" ever since.

THE PUNCH

Merckx was going for win number six in 1975. He had the yellow jersey, although not by as big a margin as in some years. Then, on the climb up the extinct volcano just outside Clermont-Ferrand called the Puy de Dôme, he was punched in the stomach by a spectator. Even though they almost crowd the racers off the road, there is very rarely any contact with spectators. Merckx was hurt and lost time. The crowd made a citizen's arrest on his assailant, and he was brought to justice and convicted of assault, although he claimed he was pushed from behind. Merckx had his bruising treated with a blood-thinning drug and he says this explains what happened next day, when after going on the attack he slowed dramatically on Pra-Loup, the final climb of the day. He was caught and passed by Bernard Thévenet of France, then other riders. It was the beginning of the end of Merckx's reign in the Tour de France.

↗ *Merckx struggles up the last few metres of the Puy de Dôme after being punched by a spectator in 1975.*

TRUE BELGIAN

Belgium is a country of two halves, divided by language and culture. The north is part of what was Flanders, and they speak a Dutch dialect called Flemish. The south is called Wallonia, speaks French and has a very different history. Cycling is far more popular in Flanders, so where Eddy Merckx comes from is important. He grew up in a French-speaking suburb of Brussels, but was born in Flanders. However, mindful of the wedge between two parts of his country, when asked where he comes from, Flanders or Wallonia, Merckx always says: "I am a Belgian."

DIGNITY IN DEFEAT

A couple of days after losing the yellow jersey in 1975, but still not out of contention, Merckx had a fall and fractured his jaw. The injury was bad enough for him to have abandoned the Tour, and he couldn't eat solids for a few days after, but Merckx carried on. Not only that, he kept attacking Bernard Thévenet. The French public had been a bit cold with Merckx when he was winning, but in defeat they really appreciated his spirit and sense of fair play.

LUIS OCANA

There was one Tour where Merckx looked fallible, and that was in 1971 when Luis Ocana of Spain made an audacious attack in the Alps when Merckx was having an uncharacteristic bad day. Ocana was a super-talented climber who could time trial too. He took the yellow jersey and Merckx reacted as he always did – he attacked. Next day was a flat stage but Merckx still went for it, winning and taking time back from Ocana. He did the same in a time trial and launched more attacks on the first stage in the Pyrenees. Merckx raced up and down the mountains, forcing Ocana to take risks, so many risks that the Spaniard crashed on the descent of the Col de Mente and was too badly injured to continue. As a mark of respect for him, Merckx, who won the Tour, wouldn't wear the yellow jersey the day after Ocana crashed out.

← *Luis Ocana had Merckx on the back foot in 1971 until the Spaniard crashed out of the Tour on the Col de Mente.*

RAYMOND POULIDOR

Every one of our legendary riders has won the Tour de France, apart from Mark Cavendish –a legendary sprinter and sprinters will never win the Tour – and Raymond Poulidor. The Frenchman could have won it, he was a strong climber who could do a good time trial, but he didn't win and never even wore the yellow jersey, not for a day. So why is Poulidor legendary? It's because French cycling fans loved him and those from other countries really respected him. They say that everyone loves the underdog, and one way or another Poulidor played that role to perfection.

TOUR RECORD

Name:	Raymond Poulidor
Nationality:	French
Born:	15 April 1936
Tour career span:	1962–76
Tours contested:	14
Green jersey:	1
Stage wins:	7

↑ *Neither winning nor losing affected Raymond Poulidor's popularity with France's passionate cycling fans.*

➡ *Strong enough to win the Tour, Poulidor found better riders in his way and bad luck when they weren't.*

ETERNAL SECOND

That was the nickname journalists gave Raymond Poulidor. The thing is, they gave it him quite early on in his career. It wasn't strictly true either, because Poulidor scored three second and five third places. Joop Zoetemelk of Holland finished second six times, but of course he won the Tour in 1980. It leaves the suspicion that Poulidor got the name because he never really looked like winning. He made tactical errors against the two superstars of cycling he raced against, Jacques Anquetil and Eddy Merckx, but they were better racers than him anyway. In the Tours between the reigns of Anquetil and Merckx, his best opportunity, Poulidor continued to either get it wrong, crash or get injured. When Raphaël Géminiani was Jacques Anquetil's team manager he once said to his rider: "Actually, we don't have to worry about beating Raymond because Raymond always finds a way to beat himself." Harsh but true.

HARD UPBRINGING

Poulidor is from Limousin, not the richest region of France even now, but his family had very little money when he was young. To teach him the value of property, after Poulidor and his brother accidentally broke a small pane of glass in their bedroom during the autumn, their father refused to replace it until the following spring. And as Poulidor says, "A Limousin winter is no joke. We blocked it up with cardboard but we often woke to a little pile of snow in the room."

FIRST NEMESIS

Raymond Poulidor is only two years younger than Jacques Anquetil, and when he turned pro he was older than Anquetil was when he did. Their biggest clash came in 1964 on the Puy de Dôme. Anquetil had the yellow jersey, but not by much, and the steep climb, which was the stage finish, really suited Poulidor. If he'd attacked quite early and decisively, Poulidor might have had Anquetil in real trouble, but Anquetil out-thought him. Instead of riding behind Poulidor he rode alongside him. Unnerved by this, instead of making an all or nothing attack Poulidor just accelerated to test Anquetil, and Anquetil stayed alongside. Poulidor picked it up again, and Anquetil didn't flinch. He kept on doing this, accelerating slightly with Anquetil matching him until, with just a few hundred metres left, Anquetil gave in and Poulidor romped away. By that time there wasn't enough mountain left for him to gain the margin he needed to win the Tour, and Anquetil beat him easily in the final time trial.

GOOD SPORTSMAN

No matter what bad luck befell him, no matter what his mistakes cost him, Raymond Poulidor never stopped smiling and never stopped being kind to fans and having time for them. This only added to his popularity, especially compared with Anquetil and Merckx, who were much more distant and aloof.

OLDEST PODIUM

In his final Tour, in 1976, Poulidor made the podium for the eighth time in his career, in third place. He was 40 years old and he is still the oldest ever top-three finisher. Next is Lance Armstrong, who was 38 when he made it to third in his comeback of 2009.

↑ *Life was never a tea party for Poulidor, but he enjoyed himself nevertheless.*

SECOND NEMESIS

Eddy Merckx was even better than Jacques Anquetil; he never had to resort to tactics when dealing with Poulidor, but there was one time when the Frenchman got the better of him. It was 1974, when Poulidor was 38. Merckx was leading the Tour but he was tired. By the time Poulidor realized it, however, there was only eight kilometres of the mountain-top finish at Pla d'Adet to go. When he finally attacked, Poulidor took 14 seconds out of Merckx for every remaining kilometre, and it wasn't enough. He took more time next day, but it was the last day in the mountains, so there was nothing left for Poulidor. He couldn't out-ride even a tired Eddy Merckx on the flat stages, so he finished second again.

TYPICAL MISTAKE

On the stage to Toulouse during the 1964 Tour, Poulidor was in a break with Jacques Anquetil and a number of others when a spoke broke in his rear wheel. The wheel went out of true, but not badly. If Poulidor had operated the brake quick release to stop the wheel's rim rubbing on the brake pads, he could have stayed where he was. Instead he stopped to change the wheel. It was a slow change and the group were going incredibly fast on the flat roads into the French city. Poulidor, on his own, couldn't catch up – he had no team-mates to help him because the stage had started in the mountains and the field was really spread out. As it turned out, he eventually lost the Tour de France to Anquetil by less time than he gave away through that wheel change.

➜ *Raymond Poulidor (right) goes wheel for wheel with Jacques Anquetil on the Puy de Dôme in 1964. He was stronger than Anquetil for once, but Anquetil out-thought him.*

BERNARD THÉVENET

Bernard Thévenet will go down in history as the man who defeated Eddy Merckx in the Tour de France. After that 1975 triumph, he was ill and had to abandon in 1976, but he won again in 1977. Thévenet was good but he wasn't a natural champion like Eddy Merckx. Bernard Thévenet was more of a Louison Bobet, a strong racer who studied his métier until he became a champion. Like Bobet he won at 28 after five attempts. He also emulated Bobet's crowning glory by wearing the yellow jersey to lead the Tour across the Col d'Izoard.

TOUR RECORD

Name:	Bernard Thévenet
Nationality:	French
Born:	10 January 1940
Tour career span:	1970–81
Tours contested:	11
Stage wins:	10
Tour wins:	2 (1975, 1977)

← *Bernard Thévenet goes down in Tour history as the man who brought the Eddy Merckx era to an end.*

FIRST TOUR

Thévenet turned pro in 1970 but wasn't selected for his team, Peugeot-BP's Tour de France squad. Two days before the race started, Thévenet left home on his bike to meet a friend for a training ride. Shortly after he did so his team manager called to say that two Peugeot riders had fallen ill and they needed Thévenet for the Tour. Luckily his mother telephoned his friend's home, to which Bernard was riding, otherwise he would never have made it back in time to pack and get to Limoges for the start. He won a stage in his first Tour, too.

⬇ *Bernard Thévenet was a late inclusion in the Peugeot team for the 1970 Tour de France, but he still managed to win a stage that year.*

NEVER GIVE UP

Eight kilometres from the summit of the Alpe d'Huez in 1977 it looked as if Lucien van Impe would repeat his 1976 Tour win. He had attacked on the Col de Glandon, the penultimate climb, and gained time with every pedal turn up and down that pass and in the valley before the Alpe d'Huez. Then he did the same on this final climb until he was three minutes ahead of a group of favourites led by Thévenet, who was the yellow jersey, but now in name only. Van Impe was three minutes ahead so actually led the Tour by two and half on the road. No one would help Thévenet, they just followed as he rode as hard as he could. But Van Impe had overestimated his strength, and just three miles from the summit he slowed dramatically. It was terrible to see, Van Impe could hardly keep moving, and hearing about his near collapse the rivals who had been content to shadow Thévenet now attacked him. He had to dig deep and chase them. He couldn't catch Hennie Kuiper, who won the stage, but he saved the yellow jersey. He also passed a huge test of character, one that all Tour legends have to pass at some time or other.

WHERE AM I?

In 1972 Bernard Thévenet crashed on the descent of the Col d'Aubisque and was knocked unconscious. When he came round he didn't have a clue who or where he was, he said later. "My manager and mechanic put me back on my bike, but I couldn't balance. They pushed me 200 metres down the road while I climbed the thread of my own existence to work out who I was and why I was there. I wondered why I was on a bike, but then I saw Peugeot printed on my jersey and thought I must be a racing cyclist, but in what race? Then I saw the yellow ID plate on my team car and asked my manager if we were in the Tour de France. My manager said yes and not to worry as I had only fallen on my head, and he let me go. I began pedalling and got with a group of tail-enders, but all I could do was follow, and it was an hour before everything suddenly came back to me."

After banging his head in a crash in 1972 Thévenet didn't even know he was a cyclist when he first regained consciousness.

FOUR TOURS, SIX STAGE WINS

Big stage races suited Thévenet, who seemed to get stronger as they went on, and he was a very solid climber. Not flashy fast maybe, but hard to break. He won a mountain stage in 1971; two in 1972, including one on top of Mont Ventoux; and one flat and one mountain stage in 1973, when he finished second overall.

BORN IN THE HANDLEBARS

Thévenet comes from the Burgundy region of France, from a tiny village called Le Guidon, which happens to mean handlebars. He was French amateur road race champion in 1968, but steady rather than spectacular results meant he was passed over for national selection sometimes for amateur riders with better results.

PRESIDENTIAL VISIT

The day Bernard Thévenet won the 1975 Tour was a great one for France. For the first time the race finished on the Champs-Elysées, in front of thousands of ecstatic fans, after a finale of several laps in the very heart of Paris. It was only seven years since the last French victory, but the country had been stung by the dominance of Belgium's Eddy Merckx. National pride was restored, and President of France Valéry Giscard d'Estaing was there to welcome a new hero and give him the final yellow jersey.

Thévenet is presented with the yellow jersey by the French President, Valéry Giscard d'Estaing, in Paris in 1975.

PHILIPPE THYS

Philippe Thys of Belgium was the first man to win three Tours de France, as well as being the first to have his career interrupted by war. In many ways professional cycling came of age during the Thys era, with more races, well-organized teams, serious training plans and some of the tactics we see today. Thys was a clever rider who raced like a modern Tour champion to some extent. He didn't go all out to win from stage one, but used his rivals' strengths by shadowing them when they made their moves to gain time. Then he would focus on distancing himself from each of those rivals until he ran out the winner.

TOUR RECORD

Name:	Philippe Thys
Nationality:	Belgian
Born:	8 October 1889
Died:	16 January 1971
Tour career span:	1912–25
Tours contested:	10
Stage wins:	13
Tour wins:	3 (1913, 1914, 1920)

➡ *Thys was the first triple winner of the Tour de France, winning twice before the First World War and once after it.*

⬆ *Philippe Thys is congratulated after winning the 1920 Tour de France, the second after the First World War.*

POST-WAR TOUR

The first Tour after the First World War was held in 1919. Only 67 riders started it and many of them were unfit, because it was impossible for them to train during the conflict. Thys didn't even make it through the first stage, but his retirement was due to illness rather than unfitness because he had won some big races in 1917 and 1918, including the Tour of Lombardy and the Paris–Tours race. The northern stages were raced over what had been the First World War battlefields and the roads were so bad that a journalist called one stage the Hell of the North. The name stuck, and part of the route of the great single-day Classic, Paris–Roubaix, is still referred to as the Hell of the North.

FAN BASE

Belgian bike fans were so happy that their hero had returned to top form in 1920 that no fewer than 20,000 of them swarmed into the Parc des Princes stadium to celebrate his victory in Paris.

SPORTS SCIENCE

Philippe Thys had a good understanding of how his body worked. He trained hard, ate the right things and had a good constitution. In an interview after the 1920 Tour he said that a mark of fitness and good form was for a rider to finish the Tour at the same weight as he started it. Thys had started and finished that Tour weighing 69 kilograms. This shows that he must have been drinking enough to rehydrate between each stage, and eating enough of the correct balance of food to recover and maintain his muscle mass.

PENALTY

To get some idea of the draconian rules imposed by Henri Desgrange, the Tour's first organizer, Thys was penalized 30 minutes in 1914 for receiving help to repair a damaged wheel. It happened on the penultimate stage, so going into the final run to Paris, Thys led the Frenchman Henri Pélissier by just two minutes instead of the 32 he had before. Everyone thought the Frenchman would win and they lined the route to see it, spilling out on to the road in the places where Pélissier was most likely to attack. The crowds proved Pélissier's undoing: they were so thick that he couldn't attack as he kept having to slow to avoid hitting anyone.

➜ *Even having someone hold your bike could attract a penalty in the early Tours de France.*

CYCLO-CROSS CHAMPION

Belgium is a world force in cyclo-cross, which is cycling's winter sport played out around parks, fields and woods, just like cross-country running. Cyclo-cross has always been popular in Belgium, and Philippe Thys was their first national champion, way back in 1910. He was 21 and it was his first big victory.

STUNG BY CRITICISM

Henri Desgrange never let the facts get in the way of a good story. He wrote after Thys's retirement on the first stage in 1919 that the Belgian was "a petit-bourgois who no longer loved his bike". That hurt Thys, and when he won in 1920 he was less tactical than before and took four stage wins as well as the yellow jersey.

YELLOW CONTROVERSY

Official records state that the first yellow jersey was awarded to Eugène Christophe in 1919, but in the late 1950s an article appeared in a French cycling magazine containing an interview with Philippe Thys in which he said he was asked to wear a yellow jersey when he led the Tour in 1914. He said he refused at first, knowing that the jersey would make it easier for his rivals to pick him out, but he agreed to do it when his Peugeot team, seeing the marketing opportunities of wearing the race leader's jersey, offered to pay him extra. The story cannot be verified, because all of the Tour records for this era were lost during the Second World War, but Thys's 1950s account, which included how they had to enlarge the neck and arms for him to fit, is believable.

HONORÉ BARTHELEMY

Honoré Barthelemy, a tough French racer and a fierce rival of Thys in 1920, crashed on stage 9, injuring both his back and his eye, to the extent that surgeons had to remove the eye. He still stayed in the Tour, finishing eighth overall and riding every stage with cotton wool wedged in his empty eye socket. After the Tour, Barthelemy had a glass eye fitted, but it fell out so many times in subsequent races that he claimed he was spending all his winnings on new ones. Back went the cotton wool, and for the rest of his career Barthelemy would remove his eye before a race, insert his cotton wool, and afterwards swap them over for the prize presentation.

← *Honoré Barthelemy was a tough competitor to Thys; not even the loss of an eye following a crash on stage 9 could stop him finishing the 1920 Tour.*

PART 4
THE GREAT CLIMBS

The Tour de France is three weeks long, but its outcome is decided on a handful of stages in the mountains. Ever since those pioneer racers climbed into the Pyrenees in 1910, the Tour has sought out the highest and most spectacular settings for its key acts to be played out. Just their names, Izoard, Galibier, Huez, Tourmalet and Ventoux, conjure images of battles fought out on their slopes in front of baying crowds on a ribbon of road that climbs through jaw-dropping splendour. If you are going to see the Tour de France once, go to the mountains; and not just any mountain, but one of the great climbs. They don't all feature in every Tour, but do so often enough to have helped write the crucial chapters of the Tour. No one pays to stand on the great climbs and watch the Tour go by; these are places of pilgrimage, and pilgrims journey back again and again. Up to half a million fans pack the slopes of the Alpe d'Huez. Anticipation builds as the riders approach, and the noise rises with them, building like a tsunami until it washes over you.

L'Alpe d'Huez is one of the most famous climbs of the Tour de France. Riders ascend almost 1,100 metres riding on less than 14 kilometres of winding, treacherous, twisty roads.

COL D'AUBISQUE

The road over the Col d'Aubisque was created for the Tour de France. When Alphonse Steines, a journalist who worked for *L'Auto*, visited the proposed route for the Tour's visit to the Pyrenees in 1910, he was nearly killed trying to cross them in a car. The roads were bad on most of the climbs, but on the Aubisque they were non-existent. Steines had to contact his boss saying he needed funds to repair some roads, when in fact most of the money went to build one over the Aubisque.

RECORDS

Length:	30 kilometres
Summit height:	1,709 metres
Height gain:	1,247 metres
Average gradient:	4.1%
Maximum gradient:	13%
Tour appearances:	43

↑ *Eddy Merckx on the Aubisque in 1969 on his way to doubling an already eight-minute lead in a single day.*

CLIMATE BOUNDARY

The summit of the Aubisque marks the boundary between the wetter climate of the western Pyrenees, which is heavily influenced by the Atlantic Ocean, and the drier east. Even the name Aubisque underlines this wetness: it comes from a local dialect word for a kind of sedge that grows on its slopes, and sedges only grow where it's wet.

EDDY'S GLORY

Eddy Merckx already led the 1969 Tour by eight minutes before the climb of the Aubisque, but he attacked alone just before it and crossed the top with nearly as much of a lead again. He went on to win the stage by eight minutes and the Tour by 20, plus every other classification.

DUBOC IS POISONED

In 1911 the race leader, Paul Duboc, accepted a drink from a spectator on the Aubisque – and within minutes he collapsed with violent stomach cramps. Somehow he managed to finish the stage, but lost three hours 47 minutes and any chance of winning. Duboc was from Normandy, and his fans believed that his rival Garrigou, who took over the lead, was behind the poisoning. They planned to get their revenge when a stage passed through Rouen, but the Tour organizers heard about the plot and asked Garrigou to change his jersey and wear a false beard to ride through the city so he couldn't be identified.

ASSASSIN!

The Aubisque was the last climb on the first ever big mountain stage, so it was where Alphonse Steines chose to watch the riders go through. The stage was brutal, 326 kilometres from Luchon to Bayonne, over the Peyresourde, Aspin and Tourmalet before the Aubisque. First over was a local racer, François Lafoucarde, and then came two Tour favourites, Octave Lapize and Gustave Garrigou. They were pushing their bikes, and when Lapize saw the man responsible for the route, he called him an assassin. Lapize went on to win the stage in Bayonne, but some riders finished almost a day behind him.

← *Octave Lapize pushed his bicycle to the summit of Aubisque in 1910, but still won the Tour, the first time the highest mountains were included in the route.*

STEEP SECTION

About halfway up the western ascent there is a section of 13 per cent climbing. After that the average gradient for the climb, another eight kilometres, is eight per cent, although the road never stays that way for very long. A local pro racer who rode the Tour de France from the early 1980s to the '90s says, "The middle section of the climb and well into the second half is the hardest. There is no let-up after the 13 per cent really, it's always between eight and ten, and you are always shifting gear, otherwise you have to be in and out of the saddle. It's very easy to go into the red here. But that's disastrous, because although the gradient lessens gradually towards the top, it's only the last two kilometres where it gets any easier."

STEPHEN'S TIME TRIAL

By 1985 Stephen Roche had been a pro for four years. He'd won some good races, some of them brilliantly, but the lack of consistency that dogged his career was already showing. He was under pressure and needed a result from this Tour, so he set out to get one. The stage was a 52.5-kilometre road race from Luz-St-Sauveur to the Aubisque summit. At the start Roche caused amusement by lining up in a skinsuit, the kind worn by racers in a time trial. "This isn't a time trial," some of the peloton told him. "You reckon?" Roche replied. Then the flag dropped and he attacked, getting a lone lead and proceeded to time trial to the finish and won the stage.

TWO FOR THE PRICE OF ONE

The eastern ascent of the Aubisque involves climbing the Col de Soulor first. Then there is a short descent before the last ten kilometres of tough climbing. Sometimes the Tour only calls this part of the climb the Aubisque; generally, though, the Aubisque and Soulor are lumped together and listed as one climb.

LA CORNICHE

There is a section just before the summit of the Aubisque where the road has been cut into the rock face. It feels very exposed and is quite an experience to make this traverse in a car, let alone on a bike.

← One of the scariest roads in the Tour, La Corniche on the Aubisque.

COL DE LA COLOMBIÈRE

The Colombière didn't make it into the Tour until 1960, but it has played a big part since. Its northern location, about 50 kilometres south-east of Geneva, means it's often the first or last climb in the Alps, depending on the direction the Tour stage comes from. The northern ascent is the harder one, with two six-kilometre stretches of tough climbing separated by an easier middle section. The easier south side has a gradient of around six per cent for almost the whole of its length, with only the top two kilometres a bit steeper.

RECORDS

Length:	16.3 kilometres
Summit height:	1,613 metres
Height gain:	1,108 metres
Average gradient:	6.8%
Maximum gradient:	11%
Tour appearances:	20

↑ *Britain's Barry Hoban wins the stage at Sallanches after climbing the Colombière alone in 1968.*

TROUBLED DOUBLE

A French climber who won the King of the Mountains title in 1990, Thierry Claveyrolat is the only rider to have led the Tour over the Colombière more than once. What's more, he did it two years in a row and from both directions. The first was in 1990, when he climbed the tough north side before winning in St-Gervais. The second was in 1991, when he scaled the south side to win in Morzine. Claveyrolat was born in the Alps. Local fans called him the "Eagle of Vizille", and when his career ended he bought the Café de la Gare in Vizille, which is just south of Grenoble. Sadly, for various reasons his business wasn't a success and he found that difficult to deal with. Then in 1999 he had the misfortune to be involved in a car accident after he'd been drinking, in which a child lost his sight. This was too much for Claveyrolat and he committed suicide shortly after.

HOBAN'S MOUNTAIN

Barry Hoban is a British racer who won eight Tour stages in the 1960s and '70s. He was Britain's Tour stage record holder before Mark Cavendish and has often been compared to Cavendish, but Hoban was a different racer. He won sprint stages, as Cavendish does, but in 1968 he won a mountains stage to Sallanches, and he used the Colombière as his springboard to victory.

← *Tragic Thierry Claveyrolat climbs to happier times in the Tour de France.*

INFAMOUS STAGE

American rider Floyd Landis punctured on the Col de la Colombière in 2006. It was the day of his amazing resurrection when, after looking as if he'd lost any chance of winning on the previous stage, he went on a long lone break and hauled himself back into contention. Landis won the Tour but was stripped of his title as a result of the positive drugs test he supplied after this stage.

➡ *Floyd Landis on the Colombière in 2006.*

THE MOMENT OF 2009

The 2009 Tour was designed to be close, and it was. The penultimate stage finished on top of Mont Ventoux, but the wind negated that as a spectacle. Instead it was the third last stage that climbed the north side of the Colombière that provided the excitement. The organizers replaced the first steep ramp with an even steeper one, a new climb called the Col de Romme. This acted like a ladder leaning on to the Colombière, joining it just before its second steep bit. It saw some great racing, and the battles for first and second, between Alberto Contador and Andy Schleck, and for third and fourth, between Lance Armstrong and Bradley Wiggins, were both settled here.

COLOMBIAN KING

The Colombian climber Luis Herrera pranced away from the front of the race to collect the first-place points on top of the Col de la Colombière on stage 12 in 1985. Having won the previous day's stage he was well on his way to the first of two King of the Mountains titles. The stage was a monster, with seven climbs and 269 kilometres of racing that took the leaders over eight hours, before fellow Colombian Fabio Parra eventually beat Herrera to the line at Lans-en-Vercours.

STANDING STILL

German racer Linus Gerdemann showed just how steep the north side of the Colombière is when he won a stage to Le Grand Bornand in 2007. The Colombière was the final climb of the day and Gerdemann had a good lead at the start, enough to take the yellow jersey, but he looked exhausted as he neared the top. He slowed to an agonizing crawl, and at one point he wobbled and nearly collided with a photographer's motor bike. He pulled back some time with a hair-raising descent to Le Grand Bornand, which is on the southern side of the climb. It was enough to secure the stage and the yellow jersey for Gerdemann.

⬅ *Linus Gerdemann pushing hard near the summit in 2007; a breakneck descent secured him the stage and gained enough time to take the yellow jersey.*

COL DU GALIBIER

The Col du Galibier is a Tour de France giant in so many ways. It was first used in 1911, so it has a lot of history. It was the highest mountain pass the race ever climbed for many years. It's long, it's hard and some of the best moments of racing have been played out on its slopes. The Galibier represents the beating heart of the Tour de France, with the continuity of over a century of history, and still has the impact to inspire awe today.

RECORDS

Length:	34.8 kilometres
Summit height:	2,646 metres
Height gain:	2,096 metres
Average gradient:	7%
Maximum gradient:	10%
Tour appearances:	58

NORTH SIDE

The north side of the Galibier is the hardest and most spectacular. It is two climbs really, beginning with 12 kilometres of the Col du Télégraphe, rising out of the Maurienne valley. After a four-kilometre descent to Valloire, the Galibier starts with a long, straight section that climbs through a huge and very remote valley. All that can be seen ahead is a wall of mountains with apparently no way through, but at a place called Plan-Lachat the road suddenly swings right and climbs a series of hairpins that are like a ladder to the Galibier's summit. Until 1978 all traffic went through the tunnel at the top, which was dug in 1891, but only cars do that now. Bikes must climb over the tunnel on to the ancient pass that was made by shepherds and foot travellers. In 2011, the stage finished at the top of the pass; at 2,645 metres, it was the Tour's highest ever stage finish.

SPREADING THEIR WINGS

After taking the yellow jersey the previous day, Luis Ocana attacked on the Galibier in 1973 with fellow Spaniard José-Manuel Fuente. They stayed away all day, with Ocana winning the stage and establishing an unassailable lead in the Tour. It was truly spectacular to see two Spanish climbing geniuses romp up the famous slopes. A perfect setting for the perfect exploit.

← *Luis Ocana (left) and his Spanish compatriot José-Manuel Fuente fly up the Galibier in 1973.*

ANQUETIL AND POULIDOR'S LAST BATTLE

Jacques Anquetil and Raymond Poulidor had both lost the Tour by the time they hit the Galibier in 1966. Anquetil had taken his fifth victory in 1964, but he suspected that Poulidor had the legs to beat him. Poulidor should have attacked from the off in 1966, but instead he fixed his race on his old rival, and Anquetil suckered him into letting his team-mate, Lucien Aimar, get away in the Pyrenees. Anquetil's job was done, one of his team would win the Tour, but when Poulidor attacked on the Galibier, Anquetil couldn't resist one last dig at him. He had nothing to gain by doing it, as another team-mate, Julio Jimenez, was long gone and would win the stage, but Anquetil rode at Poulidor's side. Poulidor piled on the pressure but couldn't shift his nemesis. It was the last act of a rivalry that had divided a nation.

➔ *Neither was in a position to win the Tour in 1966, but Jacques Anquetil (left) took on and beat Raymond Poulidor on the Galibier stage simply because he could.*

JULIO JIMENEZ

First over the Galibier in 1966 and 1967, Spanish climbing legend Julio Jimenez was never a threat to win the Tour because he couldn't time trial. However, Jimenez had the credentials to be judged as one of the best climbers in history. Stick thin, he danced up climbs where others looked as if they were pushing a barrel in front of them. Jimenez was King of the Mountains three times in a row from 1965 to 1967.

GOING DUTCH

No one who witnessed it will ever forget the sight of the tall, slim Dutchman, Gert-Jan Theunisse, his long hair falling about the shoulders of his polka-dot jersey, on the day in 1989 when he won at the Alpe d'Huez. The stage climbed the easier south side of the Galibier, but Theunisse's effort deserves inclusion in the Galibier story because he attacked almost from the start of the stage and stayed away over the Galibier, then the Croix de Fer and finally the Alpe d'Huez.

PIRATE RAID

They called Marco Pantani "The Pirate" because of the bandana he wore when he raced. In 1998 he attacked on the first slopes of the Col du Télégraphe on the rain-soaked 15th stage. Jan Ullrich was the yellow jersey and until that moment had looked set to take his second successive Tour victory, but Pantani took time from him all the way to the top of the Galibier. The little Italian dropped down the other side of the Galibier like a stone, then romped up the final climb to Les Deux-Alpes and took over the race lead. He'd done what only the very greatest climbers can do, won the Tour with one single brave attack in the terrain that suited him best.

← *Marco Pantani launches the attack on the Galibier that would win him the 1998 Tour de France.*

ALPE D'HUEZ

This is perhaps the most glamorous mountain-top finish; partly because it was the first, but also because of its setting. The road to the Alpe d'Huez from Le Bourg-d'Oisans, the town at its foot, climbs an almost vertical rock wall in 21 bends between ramp-like straights that pile one on top of the other, like seats in a theatre. And to maintain the theatrical effect, each bend is dedicated to an Alpe d'Huez winner, their names written on bold plaques above the road, like actors' credits.

RECORDS

Length:	13.9 kilometres
Summit height:	1,860 metres
Height gain:	1,100 metres
Average gradient:	7.9%
Maximum gradient:	11.5%
Tour appearances:	28

PANTANI'S RECORD

Italy's Marco Pantani won on the Alpe in 1995, and he won again in 1997, after recovering from a collision with a car. Pantani attacked right at the start of the climb. At first Jan Ullrich, the Tour winner that year, managed to follow him, but as Pantani continued to accelerate, even Ullrich couldn't hold him. He romped up the climb, setting a record of 37 minutes and 35 seconds, which is still the fastest the Alpe has ever been climbed. However, his time probably has to be qualified, as it now seems certain that Pantani was taking the blood-boosting drug EPO, as were many other racers at the time. Pantani was a very troubled person outside sport and he died in 2004 of an apparent cocaine overdose.

↑ Dutch fans turn the side of the road up to the l'Alpe d'Huez a colourful shade of orange as they cheer the riders by.

DUTCH MOUNTAIN

That's what the Alpe d'Huez is called, and the reason is a combination of one man's passion for the place and the fact that there were some very good Dutch climbers around in the 1970s and '80s. Father Jaap Reuten first visited the Alpe d'Huez as an enthusiastic skier in 1964, but he was amazed to find that there was no church in the village, so he stayed and set about building one. Reuten raised the money he needed, even becoming the representative for a Dutch beer company in the area, and Notre Dame des Neiges (Our Lady of the Snows) was opened in 1969. When a compatriot, Joop Zoetemelk, won on the Alpe d'Huez in 1976, Father Jaap rang the church bells in celebration. He did it again when Hennie Kuiper won there the following year, and the tradition was reinforced when Dutch riders won another six times out of the next 11 Tour visits to the Alpe d'Huez, all to the sound of the chapel bells.

FIRST SUMMIT FINISH

The spectacular setting of the Alpe d'Huez inspired a local artist, Jean Barbaglia, the first to visualize a bike race on the Alpe. He approached Georges Rajon, who owned the biggest hotel in the resort, the Christina, and suggested that the Alpe d'Huez would be ideal for a Tour de France stage finish. Rajon was hooked, and very persuasive. The Tour had not had a mountain-top finish until Rajon approached them, but they agreed to have one at the Alpe d'Huez in 1952. On a sporting level it was a success, Fausto Coppi winning, and opening the Alpe to cycling in style, but summit finishes are demanding logistically, so the race didn't return until 1976.

← L'Alpe d'Huez was the first summit finish of the Tour. It's still the best.

MEMORIAL

Joachim Agostinho was 36 when he won on the Alpe d'Huez in 1979. He was a tough old rider, a former soldier who'd seen active service, and one of those racers who would have done better had the Tour been four weeks long instead of three. He was always good in the final week, and he dropped his breakaway partner Robert Alban with three kilometres left of the Alpe. Agostinho was still racing in 1984 when he was killed in a crash during the Tour of the Algarve. There's a memorial stone to him on the Alpe d'Huez located close to where he attacked in 1979.

DOWN AND BACK UP

The Alpe's first double winner, Joop Zoetemelk won there in 1976 and 1979. The 1979 win was on a very strange stage. It was the second of two stages that finished on the Alpe that year, and this one started there too. The riders descended the Alpe, shot down the Romanche valley and rode up a climb called La Morte. Then they turned around and raced back up the valley to climb the Alpe d'Huez again. Just to add to the weirdness of it, Zoetemelk was wearing the green jersey, which is normally the sprinters' domain, because he was second on points to a dominant Bernard Hinault, who also had the yellow.

ERIK

In 1999 Giuseppe Guerini was leading by a good margin near the top of the Alpe when a spectator decided to take a snapshot. The fan, who was a German called Erik, stood in the middle of the road as the Italian rider headed for the top in lone splendour. Unfortunately, through the viewfinder of Erik's camera Guerini looked further away than he actually was. They both took evasive action at the last moment, but it was the same evasive action and Guerini collided with Erik and fell. He still managed to get up and win the stage, and that night Erik waited in the lobby of Guerini's hotel to apologize.

← *Giuseppe Guerini enjoys his moment on Alpe d'Huez, winning despite a short-sighted fan.*

THE LOOK

Lance Armstrong looked as though he was struggling on the Madeleine and Glandon climbs in the 2001 tour, but he was just trying to lull his opponents into a false sense of security. Jan Ullrich took the bait and got his team-mates to ride hard on the front in an effort to drop Armstrong. It didn't work; in fact all it did was exhaust Ullrich's men, so they were dropped. Armstrong moved to the front as they started to climb the Alpe d'Huez, and as they passed through a hamlet called La Garde he turned to stare Ullrich in the face. All of a sudden, just as Ullrich realized his mistake, Armstrong attacked and the German had no answer.

→ *Jan Ullrich (in white) begins to realize he has misjudged Lance Armstrong's form on Alpe d'Huez in 2001. Minutes later his suspicions were confirmed.*

COL D'ISERAN

The Iseran is big in every sense of the word. The top of the pass is at 2,764 metres, and the road over it was the highest in France until 1961. First used in 1938, it was also the highest the Tour had ever been until 1962. The Iseran is long; the north side is a staggering 48 kilometres uphill, with a height gain of 2,028 metres. It's located in the Vanoise, in the north-east corner of the French Alps, close to the Italian border.

RECORDS

Length:	48 kilometres
Summit height:	2,764 metres
Height gain:	2,028 metres
Average gradient:	4.3%
Maximum gradient:	10%
Tour appearances:	8

↑ *Italian rider Claudio Chiappucci climbs the Iseran in 1992, the first time the summit was reached from the north side.*

THREE IN A DAY

Racing in high places like the Iseran must have been scary in the 1930s. The top part of the climb, above Val d'Isère, is wild, even today. Imagine being confronted with something so vast, high and inhospitable as the middle leg of a triple-stage day, because that's what the Tour riders faced in 1939. The first leg was a 127km road race from Briançon to Bonneval-sur-Arc, crossing the Galibier. The second was a 64.5km time trial, up and over the Iseran, finishing at Bourg-St-Maurice. And the day was rounded off with 103km to Annecy, climbing Mont Tamie. It was the second triple-stage day in a Tour de France that also had six double stages out of 18 days' racing. The riders started the first leg at five in the morning, when the temperature was still below zero. The Belgian Sylvère Maes won the Iseran time trial, tying up his second Tour de France.

SIDE SWITCH

The first Tours climbed the Col d'Iseran from the south, from Bonneval-sur-Arc, and descended to Bourg-St-Maurice. The last ascent from that side was in 1963, and the Iseran didn't return to the Tour until 1992, when it was climbed from the north side, as it has been ever since. The northern ascent is the longest one. It's not steep at first but goes through a number of dark tunnels. The climb gets much steeper after passing through Val d'Isère, the famous ski station, and there is a real feeling of high altitude approaching the top. The final slog traces the top of a rocky crest beside the Vallon d'Iseran, up to the natural gap between two 3,000-metre peaks, which is the Iseran pass. This part is brutally steep, cold, windy and exposed. It feels like climbing Mount Everest on a bike.

BOBET'S FINAL HOUR

In 1959 Louison Bobet was 34 and still part of the French team, because of his giant status, but in truth well past his best. He was out of form before the Tour, struggled through it and was dropped by almost the whole field on the Iseran. He wouldn't stop, though, not on the slopes. If he had, the mountain would have beaten him, and Bobet was too proud to let that happen. Instead he reached Iseran's summit, where he got off his bike and into the French team car. As he did so he asked a journalist for his hat, so the fans wouldn't see his face as he was driven off the mountain and out of the Tour de France for ever.

← *Lousion Bobet ends his Tour de France career on top of the Iseran in 1959.*

WORLD'S HARDEST LABRADOR

In 2007 a stray dog ambled across the road right in front of Marcus Burghardt, who crashed into it. The dog hardly seemed to notice and continued on its way as though nothing had happened. Next day the *Guardian* newspaper called it "the world's hardest Labrador".

➜ *Marcus Burghardt has a nervous look over his shoulder to see if any more dogs want a piece of him.*

LOST TITLES

The highest point in any Tour de France is called the roof of the tour, and the rider who leads there wins the Souvenir Henri Desgrange. Whenever the Iseran was included, it was here that the prize was won, because it was the highest natural pass in France. The Col de la Bonette was the second highest, at 2,731 metres, but in 1961 the local authority there decided to build a road around the peak that stands above that pass, and the high point of that road was 2,802 metres, so it became the highest in France. It was called the Cime de la Bonette, and the Tour used it for the first time in 1962. The Iseran thus lost both its titles, as the highest road in France and as the highest point in the Tour de France.

BROKEN TOOTH

Riding for the French regional team, Ile de France, Pierre Tacca made a bid for glory on the stage to Aosta in 1949 by attacking on the second climb, Mont Cenis. Unfortunately he chose a freezing cold day, but although it was his undoing it won him a place in Tour de France folklore. He led over Mont Cenis and was climbing the south side of the Iseran alone when he punctured. With no support car, he had to change his own tubular tyre, but his hands were so numb from the cold that he couldn't prise it off the rim, so he used his teeth, breaking one in the process. He continued over the Iseran in the lead, but was caught by Coppi and Bartali, before dropping to 21st on the stage, over 28 minutes behind.

↑ *Gino Bartali (leading) struggles up the Col d'Iseran in 1938. Only a daring and incredibly skilful descent will save his yellow jersey.*

BARTALI'S SAVE

The first time the Iseran was used was the day after Gino Bartali dominated over the Col d'Izoard in 1938. He'd given everything and his rivals knew it, so they piled on the pressure up this new giant climb. Bartali was behind at the summit, but he was saved by the unusually long north descent, where he took incredible risks to catch his rivals and save his Tour de France. Bartali coped with the problem posed by the tunnels of riding from daylight into darkness and out again by using a technique that Tour riders still use. He kept one eye shut outside, thus keeping it used to the dark, and opened it in the tunnel. That way he didn't have to slow down in every tunnel until both eyes grew accustomed to the darkness.

COL D'IZOARD

The Izoard is in the Queyras, one of the last areas of the Alps to be opened up to tourists. It's a region of high peaks and wild landscapes, but the wildest is the incredible Casse Déserte, which lies towards the top of the Col d'Izoard. This other-world of shattered boulders, guarded by improbable rock towers, has been part of the Tour de France since 1922, when Philippe Thys was first to the top. More than any other Tour climb, the Col d'Izoard has about it an aura of a bygone age of bike racing. It's not used much in modern Tours, but the Izoard has witnessed some iconic moments, and did so again when the Tour made a long overdue visit in 2011.

RECORDS

Length:	15.9 kilometres
Summit height:	2,361 metres
Height gain:	1,095 metres
Average gradient:	7%
Maximum gradient:	12%
Tour appearances:	32

↑ *Jean Robic forges a lonely path upwards through the Casse Déserte in 1947. Although René Vietto won the stage, it was Robic who won the Tour.*

SECRET PASS

The road over the Izoard travels in a huge double dogleg from the village of Guillestre in the south to the highest town in France, Briançon, in the north. At first there doesn't appear to be a way though the mountains that separate the two places, especially since the Durance valley links them by a longer but easy route. It was local poachers and smugglers, in need of an alternative, who pioneered the Izoard pass and kept it secret. Their route was only turned into a road at the beginning of the 20th century.

CASSE DÉSERTE

The first part of the climb goes through woods or across wide meadows, but where the grass and the trees end, the Casse Déserte begins. The name means desert fell, and it's a world of shattered rock in which towers stand like sentinels dotted along the route. They are the withered pinnacles of extra-resistant rock that have stood the erosive test of time. Higher mineral concentrations give the towers colour: pink in the morning, bleached yellow in the midday sun. In the evening they assume ghostly shapes, and by moonlight a vivid imagination can almost breathe life into them.

COPPI AND BOBET

Fausto Coppi and Louison Bobet, who were great friends, had some of their finest Tour de France moments on this climb. They are remembered by a plaque on one of the rock pinnacles on the left side of the road, not far from the top. It's easy to pick out as there are always floral tributes in front of it.

← *The memorial to Fausto Coppi (left) and Louison Bobet stands near to the summit of Col d'Izoard.*

SCHLECK'S ATTACK

The 2011 Tour de France climbed the Izoard from its classic south side. It was stage 18 from Pinerolo in Italy to the top of the Col du Galibier. Andy Schleck made a devastating attack on the Izoard, and with the help of a couple of team-mates who had gone ahead in earlier moves he established a lead on the descent into Briançon and in the valley towards the Col de Lautaret. Then he attacked again, going alone to the top of the Galibier to win the stage and move to within a few seconds of the yellow jersey. Schleck got it next day, but not with enough time advantage to prevent Cadel Evans taking it from him in the final time trial. It was a great attack, though, and one reminiscent of the days when Coppi, Bobet and Merckx won Tours with similar moves.

THE BROTHERS RIDE AGAIN

Louison Bobet wanted to ride the Izoard to celebrate his 50th birthday and invited his brother Jean to go with him. Louison was in less good shape than Jean and could only ride behind him on the nearby Col de Vars, which they did as a warm-up, and it was the same on the Izoard – until the Casse Déserte. Then, in Jean's words: "In his domain Louison came alive. He rode alongside me for a while, then he was gone, a few metres in front at first but then 200 metres. I'll not say what I thought of him after leading all that way and then him dropping me near the top, but now I realize that the champion inside Louison just took over."

↑ Andy Schleck attacks in a brave attempt to win the 2011 Tour. He fell just short, but his quest for a first Tour victory came in February 2012, when Alberto Contador was stripped of his 2010 success after a failed drugs test.

MUSEUM

Right at the top of the Col d'Izoard there's a Tour de France museum containing a brilliant photographic record of the exploits and battles on the climb.

TRUCE

Up until 1949 Fausto Coppi and Gino Bartali were fierce rivals. Theoretically they were obliged to ride together if they were selected for the Italian team, but they refused to do it, for which they were disciplined by the Italian cycling authorities. However, their war ended on the Izoard in 1949. They were riding well clear of the rest when Coppi's rear wheel hit a pot-hole and he punctured and crashed. Bartali stopped to help him up, and they continued together. Later Bartali had to ask Coppi to slow down. The older man had finally accepted the younger man's superiority. It was Bartali's birthday, so Coppi did slow – and even let him win the stage. Coppi won the 1949 Tour by nearly 11 minutes from Bartali.

← Fausto Coppi leaves the rest struggling in his wake as he dances up the Col d'Izoard in 1949.

COL DE PEYRESOURDE

The Col de Peyresourde was the first high pass to be climbed by the Tour. On that epic day in 1910, the Tour proved that cyclists could race over passes that rose more than a mile high. The Pyrenean peak was the first climb that day, and it is part of a classic Tour route that takes in the Peyresourde, Aspin, Tourmalet and Aubisque. The descent of one ends at the start of the next climb, so this saw-tooth route has been used by the Tour more times than any other section of road in France. It's so forbidding that it is called the Circle of Death.

RECORDS

Length:	15.2 kilometres
Summit height:	1,569 metres
Height gain:	944 metres
Average gradient:	6.2%
Maximum gradient:	10%
Tour appearances:	61

IRON JENS

In 2010 Jens Voigt's front tyre blew out at 70 kph on the descent of Peyresourde and he crashed on to the granite-chipped road. Torn, bloodied and bruised, he was given another bike and he carried on. He had grazes all over his body, stitches in his arm and cracked ribs, but he finished the stage. That night Voigt got a telephone call from Chris Boardman, his one-time team-mate, who recalls the conversation: "The first thing Jens says is, 'Hi Chris, how are Sally and the kids?' I mean, I'd still be sobbing, telling anyone who'd listen how much it hurts. Not Jens, he is the most positive person I ever met. Being in the same team as him added an extra two years to my career."

LICENSED TO THRILL

There is an airport close to the summit of the Col de Peyresourde (officially it is called Peyresourde Balestas airport), and a dramatic one it is too. So dramatic, in fact, that it was used to shoot the opening scenes of the James Bond film *Tomorrow Never Dies*.

MOUNTAIN IMPASSE

Michael Rasmussen and Alberto Contador were by far the best climbers of the 2007 Tour. Rasmussen had the yellow jersey with Contador in second place. The fight between them came to a head on the Peyresourde, when Contador tried to drop Rasmussen in a game of reverse cat and mouse. After Rasmussen nullified Contador's first attack, the Spaniard and the Dane slowed to a crawl. Contador went again, and Rasmussen clawed him back. Contador launched another attack, and once again Rasmussen chased him down. Then they almost came to a stop, with Rasmussen leading, Contador behind. Suddenly Contador accelerated, but Rasmussen still hauled him back just before the summit. It was a total impasse.

← *Michael Rasmussen, in yellow, hauls himself back up to Alberto Contador as they play out their 2007 Peyresourde duel.*

Van Impe's solo

This is where Lucien van Impe changed the way he raced. Previously he had limited himself to winning mountains stages and the King of the Mountains title, fearing that he wasn't a strong enough all-rounder to take on Eddy Merckx. But then Merckx was beaten by Bernard Thévenet in 1975 and, by coincidence, the 1976 Tour route was very hilly. "As soon as I saw it, I knew I could win," Van Impe says now. He needed to be brave and attack early on the most mountainous stage, then go for it alone to the finish to gain a stack of time, and that's what Van Impe did on the Col de Peyresourde. He danced up the climb, quickly catching two early leaders and leaving the other favourites for dead. Van Impe pressed home his advantage on the next climb, the final one, to win the stage and take the yellow jersey by well over three minutes.

→ *Lucien van Impe won the Tour de France in 1976 his attack on the Col de Peyresourde being a key factor.*

Ullrich payback

The descent of the Peyresourde has caught out more riders than Jens Voigt. His countryman Jan Ullrich crashed here in 2001, when he was lying second to Lance Armstrong, and Armstrong waited for him to remount and catch up. Fast forward to 2003, and Armstrong crashed when wearing the yellow jersey again, but this time Ullrich was a lot closer to the American in the overall standings of the Tour. They were climbing to the ski station of Luz-Ardiden when Armstrong's handlebars were knocked by a spectator and he fell. Ullrich could have really profited from Armstrong's bad luck, but instead he waited. Further up the climb to Luz-Ardiden, Armstrong attacked to win the stage and gain time on Ullrich.

Lance's last stand

Lance Armstrong came back to the Tour de France in 2009 with third place overall, and despite being almost 40 he wanted to do more in 2010. He started the race well, but the luck he'd had during his run of seven victories, aided in no small part by his superb reactions and the way he always read correctly what was happening in the peloton, deserted him. He had several crashes and was delayed behind several more. Armstrong still wanted to do something in the race, so he seized his chance on the 17th stage by attacking on the first climb of the day, the Col du Peyresourde. For one last time the Tour saw Armstrong flying, but even though he fought all day for a stage victory, sixth was the best he could do.

Back in contention

The Tour de France is too close a contest for it to happen now, but years ago riders could look out of contention then ride right back into the frame. Before stage 15 in 1947, Jean Robic was sixth overall, over 23 minutes behind the leader. He attacked on the Peyresourde and led over the summit, then forged on to lead over every climb in the Circle of Death, winning the stage by ten minutes and almost halving his deficit to the leader René Vietto. Robic stealthily cut Vietto's lead over the next seven days to run out the winner in Paris.

← *Jean Robic begins to drag himself back into contention on the Peyresourde in 1947.*

COL DU TOURMALET

The Col du Tourmalet was first ridden in the 1910 Tour, and is the Tour's most visited climb. It's a classic pass, a V-shaped notch between two mountains, with a knife-edge summit. The Tourmalet, one of the most iconic climbs in Tour history, is the king of the Pyrenees and the most famous Tour climb of the whole range. The Pyrenees are different from the Alps. The roads over them are older and tend to be less well engineered, using natural rather than man-made paths up the mountains. The Tourmalet is all that and more: all of the character of the Pyrenees rolled into a single climb.

RECORDS

Length:	17.1 kilometres
Summit height:	2,115 metres
Height gain:	1,275 metres
Average gradient:	7.5%
Maximum gradient:	11%
Tour appearances (both sides):	79

THE GIANT

There is a huge sculpture on the Tourmalet summit. It's called the Giant of the Tourmalet and it soars above the road on top of a memorial stone to Jacques Goddet, who took over from Henri Desgrange as Tour director in the 1930s. The sculpture is a polished steel representation of a cyclist riding out of the saddle. His look is focused resolutely upwards, caring nothing about what is behind. It is the spirit of a true climber in a true climber's spiritual place.

⬆ *Art on the mountain; the Jacques Goddet memorial and a sculpture that depicts the spirit of climbing grace the summit of the Tourmalet.*

GEOGRAPHY

The road over the Tourmalet runs north-east to south-west, connecting the Adour and Luz valleys. The north-east ascent starts easily but becomes very tough towards the top, whereas the south-west climb is hard all the way up, but with lots of little variations in gradient. Before the road was built over it, the Tourmalet was a place where local guides had to help tourists travel. There are even stories of rich people being carried over the Tourmalet on Sedan chairs.

⬇ *Injured in a crash at St-Etienne a few days earlier, Bernard Hinault (right) struggles on the Tourmalet in 1985. Miki Ruttimann is to his right and Joop Zoetemelk just behind.*

CONSPIRACY

Bernard Hinault was injured in a crash at St-Etienne during the 1985 Tour and was really struggling on the Tourmalet. Greg LeMond went ahead with a break on Hinault's instructions to mark Stephen Roche. LeMond says that he felt good, so he asked their team manager Paul Koechli if he could attack, but Koechli told him not to because Hinault was only 40 seconds behind and closing. In fact he was one minute behind and not gaining a metre. LeMond still feels that if he had attacked he could have won the 1985 Tour.

MILLAR TIME

In 1983 the Tourmalet saw a group of young Tour first-timers, all with great futures, go clear of the rest. They were Pedro Delgado, Laurent Fignon, Patrochinio Jimenez and a Scot, Robert Millar. Millar attacked shortly before the summit, taking the Colombian, Jimenez, with him. Jimenez took the summit points and the pair built a lead on the descent and over the Aspin and Peyresourde. Millar went ahead alone towards the top of the final climb to take his first Tour de France stage win. Millar was again first over the Tourmalet on another brilliant day in 1989, when he took top points on every climb and won the stage at Superbagnères.

NO PROBLEM FOR CYCLISTS

When he reconnoitred the route for the organizers to see if racing over the Pyreneean climbs was feasible, Alphonse Steines almost perished on the Tourmalet. He worked for the organizers, *L'Auto* and it was his dream for this stage to work. He went to the area in May, and at first couldn't find a guide prepared to take him over the giant climb. Eventually an old guy volunteered, so long as he could drive Steines's car, but that quickly got stuck in the snow and the guide returned to Ste-Marie-de-Campan. Steines pressed on, dressed only in his city clothes, eventually walking off the track and getting lost. It was dark by now and not knowing where he was anything could have happened, but then Steines came across some shepherds and one of them took him to the summit of the pass, showing him the way down the other side. He made it to Barrèges at the western foot of the climb at three o'clock in the morning. Next day he sent a telegram to Henri Desgrange, which read: "No trouble crossing Tourmalet. Roads satisfactory. No problem for cyclists".

Britain's greatest climber, 1984 Tour de France King of the Mountains Robert Millar in 1989.

TASTE OF THE ANDES

A big flock of llamas graze freely towards the top of the north-east ascent, in the meadows just after the ski resort of La Mongie. Several stages have finished at La Mongie. It's where Bernard Thévenet won his first stage in his first Tour. Just to emphasize what a surprise that would have been, Thévenet's bike was equipped with a spare tyre and a pump. If they made him carry those, his team must have thought he'd get dropped and finish behind the team cars.

INSPIRED BY FEAR

Marcel Queheille was by no means the worst rider ever to race in the Tour – he won a stage in 1959 – but he never represented France in the days of national teams and only raced as a regional selection. One of the things that held Queheille back was the fact that he hated big mountains. He hated their height, the feeling of exposure on roads that cling to rock faces, and especially the Tourmalet. "Everything about it frightens me, and I breathe a sigh of relief every time I cross the summit," he explained to reporters after a stage in 1961 when he had clearly conquered his fear – he had found himself in a group at the front of the race and was first over the Aspin and the Tourmalet, before finishing third on the stage in Pau.

Marcel Queheille overcomes his fear on the Col du Tourmalet during the 1961 Tour.

MONT VENTOUX

Mont Ventoux always delivers drama. In summer its capricious weather can swing from furnace-like heat to menacing cold. Tour racers have collapsed here, one even died, and those that triumph are among the biggest names in bike racing. Unlike the other legendary climbs, the road over Mont Ventoux isn't a mountain pass, a place to cross a range between two peaks; it serves no other purpose than visiting the top of the mountain.

↑ *The overhead banner indicates one kilometre to go for the new hope of France, Jean-François Bernard on Mont Ventoux in 1987.*

RECORDS

Length:	21.5 kilometres
Summit height:	1,909 metres
Height gain:	1,609 metres
Average gradient:	7.6%
Maximum gradient:	10.7%
Tour appearances:	14

BALD MOUNTAIN

Mont Ventoux can be seen from a large area of Provence, not only because of its vast bulk but also because of its white summit. This looks like snow, but in summer it's the whiteness of the rock of which the mountain is formed. The white summit came about because trees were cut down on the Ventoux for shipbuilding in Toulon, and on the south side of the mountain they never grew back above a certain height. The Ventoux is sometimes called Mont Chauve, the bald mountain.

RED ZONE

When Bernard Hinault retired, the weight of his success, and French cycling's expectations, fell on the young shoulders of Jean-François Bernard. He became the leader of the La Vie Claire team, and he says now that he felt immense pressure to perform and gain his team-mates' respect. He had a chance of winning the 1987 Tour, but bad luck beat him, and so maybe did his amazing climb of the Ventoux. It was part of a time trial from Carpentras, a town about 16 kilometres from the start of the climb, to the top of Mont Ventoux. Bernard won it with a ride of huge power, and he took the yellow jersey. He crashed next day and lost the lead, and he never seemed the same rider after that. It was as if he had put his whole career into one day. Some say that when a rider goes beyond his limits, into what they call the red, he shortens his career. As Bernard flogged himself up the Ventoux, his face a constant grimace of pain, he appeared to be in the red all the way.

THREE WAYS TO THE TOP

There are three ways to the top of the Ventoux by road. One is from Malaucène, using the northern side. Another is from Bédoin to the south. The third is from Sault to the east: this is the longest route and it joins the Bédoin road just south of the Chalet Reynard, a cafe six kilometres from the summit. The Tour de France always climbs from Bédoin.

← *The summit of the Ventoux has been likened to the surface of the moon. It's easy to see why.*

ARMSTRONG'S INSULT

In 2000 Marco Pantani and Lance Armstrong were head and shoulders above the rest on the Ventoux. Pantani launched a series of attacks to whittle down the lead group, then made a very big attack. Only Armstrong could follow this one, and it took him a kilometre of out-of-the-saddle chasing to close the gap. Once with Pantani, Armstrong set a relentless pace, occasionally glancing behind to see where Pantani was. After three kilometres with Armstrong leading, Pantani attacked late to win the stage, and Armstrong didn't answer his attack. He was content that he'd distanced his closest rivals and made winning his second Tour a little more certain. However, the fact that Armstrong didn't sprint offended Pantani. He thought Armstrong had given him the stage, and by doing so had failed to show proper respect for a former Tour winner.

↑ *Marco Pantani (right) sprints to win on the Ventoux in 2000, but Lance Armstrong clearly isn't trying. Proud Pantani never forgave him for that.*

THE SIMPSON MEMORIAL

When Tom Simpson set out on stage 13 of the 1967 Tour he was lying in seventh place overall. A career still unequalled by any British racer made Simpson one of the stars of 1960s pro bike racing. He won some of the best races in the world, but he wanted to win the Tour de France. The 1967 race, in which he led the British team, started well, but Simpson fell ill during an Alpine stage and was still unwell with a stomach virus on stage 13. Unable to eat solids, Simpson was in no fit state to fight for his overall position on the Ventoux, but he wouldn't back down. He dosed himself with amphetamines in an effort to stay competitive, but in his already dehydrated state and in temperatures of over 40 degrees Celsius that proved fatal. Simpson collapsed and died, still fighting to stay near the front, two kilometres from the summit. There's a memorial stone to him there now, paid for by British cyclists, where thousands stop each year and leave some memento of their visit – a flower, a cap, a bottle – or they write a message on a piece of the white scree that covers the summit. This truly is one corner of a foreign country that will forever be England.

COLLAPSE

In 1955 the Breton racer Jean Malléjac collapsed in incredible heat on the 11th stage of the Tour de France. He was delirious, and when he was placed in the race ambulance he began to fit. Malléjac wasn't the only rider in trouble that day, and what happened convinced Pierre Dumas, the race doctor, to call for anti-doping controls. However, no one was listening – yet.

SUFFERING

Racing on the Ventoux is full of stories of suffering. In 1955, when the 1950 winner Ferdi Kubler of Switzerland was leading on the climb with Raphaël Géminiani, instead of riding steadily with his French breakaway companion, he kept attacking. Géminiani told him to be careful, that the Ventoux was no ordinary mountain. To this Kubler replied, "And Ferdi is no ordinary racer" – and attacked again. A few kilometres later, Géminiani passed Kubler, who was now crawling up the climb. He was very strong but had overestimated his strength, and the Ventoux had got him. Even the great Eddy Merckx was so shattered when he won at the top of the Ventoux in 1970 that he almost passed out afterwards and had to be put on oxygen.

↑ *Raphaël Géminiani tries to warn Ferdi Kubler that the Ventoux is unlike any other mountain, but he will not listen.*

INDEX

Picture Credits

All photographs in this book: © Presse Sports / Offside Sports Photography

Special thanks are due to Mark Leech and David Wilkinson at Offside Sports Photography, who showed speed, stamina and determination to deal with the mountains of picture requests put their way throughout this project.

About the Author

Chris Sidwells, the nephew of British cycling legend Tom Simpson, is a journalist, photographer and author who has covered cycling for more than a decade. His writing and photographs feature in every issue of *Cycle Sport* and *Cycling Weekly* magazines. He also writes for *220 Triathlon* magazine and has contributed to *Bicycling, Cycling Plus, Running Fitness, Men's Fitness* and *GQ* magazines as well as broadcasting and speaking about cycling on radio and television. His books (which have been translated into 24 languages) include biographies of his uncle, *Mr Tom*, and of cyclist Allan Peiper, *A Peiper's Tale, The Complete Bike Book, Bike Repair Manual, Cycling for Fitness, Tour Climbs* (a best-seller in the summer of 2008) and *A Race for Madmen*. He lives in Devon, south-west England.